THE
MONEY
DIET

THE ULTIMATE GUIDE TO SHEDDING POUNDS OFF YOUR BILLS AND SAVING MONEY ON EVERYTHING!

MARTIN LEWIS
Money Saving Expert

Vermilion
LONDON

19 20 18

First published in the UK in 2004 by Vermilion, an imprint of Ebury Publishing
This revised an updated edition published by Vermilion in 2005

Ebury Publishing is a Random House Group company

Copyright © Martin Lewis 2004, 2005

Martin Lewis has asserted his right to be identified as the author of this Work in
accordance with the Copyright, Designs and Patents Act 1988.

The Random House Group Limited Reg. No. 954009

Addresses for companies within the Random House Group can be found at
www.randomhouse.co.uk

A CIP catalogue record for this book is available from the British Library

The Random House Group Limited supports The Forest Stewardship
Council (FSC), the leading international forest certification organisation.
All our titles that are printed on Greenpeace approved FSC certified paper
carry the FSC logo. Our paper procurement policy can be found at
www.randomhouse.co.uk/environment

Mixed Sources
Product group from well-managed
forests and other controlled sources
www.fsc.org Cert no. TT-COC-2139
© 1996 Forest Stewardship Council

Designed by seagulls

Printed in the UK by CPI Cox & Wyman, Reading, RG1 8EX

ISBN 9780091906887

Copies are available at special rates for bulk orders. Contact the sales development
team on 020 7840 8487 or visit www.booksforpromotions.co.uk for more information.

To buy books by your favourite authors and register for offers, visit
www.randomhouse.co.uk

Paul Lewis, BBC Radio 4's *Moneybox*

'The UK's Tightest Man' Philip Schofield, *This Morning*

'If anyone can help, it's this man, Martin Lewis knows more
about credit cards than possibly anyone else in the country'
Justin Rowlatt, BBC1 *Panorama*

Dedicated to the memory of my mother, Susan Lewis

Acknowledgements

Huge thanks to the whole MoneySaving community of www.moneysavingexpert.com. Their contributions, suggestions and thoughts are an inspiration. There are too many individuals to thank, so to represent them I've picked those contributors currently with the most postings in the chat forum. Thank you to Rushnowt, Trafalgar, Foxy, 16011996, Savvy, Fran, M.E.2, Lola G, Elfmay and Elvis Bloggs.

Kind thanks for their astute comments on the relevant sections of the first edition to Peter White and the Consumer Credit Counselling Service, Jill Stevens and Experian, Rudi Schlenker and London & Country Mortgages, Anna Bowes and Chase de Vere, Steve Playle and Trading Standards, Ray Boulger and Charcol. Special thanks to my uncle, Tony Tesciuba, for stepping out of the tax accountancy world and providing hardcore comment and number checking for the entire diet.

And a big thank you to my MoneySaving team. When I wrote the first edition, I was on my tod; now with the website growth I've built a wonderful team to help me. Huge thanks to Andrea, Brendan and especially Archna for keeping track of my scribblings as I put this new edition together and Dan for checking the numbers on this edition.

And unexpected thanks to Starbucks. You may be shocked by this – after all, up to three quid for a cup of coffee ain't no MoneySaving. However, when I needed time and space to turn the mobile off, disconnect from the net and just think and write, Starbucks it was. It may be overpriced, but it provides plugs for my laptop, so on many occasions I wrote there for a whole day, buying just two cups of coffee. In other words, six quid for office rental. Bargain!

VERY IMPORTANT: THE MONEY DIET CALORIE COUNTER

For a quick guide as to how much The Money Diet can save you and how to prioritise your MoneySaving, turn to page xiv for The Money Diet Calorie Counter

CONTENTS

contents

contents

contents

Part 3: Healthy Eating

contents

The Money Diet Calorie Counter

Use the following Calorie Counter to prioritise your MoneySaving. It brings together all the specific products detailed in the Crash Diet and Healthy Eating sections of the book. Find what you want, turn to the page, read the recipe, save the cash – it's as simple as that. Don't forget the Financial Fitness section though – read that and you'll permanently hone your MoneySaving muscles.

TERMS EXPLAINED

Time taken: A rough guide, the purpose of which is to help you prioritise your time.

Typical savings: The savings, of course, vary widely. The amount listed is typical for someone to whom the specific recipe applies. For example, international phone calls: many people don't make any calls abroad, yet those who do tend to do so regularly, and could save £300 a year. Don't think of the amounts as an accurate guide, more as a rough scale of savings available for each recipe.

Difficulty level: Incorporates both the practical difficulties and how complex it is to understand.

Subject	Details	Section	Page	Typical Saving/Gain	Time Taken	Difficulty Level
Balance transfer cards	Cut existing credit card debt costs	Healthy Eating	372	£2,500 until balance is cleared	30 minutes	Easy
Broadband	Save on a speedy connection	Crash Diet	196	£100 per year	45 minutes	Mid
Calling overseas	Cheapest way to phone abroad	Crash Diet	200	£75 per year	30 minutes	Easy/Mid
Car insurance	The drop, shop double and haggle method	Crash Diet	284	£300 per year	1 hour	Easy/Mid
Charity credit cards	Give more by being savvy	Healthy Eating	382	£220 per year	30 minutes	Mid
Charity giving	Give more for no extra cost	Crash Diet	279	£80 per year	15 minutes	Easy
Child savings	Save for your kids & sneaky tax saving for you	Crash Diet	219	£40 per year	20 minutes	Easy/Mid
Contact lenses	The same lenses for less	Crash Diet	248	£100 per year	30 minutes	Easy
Credit card shuffle	Cut interest even if you can't get new cards	Healthy Eating	391	£500 per year	90 minutes	Mid/Hard
Current accounts	More interest or cheaper overdrafts	Crash Diet	238	£175 per year	30 minutes	Easy/Mid
Discount brokers	Buy unit trusts or shares ISAs for less	Crash Diet	233	£250 per year	25 minutes	Easy
Existing cash ISAs	Improving the returns	Crash Diet	225	£100 per year	20 minutes	Mid
Fixed-rate cash ISAs	A loophole to fix the rate and allow escape	Crash Diet	228	£100 per year	30 minutes	Mid/Hard
Flights	Get the cheapest	Crash Diet	264	£100	15 minutes	Easy
Foreign currency	Get the cheapest	Healthy Eating	384	£20 per trip	20 minutes	Easy
Free calls worldwide	Via your PC	Crash Diet	203	£300 per year	20 minutes	Mid
Gas & electricity bills	No difference, just cheaper bills	Crash Diet	175	£150 per year	10 minutes	Easy

Subject	Details	Section	Page	Typical Saving/Gain	Time Taken	Difficulty Level
Healthcare cashback plans	Little-heard-of policies that pay for your healthcare	Crash Diet	245	£350 per year	30 minutes	Mid
Home insurance cost cutting	The drop, shop, double and haggle method	Crash Diet	291	£250–350 per year	1 hour	Easy
Home phones	Slash your phone bills	Crash Diet	183	£350 per year	60 minutes	Easy/Mid
Internet access (dial-up)	Cut the cost of getting online	Crash Diet	193	£150 per year	45 minutes	Mid
Level-term life assurance	Cut the cost of protecting your family's income	Crash Diet	275	£240 per year	20 minutes	Easy
Loan insurance	Get separate insurance for your loan to cut the costs	Crash Diet	282	£200 per year	30 minutes	Mid
Medications	Beat prices by busting the brands	Crash Diet	254	£75 per year	5 minutes	Easy
Mini cash ISAs	Best tax-free savings	Crash Diet	223	£80 per year	20 minutes	Easy/Mid
Mobile calls at landline prices	Bypass your network's charges	Crash Diet	181	£350 per year	45 minutes	Mid/Hard
Mobile phone contract, batter down the price	An easy haggling technique to slash the price	Financial Fitness	124	£120 per year	30 minutes	Easy/Mid
Mortgage	Cheapest mortgage possible	Healthy Eating	322	£1,200 per year	3 hours	Mid
Mortgage life assurance	Ensure your house is passed on to your dependants	Crash Diet	279	£200 per year	20 minutes	Easy
Mortgage payment protection insurance	Cover your repayments in the event of accident, sickness and unemployment	Crash Diet	273	£240 per year	30 minutes	Easy
Online shopping	Shop for less	Crash Diet	206	£250 per year	10 minutes	Easy
Overseas spending credit card	Cheapest way to spend when abroad	Healthy Eating	383	£75 per year	30 minutes	Easy/Mid

Package holidays	Special techniques for bagging bargain holidays	Crash Diet	262	£600 off brochure price	2 hours	Mid
Pensions	Get a stakeholder pension the right way and it'll grow faster (or shrink slower)	Crash Diet	256	£9,000 on a lifetime pension fund	60 minutes	Mid/Hard
Personal loan – half-price plastic version	Use credit card to get a cheaper loan	Healthy Eating	406	£3,500 over life of loan	2 hours	Mid/Hard
Personal loan (existing customers)	Cut the cost of existing loans	Healthy Eating	409	£1,000 over life of loan	1 hour	Mid/Hard
Personal loan (new)	Avoid the hurdles and get the real cheapest	Healthy Eating	398	£3,000 over life of loan	45 minutes	Easy/Mid
Prescriptions	Reduce regular prescription costs	Crash Diet	251	£100 per year	10 minutes	Easy
Purchases credit card	Cheapest way to borrow for new spending	Healthy Eating	369	£500 per year	30 minutes	Easy
Regular savings account	Special account that beats the best buys	Crash diet	217	£120 per year	30 minutes	Mid
(Re)Mortgage advice for free	Independent advice at no cost	Crash diet	269	£750 per year	20 minutes	Easy
Repensioning	Increase the returns on existing pension funds	Crash diet	259	£4,500 on final fund	2 hours	Hard/Very hard
Roadside Recovery	Peace of mind at rock-bottom prices	Crash diet	289	£120 per year	30 minutes	Easy/Mid
Roam, use your mobile abroad	Cut the cost of calling home when abroad	Crash diet	189	£200 per year	30 minutes	Mid
Savings accounts	Earn more interest	Crash diet	215	£150 per year	20 minutes	Easy
Shares	The cheapest way to buy, hold and sell	Crash diet	236	£130 per year	30 minutes	Easy/Mid
Student bank accounts	Swot up on your finances	Crash diet	242	£150 over the course	20 minutes	Easy
Travel Insurance	Get the same cover for less	Crash diet	266	£150 per year	30 minutes	Easy
Water bills	Meter or bills	Crash diet	179	£100 per year	10-25 minutes	Easy/Mid

INTRODUCTION

If you've just bought this book, why on earth didn't you borrow it from the library instead? If your answer is 'a book like this is so important I need it close by all the time', great. This is the key to the Money Diet – making smart and rational consumer decisions while understanding others' agendas. If you bought this book on impulse, luckily it's a good buy anyway, as the money saved should easily exceed the cover price. And, it shouldn't be forgotten, it enables me to continue to make a living!

Let me set out m'stall.

The Money Diet isn't Hard Work –
All the Work is Done for You

The Money Diet involves as little or as much work as you want: you decide how far you're willing to push it. Those who want a quick cost-cutting hit will find the work's been done so it is immediately possible. And hardcore Money Dieters who want to become 'loophole spotters' and 'system screwers' (see pages 150 and 151) will find techniques to tone their MoneySaving muscles, too.

The Money Diet is not about Being Tight

It's about getting the best value. It isn't about 'stopping spending'; it's about 'spending better'. It's about preventing companies taking too many of your hard-earned shillings, about not spending more than you need.

The Money Diet is for Everyone, not just Those who are Skint

It's *not* a 'what to do if you've got no cash' system. It's all about saving pounds without tightening your belt. If you've very little cash, it should stretch your money further. For those who are comfortable, it should enable you to buy or to save more. It's all about putting more money in your pocket.

The Money Diet is a Way to Get Your Own Back

Making rational decisions and understanding others' agendas are the engines powering the Money Diet. Without wanting to get too militant about it, most people have been taken for a ride for a very long time. We spend our lives being screwed by companies for their profit. My aim is simple: I want to show you how to screw them back.

ADDITIONS TO THE SECOND EDITION

The longevity of *The Money Diet*'s first edition surprised me. When I originally wrote it, I told my publisher it'd have a maximum shelf life of 18 months, as the world of money is viciously fast-moving.

When I sat down to re-read it in its entirety for the update, I actually discovered most of the book was still relevant, and anyone using it would still be saving. So, with a throaty gulp, I decided it had to be more than just an update, and in the end my passion rekindled – there are 100 new MoneySaving pages.

Much has happened, both to me and the MoneySaving world, in the past 18 months. Consumers are getting more active, rate tarts are on the rise, and there's a growing realisation that you have to do it yourself to survive – television producers now tell me 'debt is the new property, darling'.

For me, it has been a change of profile and scale – both in my broadcast work, but most notably in the fact that my little website ain't so little any more. It's breadth, depth and store of information – both from the body of my work and the combined research and instincts of the hundreds of thousands of regular MoneySavers – has seen the MoneySaving standards step up a notch further.

Companies, you can begin quaking now!

What's New?

The Adversarial Consumer Society. Perhaps my greatest indulgence was adding this new section. The adversarial consumer society is my philosophy, my passion and my politics. It drives me and MoneySaving.

This time I wanted to briefly go behind the Money Diet and

explain why we must become savvy consumers, and that's what this is all about.

New Ways To Save. There is a raft of new stuff in this book. Added Crash Diet topics include home insurance (page 291), roaming mobile phones (page 189), where to start with saving (page 209), medicines (page 254), broadband (page 196) roadside recovery (page 289) and free PC-to-PC international calls (page 203).

Throughout the rest of the book there are new bits too: the list of 101 ways to cut back (page 42), a very expanded debt crisis section (page 411), haggling for your mobile phone (page 124), buying on eBay (page 137), 'should I cut up credit cards?' (page 380) and even a 'Sad Fart' thrown in for good measure (page 131). Plus a smattering of new Martin's Money Memories, including Rosie Millard (page 30), plus First Direct and 'Consumer Terrorism' (page 157).

The Stuff that Really Counts. The most important addition is, of course, the actual updating of the information. Things have changed in many areas: 18 months ago credit card balance transfer fees didn't exist; ISA rules have changed; new cut-cost telephone providers have entered the marketplace and technology and top providers have shifted. So everything has been updated to be as current as possible.

Plus to help future-proof this book, each Crash Diet section now has a specific web link which will take you to the exact page on my site where you can find the latest updated information – so the savings never stop!

I hope you enjoy the book, but most of all …
I hope you save some money!

Martin Lewis, MONEY SAVING EXPERT

WHAT IS THE MONEY DIET?

Money affects every element of our lives. To get a cab or a bus? To get a pension or an ISA? To buy or rent a DVD? All are money decisions. Every time you spend, you can save, so the Money Diet's scope is huge. For most people the Money Diet is just about how to get more for less. Yet, let's be honest, many people simply outspend their income. This is why it's a two-part plan. The first part comprises the pain-free steps to becoming a smart consumer – saving you thousands of pounds without any need to change your lifestyle. If, after that, there are more savings to be made, then I make no apologies for saying it may hurt and an effort is needed.

Now, I admit, grandiose money-making promises are common, usually in con-artists' adverts in shop windows or spam e-mail. This book doesn't promise to make you millions – that's impossible. Its aim is to make the money you've got go further, just by showing you how to use it better. For me, that really is making you rich. A magazine once asked me to save its definition of an average family as much as possible, by tackling 10 mainstream consumer finance products – the big, popular ones – in one go. For a family of two adults, each earning £24,000, the spending on these 10 products was estimated at £17,000. By using 'Money Diet' techniques it was possible to reduce this to £9,000. All in all, once you take into account the impact of tax on their salaries, this is actually the equivalent of a £6,000 salary rise each.

I will say now that the Money Diet does require some action on your part – but it will be worth it. Your finances will be better. You will have the peace of mind of knowing that no one is taking you for a ride. But most important, think about the benefits. What would you give for a 10, 20, or even 30 per cent pay rise? By spending your money more efficiently, you can make the equivalent of that gain. Think how many hours you'd have to work for 30 per cent more pay ... A little bit of time spent taking on the banks, building societies, retailers, service companies (and virtually anyone else who is trying to make a profit from you) is therefore time well spent.

HOW TO DO THE MONEY DIET

L ike any diet, the recipes depend on what you like – and how
quickly you need it to work.

There are three main options:

1. The Financial Blitz

If you're roaring keen to save a huge pan of cash or in dire
need of sorting out your spending and debts, do it all in one go.

2. The Slow Burn

If you'd rather spend the day listening to fingernails being
scraped down a blackboard than deal with your money, this is
for you. Do it right and you'll hardly notice, but after a year
you'll end up having massively cut your expenditure.

3. Blitz and Pieces

Politicians would call this 'the third way'. Start with the big and
easy savings, then just take it one step at a time over the year.

A MONEY BUDDY

Whichever regime you choose, it doesn't have to be a solitary
affair. The Money Diet is a perfect example of a problem

shared being a problem halved. Start the Money Diet with a friend – it makes the research easier and perhaps adds a level of competition about who can save the most. Money can occasionally be tricky; it has to be understood. I hope that by reading this book everything will quickly become clear. But if you do get stuck, you should be able to talk through any tricky bits together.

BEFORE YOU START

It's important to know what the Diet's different parts do and how and when to use them.

Part 1: Financial Fitness for Life

This is about how to mould your MoneySaving muscles to save cash on anything and everything. It's a journey through your money, how to deal with it, and how to stop companies getting one up on you. This was the most difficult section to write. My father tells the story that, as a little boy, I knew all my times tables only weeks after starting infant school. Yet for years after, while I got the sums right, I struggled to explain how. Until now, saving money's always been 'telling the answer'. Yet

'Financial Fitness' aims to show you how to think like a MoneySaver with the Money Diet's 10 Golden Ingredients (see page 16).

Part 2: The Crash Diet

Here it's all done for you: a practical product-by-product guide to getting the best deal, how much you can save, and how long each will take. The Calorie Counter on page xiv details all this in a simple table. With it you can start the big savings straight away.

Part 3: Healthy Eating

Mortgages, credit cards and personal loans – 'Healthy Eating' covers debt from all angles, from debt crisis to how to make a profit out of credit cards. The reason I wanted to dedicate an entire section to this is simply that debt is paying money for money itself, rather than any greater purpose, so cutting its cost is the purest form of MoneySaving.

Now let's take a closer look at your three Dieting options.

1. THE FINANCIAL BLITZ

The idea of sitting down and spending a day rummaging through paperwork and finances to find the best deals makes *me* salivate with glee. For some bizarre reason, this isn't a commonly shared feeling. For those of you for whom tackling finances is the emotional equivalent of watching paint dry, don't worry. A few simple steps will make it as painless as possible.

PLANNING
Read 'Financial Fitness for Life'. The 'Money Diet Budgeting Technique' is a very good way to start. After that move on to

'The Crash Diet' to ensure you take product providers to the very extreme and get the best deals. 'Healthy Eating' will advise you if you are in debt; if you're debt-free, it will show you how to profit from lenders.

Gather your papers. Collect all the paperwork and documents relating to your different money matters, so everything is in one place.

Establish current rates and prices. Make some phone calls and establish the rates and credit limits you are paying, so you have as much information as possible to hand when you start.

Choose the day. Every day isn't equal. The most important thing is that businesses should be open, ready and able to talk to you. Thus the very best day is a weekday, and the best time to make your calls is mid-morning or mid-afternoon when the phone lines are least busy. If you can't do the Financial Blitz on a weekday – after all, time is money – the next best day is a Saturday. Then again (he writes smiling) there's still a lot you can do on a Sunday … any day is better than none.

Time and travel. For some things you might need to head out to the high street, so make sure you've got time to be able to get there. If it's all too much, split this task over a couple of days.

PREPARATION

Paperwork. Lay out the paperwork, and compile and collate everything so that it's all to hand and nice and easy to see.

Use a 'to do' list. Prioritise the areas you want to tackle. The

'Calorie Counter' on page xiv shows you the potential savings on different types of products.

Facilities. A phone is incredibly important, but if possible also use an internet connection to speed up the research (see 'Talk to People', page 103).

EXECUTION

Big 'n' easy. Why not alternate big savings with easy savings? This way, once you've got a big saving under your belt, you can take a breather with an easy one next. This should keep you going – though regular breaks and a little food are helpful, too.

Running total. As the money saved starts to flood in, keep a running list of the savings so far. It may sound like an extra effort, but when you can see the amount of extra cash you'll have, it will enthuse you and motivate you to keep going. Think about what you could spend the money on, or simply how much money you will have in your bank account. It's empowering and stimulating and helps keep your resolve firm.

2. THE SLOW BURN

Whereas the Financial Blitz is like circuit training in a gym, the Slow Burn is more like a couple of lengths in a pool every fortnight.

PREPARATION

Understand. The most important thing about starting the Slow Burn is understanding the philosophy of the Money Diet. When you have the time (on the train, bus, plane, beach, waiting to pick the kids up, when there's nothing on the telly), read through 'Financial Fitness for Life'. While the Slow Burn doesn't advocate looking backwards to repair all the problems in your money matters, it does encourage you to say, 'From now on, I am always going to get the best possible deals.'

EXECUTION

Stop and think. Every time a bill pops through the letter box, every time you sign up for something new, every time you buy something – rather than just automatically renew, pause. Say, 'Today I am going to improve my finances.' Do this with every product and gradually the overall picture changes. As a rule of thumb, always tell yourself, 'I will check out three providers, not just one option.' This alone can revolutionise your finances.

Keep a money diary. Make a list of when and how much you save every time you've done a transaction. Use this to keep a running total and you will be amazed at the end of the year.

Things change. Do remember that situations sometimes change. Even if you've already switched a product, when each bill comes through from one quarter to the next, it's worth looking at it and asking, 'Am I still doing the right thing?'

3. BLITZ AND PIECES

When you've just bought this book and still have the Money Diet ethos running through your veins, do a Mini Blitz.

PREPARATION

Follow the 'Financial Blitz' guide for preparing to save. As for what to tackle, I would choose a mix of big and easy savings. Take on the big ones and save immediately; take on the easy and quick for a few extra pounds. Always base your choices on your own priorities, but if you're not sure, here's a selection.

- Gas & electricity ('Crash Diet', page 175)
- Credit card balance transfer ('Healthy Eating', page 372)
- Mortgage/remortgage ('Healthy Eating', page 322)
- Savings accounts (cash ISAs) ('Crash Diet', pages 215 and 223)
- Water bills ('Crash Diet', page 179)

EXECUTION

That's the 'Blitz' bit, and after seeing the scale of savings, you'll have bags of enthusiasm for the 'Pieces' part. Now follow the Slow Burn and change everything in simple and easy stages.

PART 1

FINANCIAL FITNESS FOR LIFE

HOW TO SAVE MONEY ON ANYTHING

THE 10 GOLDEN INGREDIENTS

Ensuring financial fitness for life involves more than just getting the best products. That works for the short to medium term, but what really drives continued savings is changing your mentality so that every time your fingers fondle loose change, you're going to be as smart a consumer as possible. Becoming a successful Money Dieter has two sides: taking yourself on and building up your financial muscles.

The first involves throwing aside financial fears and phobias and learning that money isn't a scary monster lurking in the cupboard, but simply a tool – and one you can easily master. That's why the first five ingredients focus on taking control of yourself and your spending urges.

Building up MoneySaving muscles does sometimes involve a fight. The opposition are product providers and service companies whose goal is to make as much money from us as possible. Our task is to stop them; that's why the second five form my 'self-defence class'.

1. You're In Charge

Don't be scared. It's what they want! The easiest way to lose a game is by not knowing the rules. But they really aren't that difficult. Be confident, be informed and invest a tiny bit of thought each time you spend or make any financial decision (page 19).

2. Prepare Your Pocket

Debt and savings are two sides of the same coin. Both are paying a set amount out of your salary each month, except that debt pays for something you've already had, while savings will pay for something you will have. The big difference is: with savings they pay you a little; with debt you pay *them* a *lot* of interest (page 28).

3. Know Thyself

We're all different. And this is our secret weapon. Providers tend to base their decisions on the conglomerated masses, but by knowing yourself and finding your niche you can play against these averages, and win (page 63).

4. Be a Better Shopper

Retail therapy at a price you can afford is possible. First, control your 'gotta have' impulses with the right money mantra. This control allows you time to think, so you can have more and pay less (page 77).

5. Forget Loyalty

Fact: No one financial services product-provider is top of the table for more than one product. Therefore, by definition, having two products from one company means at least one of them isn't the best. Forget loyalty; it only pays them, not you (page 90).

6. Talk to People

We live in a time of unrivalled access to information, yet as consumers most of us simply avoid taking advantage of this. STOP! Know what you are doing and you'll be the winner. It's a question of research, evidence and simply talking about money (page 103).

7. Haggle

There's no such thing as a fixed price. The ticket price is purely an indicator of what you need to pay. Legally they don't have to accept it, so you don't need to pay it (page 116)!

8. Holler

You have rights so use them! Just because you buy cheap doesn't mean you've no right to good service. And just because you've been with a company for a long time doesn't mean you should let them take you for granted. If they do, move on (page 129).

9. Think through their Logic

Shopping around isn't enough – you may just get the best of a bad bunch. To really see through their charades ask, 'How do they make money from me?' and 'How much do they make?' (page 142).

10. Find the Loopholes

They make money out of you so always ask, 'Can I make money out of them?' Companies assume everyone is lazy and apathetic; if you're not, you can surf a wave of offers to make money. Go on, twist their terms and conditions. You've everything to gain (page 150).

The next 10 chapters will describe each one of these golden ingredients in simple terms, teaching you how to think about and act with your money.

£one

YOU'RE IN CHARGE

Don't be scared. It's what they want! The easiest way to lose a game is by not knowing the rules. But they really aren't that difficult. Be confident, be informed and invest a tiny bit of thought each time you spend or make any financial decision.

DON'T LET THEM TAKE CONTROL

I called up to book a hotel. I knew where I was going and roughly what standard I wanted. There were two hotels that fitted the bill. When I asked the cost, the first said, 'That will be £60 for the night please, sir.' The next: 'That will be £60 for the night, please, sir, including, of course, our full breakfast, porterage service and unlimited use of our swimming pool and gym.' It was a no-brainer.

But then I had a thought. So I redialled the original hotel and asked, 'What's included in the price? Do you have a porterage service? Do you offer a full breakfast? Do you have a gym and a swimming pool?' And slap me down with a wad of fivers, as I suspected, it offered all those services, and all were included in the price. The only difference between the two hotels – *the second had sold itself better.*

We must take charge and set our own agenda if we don't want companies to lead us by the nose. The sales patter the hotel used is known as 'sandwiching': as when telling a customer about a sandwich, don't just mention the filling, tell them about the bread too. So it's a beef and horseradish sandwich on freshly baked wholemeal bread straight from the oven and covered with sesame seeds.

Yet for every sales manoeuvre there's a counter-manoeuvre. When you look at a sandwich, if it matters to you always compare the bread anyway. If the packet doesn't describe it fully, find all the information to make the best choice. By taking a considered decision rather than being sold to, you take control.

All Money is DIY Money

Financial blinkers are a curse. Many people abrogate the responsibility for their own money and finances, whether formally or informally. Some hire an independent financial adviser; some simply leave it to their husband, wife, partner, child, parents, grandparents, uncle, aunt or anyone else, if they can get away with it.

Realise, though, that even if you hand over the reins to someone else, it's still your money and ultimately you must take charge. Even if that person knows more about money than you do, just let him or her guide you. Don't ever let somebody tell you what to do – not even me. This book is here to coach, guide, encourage, train, motivate and edify you; it suggests answers, solutions, methodologies and tactics – but ultimately the decision is always yours.

There's nothing wrong with taking advice, but always question it and trust your instincts. In many walks of life, advisers make mistakes. Investment advisers or stockbrokers may know more about investments than you, but they don't know your future. Think about the factors that affect you, and remember that even close family members, friends and partners have agendas, thought-processes and terms of reference that differ from yours. You must make the decisions about your life, and you must make the decisions about your money. You are in charge.

Things Change

Now let me add something unpleasant. If you are married, it may not last for ever. You may get divorced, or your partner may die before you do. In either event, if you've never taken control of your money before, you will find yourself dealing with it, alone, and probably with less income, during a stressful time. This is a tragedy you mustn't allow to happen. Take an interest in your joint financial affairs right now; build up your understanding. I hope my dire warnings above are wrong. If so, all you've lost is a little time, but you'll have gained a great deal of knowledge. And if you discover your partner isn't a cornucopia of money know-how, together you can power through more savings.

FROM ICE CREAM TO PENSIONS: DON'T BE SCARED

Go on holiday, buy the kids a prezzie, visit a friend, have a drink on the way home from work – each affects your pocket. While many people say they hate making money decisions and consciously try to avoid them, unless you're spending the day sleeping in the park, it's impossible to avoid money. Yet most

21

money decisions don't scare us because we don't think of them as being 'financial', and as we're not scared when we think the decision through, we do it correctly.

However, when we hit the big stuff – the products that affect all our lives and delineate how wealthy we are – the financial fear factor is high. You hear it all the time: 'I don't understand,' 'I never know what to do with my cash,' 'I'm the worst person in the world with money.' Often it is said as a boast. Of course, in my life I hear it more than most; people say, 'You can't help me, I'm terrible with money.' This seems slightly strange logic to me – more sensible would be, 'You can't help me, I'm superb with money.' If you are trash with your cash, fantastic – the savings available from the Money Diet are huge.

While being bad with money is one thing, not dealing with it is criminal; it's the financial equivalent of self-harm. If you always ignore the price and never think about the cost, then you're probably always struggling with money. If you throw bills away without looking at them, your finances are probably critical. That one act alone slides a knife across the neck of your credit score. If that's you – STOP. You've done well getting this book; now it's time to take a deep breath and start repairing the damage. It can, and will, get better and easier.

As you'll discover, the differences between buying a stake-holder pension and an ice cream aren't that big.

THE FIVE-SECOND MONEY MAKEOVER

Having all the necessary information simplifies and improves decision-making. Throughout 'Financial Fitness for Life' I'll be introducing techniques to aid the process, but ultimately it all boils down to a single core concept – the 'five-second money makeover'. Which is: before you carry out any transaction, think 'What are the questions I should ask?' and once you've thought of them, ask them.

Asking should be pretty easy. Simply open your mouth and start speaking. Yet many of us feel stupid asking questions. This affects everyone. As a professional know-it-all, I panic when I need to ask a question. It's the fear that everyone else will know the answer and think your question bloody stupid. The other day, a pizza menu included 'fontina' cheese, something I'd never heard of. Was it a (yuck) blue cheese? After two deep breaths I asked and it was answered without a fuss. If it's a choice between your pride and your wallet (or palate), bite the bullet. When I was first taught to be a journalist, they always said, 'Remember to check who, what, where, when, how and why.' So ask questions – and as you read on, you'll discover this book is full of the kind of questions you should ask.

This is so important I really want to stress it. Ask questions! Ask questions! Ask questions! A lack of information is the prime weapon product-providers wield to put one over on us. Questions disarm them, and empower us.

THE LIST OF THERE'S NOTHING WRONG WITH...

1... *asking your partner how good your, and their, finances are.* Knowledge of your own financial situation is crucial. You need to be assured that, independently as well as together, you would be fine. This isn't selfish. If you care about your partner, make sure their financial fitness is good too. Remember, they might not be as good with money as they think they are, and two heads are always better than one. So take charge of your future, and look out for them, too, while you're doing so.

2... *asking for a discount.* There's nothing to lose. No one ever gets thrown out of a shop for politely asking for a reduction. No one ever gets hung up on for asking to pay just a little bit less. So why not have a go, and see how much you can save? (See 'Haggle', page 116.)

3... *bringing sandwiches to work if you're on a budget.* Don't be embarrassed; do it with pride. Maybe if you start the trend your work colleagues will find financial freedom too and do the same. And if anyone asks why, don't say, 'I can't afford to go out and buy lunch every day,' say, 'I'm budgeting because I want to spend more on things that are more important.'

4... *asking for money you've lent to be paid back to you.* It was generous of you to help your friend out, so why be embarrassed to ask for your money back if you need it? One easy way, when you lend the money, is to set a time and a date for when you will ask for it back. Be upfront – it's much less embarrassing than beating round the bush. A quick 'Hey, remember that £20 you borrowed from me – any chance you've got it? I could do with it now' is more polite and easier to deal with than obfuscated hints. If they were bold enough to ask you for a loan, you can be bold enough to ask them for it back.

5... *not splitting the bill evenly.* Why do we have meals with friends in restaurants and agree to split the bill evenly, even when some drink or eat much more than others? If someone generously wants to pay for all, great, but by splitting evenly perhaps you're unwittingly making a debt-ridden, financially strapped friend pay for your wine. While technically the best solution is for everyone to calculate what they owe, that's a complete nightmare. My technique is what I call the 'Easy Honour System'. At the end of the meal, everybody should contribute what they think they owe, including the tip. Most people get it roughly right, but of course when you total up you'll almost always be short – it's human nature. So divide the shortfall by the number of people – let's say there's £50 difference and 10 friends, everybody then puts in an extra £5. It may not be completely accurate, but it's a quick and easy way for people to pay near enough what they should. It helps you budget, without losing friends or looking too mean.

6... *asking family for an interest-free loan, if they can help.* Too often people hide their debts. One guy I worked with was paying hideous rates of interest on his loans. He was only young. He spoke to me, looking for help. When we talked through the options it turned out his parents could quite read-ily pay, but he simply hadn't told them he was in trouble. As he had no other access to cheap credit I asked him to speak to his family. While there was a little bit of embarrassment, his parents lent him the money, interest-free. If necessary, it's fair for family members to charge a low but reasonable interest rate. After encouragement, the young man signed a formal document to establish that it was a loan, not a gift. This transported him out of financial trouble immediately, without losing too much family face.

When I wrote this in the first edition, the loan had only just happened. Now I'm pleased to report the debt's fully paid off. He's completely debt-free, earning more money and preparing to buy a house.

7... asking friends how much they paid for something and where they got it from. There's nothing wrong with freely trading information. The fact that we all like to keep quiet about our finances helps us all get ripped off. Friends often have similar interests, so when they do something or own something you might want, ask them, 'How much did you pay, and where did you get it from?' It sets up an easy point of reference for the future. And make sure they feel free to ask you the same. (See 'Talk to People', page 103.)

8... saying 'I don't understand'. Being confused is an easy way to get ripped off. If the person explaining something to you understands it, so can you. Make them explain it step by step until you get it. There's nothing wrong with going back to basics. Everyone should be concerned that they are making the right decisions based on the right facts, and therefore should always make time to ensure they understand them.

9... asking for a payrise. If you need more cash, ask your employer. This empowers you and puts the onus on them to

> **Martin's Money Memories: She Already Had the Lipstick On**
>
> Caroline is a WPC with London's Metropolitan Police. She's in her mid-30s, with two kids. She was one of my first 'Money Makeovers' on ITV1's *This Morning*. She described herself as being absolutely abysmal with money. But when we sat down, she started talking about her mortgage. Having watched the programme, and listened to me spouting on, she had already changed her provider. And that change alone meant a saving of over £1,000 a year. Then we came to credit cards and loans. Again the same, another annual £1,000 already saved.
>
> Now, of course, there was more I could save her. I'm not suggesting that everybody will make these kinds of savings right off the bat. The very best deals take time and some expertise. Yet even without any help from me, Caroline had saved herself a good wodge. And most people, just by taking a little time, can generate an equivalent scale of saving. It's all about deciding, perhaps for the first time in your life, to take charge of your finances and do it yourself. If it's a kick up the backside you need, then hopefully, as you read *The Money Diet*, you'll feel the thwack!

say no. And, incidentally, them saying no is about the worst that can happen. Remember you're trained, valued and experienced. Bringing in new people is costly. Giving you a bit more and keeping you happy may just be good business. If you don't ask you don't get.

10... *saying no.* Don't be sold to out of politeness, and don't accede to pressure. You're in charge. Only you know your financial situation, only you live your life, only you can decide what's right for you – don't let others browbeat you into a decision. Sense isn't common.

two

PREPARE YOUR POCKET

Debt and savings are two sides of the same coin. Both are paying a set amount out of your salary each month, except that debt pays for something you've already had, while savings will pay for something you will have. The big difference is: with savings they pay you a little; with debt you pay *them* a *lot* of interest.

'I'M ALWAYS SKINT AFTER CHRISTMAS'

Sitting in a bar one cold January evening with a well-paid friend who works in the City, I suggested we order some food. She turned to me and said, 'Would you mind if we just got drinks? I'm skint.' Now I was quite surprised by this. Why was she skint? Her answer, 'Christmas, of course.' 'And?' I asked again. 'What do you mean, and?' she said. 'It's just been Christmas. I've spent loads of money. I'm skint.'

Now, you're probably thinking, what's he going on about? Christmas is a good reason for spending. The festivities, the presents, going out, office parties, meeting people, and the excuse to spend and shop. So I'd like to point out a little fact – Christmas happens on 25 December every year; it's not unexpected. Yet many people try to pay for it out of December's money, and this is often doomed to failure – leaving a post-Christmas credit hangover to accompany alcohol's mists. This isn't just a Christmas phenomenon: it applies to tax bills, summer holidays and a lot more.

AVOID A SPIRALLING FINANCIAL DESCENT

Let's look at the potential consequences of what my friend did. All her spending on food, drink, gifts and décor was in the pre-Christmas run-up – the time when shops traditionally charge the most. When January rolls round, the sales are on and it's the cheapest time to buy. In her job she has to look good and feels the need to buy designer clothing. But she has no money left in January to take advantage of the bargains, so she has to wait and buy her clothes later in the year instead. This means it costs her a lot more, dropping her finances down yet another step. So by the time next Christmas arrives, she's still paying for the last one. And thus starts the spiral.

BIG, BOLD AND BLOODY IMPORTANT

Spend more than you earn = DEBT
Continue to spend more than you earn = WORSENING DEBT
Never deal with it = DEBT CRISIS

For more on debt crisis see page 411 (it isn't pleasant!)

Budget, Plan, Prepare

The weapons to fight downward-spiralling finances are budget, plan and prepare. These aren't necessarily easy, but are easily necessary. Even those lucky enough to have a bigger income than expenditure will benefit.

Martin's Money Memories: A Future Looking Rosie?

Presenter, buy-to-let columnist, former BBC Arts correspondent, Rosie Millard, was in trouble. Despite owning over £2 million worth of property, she was splashed across the papers as suffering from 'middle-class debt crisis'.

We share an agent and had worked together before, so when I read these reports, I sent her an e-mail asking if she needed a chat (although a bit 'jolly hockey sticks', she's a lovely woman). As it happened I needn't have bothered. Soon afterwards a call came from ITV's *Tonight with Trevor McDonald* asking if I'd do a money makeover on her.

It wouldn't have taken Hercule Poirot to deduce the problem. It slapped me like a moist kipper as I walked in – this was a pure case of poor planning. No budget, no plan, no balanced finances and thus no cash.

With a salary of around £200,000 between her and her husband, it wasn't a lack of money but a lack of available money that was the problem. The papers had blamed credit cards, but they weren't too bad. Rosie's a tart (of the credit card variety, of course), constantly shifting 0 per cent debts.

Whilst the viewers saw a piece focused mainly on the social side of debt, in practical terms I handed Rosie a 10-point plan. Some were very hard-core techniques for reducing the cost of debts. She was also over-reliant on property so I advised her to consider selling one of her four houses, but the real key was to do a budget, to control her expenditure and start piggybanking.

Rich or poor – managing your cash is a must.

Forgotten Gold – Don't Lose Your Payrise

When we get a payrise, we feel richer and we liberalise our spending habits. This means we rarely actually feel the gain. It's forgotten gold. After all, most people tend to think they should be paid roughly three times what they currently earn. Unfortunately, if we got that rise, soon afterwards we'd still believe a three-times payrise was due again. It's our own personal inflation.

The way to deal with this is 'shrink to fit'. As soon as you get a payrise, rework your money so you actually gain. Allocate increased savings, debt repayments and provisions immediately, before you adjust your expectations. Follow through the Money Diet budget plan, and put your newfound wealth towards a good financial future. Otherwise it's just fool's gold.

The Piggybank Technique

Piggybanks are an extremely clever idea. They sit in the corner of the room and you put money in them. You don't really notice the absence of the money as it disappears from your pocket. Yet gradually the coins add up, waiting for the proverbial rainy day.

My Money Diet budgeting technique is inspired by piggybanks, as will become apparent.

The Mr Micawber Corner

'My other piece of advice, Copperfield,' said Mr Micawber, 'you know. Annual income twenty pounds, annual expenditure nineteen nineteen six, result happiness. Annual income twenty pounds, annual expenditure twenty pounds ought and six, result misery. The blossom is blighted, the leaf is withered, the god of day goes down upon the dreary scene, and – and, in short, you are forever floored. As I am!' (From *David Copperfield* by Charles Dickens)

The debtors' prisons of Dickens's day may have left us, but attempting to spend within your means is as tough as ever. Remember that money is a two-sided coin – that debt and savings are opposite sides of the same coin. Know how much you can afford to spend and you win the toss. On one side is debt, which is simply paying money out of your salary after you've bought something, with the added burden of interest. On the other is saving, which is simply paying money out of your salary before you've bought something, but this time they pay you the interest.

Proper planning will help turn debts into savings, shifting the odds in your favour.

A FOUR-STEP 'HAPPINESS' PLAN

There are four simple steps to keep your expenditure below your income. You can follow these alone, or as part of a couple or family. Just be consistent – if you start them for a couple, make sure you fill in the total spending for both, down to the smallest article of clothing. Do it alone, then only put in your proportion of any rent or mortgage.

Step 1: Don't Trust Your Bank Account

Bank accounts are devious and cunning beasts. When you get paid, they seduce you into believing the cash in there is the cash you have available to spend. Yet this wanton temptation is a terrible vice. Bank accounts lie!

We spend money in many ways and over many time periods. Purchases are daily, weekly, monthly or one-offs. However, your bank account presents only a snapshot of how much money is in your account at that moment. It ignores where you are in your money cycle – receiving your salary and paying your bills don't necessarily coincide. It also forgets that though Christmas comes but once a year, its cost should be spread all year round; so should holidays. Yet knowing the logic is no protection, so let's move on to step two.

Step 2: Discover What Your Real Monthly Spend Is

It isn't as obvious as it seems, as it's important to incorporate all the real demands on your income. To help, I've developed the Money Diet Monthly Calorie Counter.

You'll see a detailed chart on page 36. All you have to do is fill it in. After each category you can choose whether to enter the spending as per week, per month or per year – just fill in whichever is appropriate. Don't panic if you don't know exactly how much you spend on something. A good guess is better than giving up.

Some pointers:

Only count things once. Some spending may overlap – if you've already counted it, don't count it again.

Overestimation is better than underestimation. Honesty pays dividends. Fight that very human temptation to lie to yourself about your spending, and if you're not sure, pick more not less. If you overestimate you'll have money left over rather than still being short.

Don't forget anything. There's bound to be something you spend on that's not on the list – have a think and make sure you fit it in, either in an 'others' section or the 'odds and sods' at the end. If you're struggling, do it over a week, as each day's activities should act as a reminder. This will help remind you where your cash goes.

Money-save while you write. As well as counting the calories as you write the numbers down, always ask yourself, 'Is this really the best deal I can get?'

Okay – now fill in just Part A of the chart. Once this is completed, work out what your real monthly spending is by filling in Part B, the 'monthly total' column. To do this you will (probably) need a calculator.

For things in the Per Week column: Multiply the amount by 4.33 (the average number of weeks in a month) and put the answer in the 'monthly total' column.

For things in the Per Month column: Move the answer straight over to the 'monthly total' column.

For things in the Per Year column: Divide the amount by 12 and put the answer in the 'monthly total' column.

Now total up each section and write the answer below.

Home total per month _____
Insurance total per month _____
Eats, Drinks & Smokes total per month _____
Transport and Travel total per month _____
Debt Repayments total per month _____
Savings & Investments total per month _____
Family total per month _____
Fun and Frolics total per month _____
Big One-offs total per month _____
Clothes total per month _____
Education, Courses and Classes total per month _____
Odds and Sods total per month _____
Total Monthly Expenditure _____

The Money Diet Calorie Counter: Now it's Mechanical!

I received an amazing e-mail after the first edition of *The Money Diet*. One reader, Tony, said 'The calorie counter's made a massive difference to me, I'd love to give something back.' As a techie, his gift was to design a fully automated version of this calorie counter, which is now available, for free of course, at www.moneysavingexpert.com/budget

It's an amazingly easy-to-use piece of kit, but read the more detailed what to do description here first.

Thanks Tony!

Money Diet Monthly Calorie Counter				PART B	PART C
	FILL IN FOR PART A			Monthly total	Monthly desired
	Per week	Per month	Per year		
HOME					
Mortgage/Rent					
Household maintenance					
Home & contents insurance					
Council tax					
Water rates/Meter					
Gas bill					
Electricity bill					
Oil bill					
Home phone bill					
Internet bill					
Mobile phone bill(s)					
Cleaning products/cleaner					
Garden maintenance					
Other home					
TOTAL HOME					
INSURANCE					
Level-term assurance					
Private medical insurance					
Healthcare cashback scheme					
Pet insurance					
Travel insurance					
Gas & plumbing cover					
Other insurance					
TOTAL INSURANCE					

Money Diet Monthly Calorie Counter	FILL IN FOR PART A			PART B	PART C
	Per week	Per month	Per year	Monthly total	Monthly desired
EATS, DRINKS & SMOKES					
Food shopping					
Eating out					
Coffee/sandwiches out					
Meals at work					
Pet food					
Drink for home					
Drinking out					
Smoking					
Other eats, drinks & smokes					
TOTAL EATS					
TRANSPORT AND TRAVEL					
Rail/bus/coach/taxi					
Car maintenance					
Car insurance					
Car tax					
Petrol					
Parking					
AA/RAC membership					
Other car					
TOTAL TRANSPORT					
DEBT REPAYMENTS (just the average amount repaid, not the total debt)					
Car loan repayments					
Personal loan repayment					
HP repayments					
Credit card repayment					
Other loan repayment					
TOTAL DEBT REPAYMENTS (REMEMBER DO NOT DOUBLE COUNT: If you've noted your spending elsewhere, then don't add it in the debt repayment column)					

Money Diet Monthly Calorie Counter				PART B	PART C
	FILL IN FOR PART A			Monthly total	Monthly desired
	Per week	Per month	Per year		
SAVINGS & INVESTMENTS (how much you pay in, not how much is in there)					
Saving schemes					
Mini cash ISAs					
Investments					
Buying shares					
Pension payments					
Other savings/investments					
TOTAL SAVINGS					
FAMILY					
Childcare/playschemes					
Babysitting					
Children's travel					
Laundry/dry cleaning					
School meals					
Pocket money					
Nappies/baby extras (e.g. baby wipes)					
Other family					
TOTAL FAMILY					
FUN AND FROLICS					
Hobbies					
Pet costs					
Fitness/sports/gym					
Shopping for fun					
Big days out					
Books/music/DVDs/ computer games					
Cinema/theatre trips					
Family days out					
NTL/Sky subscription					
TV licence					
DVD/video rental					
Other fun and frolics					
TOTAL FUN AND FROLICS					

Money Diet Monthly Calorie Counter	FILL IN FOR PART A			PART B	PART C
	Per week	Per month	Per year	Monthly total	Monthly desired
BIG ONE-OFFS (for things spent less than once a year, divide the total by the number of years and put it in the per year column)					
Cost of Christmas					
Cost of summer holiday					
Cost of winter holiday					
Cost of birthdays					
Cost of new sofa/kitchen/ TV/other electrical					
Other big one-offs					
TOTAL BIG ONE-OFFS					
CLOTHES					
New clothes					
New children's clothes					
Work clothes					
Other clothes					
TOTAL CLOTHES					
EDUCATION, COURSES AND CLASSES					
Your courses/classes					
School fees					
University tuition fees					
Other education costs					
TOTAL EDUCATION					
ODDS AND SODS (anything that doesn't fit anywhere else)					
Regular charity donations					
Tax and NI provisions (self-employed only)					
Newspapers & magazines					
Dentistry					
Optical bills					
Complementary therapies					
Haircuts					
Beauty treatments					
Other odds and sods					
TOTAL ODDS AND SODS					

Step 3: Work Out What You Can Spend Each Month

You've got your answer ... are you shocked? Don't worry – almost everyone is. It's almost always more than you thought. This is because lots of money floats away through direct debits, standing orders and cheques without really entering our consciousness. Plus those big one-offs aren't usually counted this way, so when you add them in it can hurt.

Don't panic, though. Let's see if your spending is affordable by discovering what your income is. It shouldn't be as tough, but here's a table to help. All figures should be after tax.

How much do you earn each month?	
Income	After tax monthly earnings*
Average earnings from employment/ self-employment	
Incomes taken each month from savings/investments	
Pensions and annuity payouts (state and private)	
Benefits, including child benefit, child tax credit, income support, council tax benefit	
Gifts or help from family or friends	
Other	
TOTAL	

*If the income isn't monthly, then use the same system as in the Calorie Counter (previous pages) to work out the monthly equivalent you receive.
*If you're self-employed, then use untaxed earnings and fill in the tax and NI provisions in the Calorie Counter.

At this point it's back to Mr Micawber.

HAPPINESS!

Your income is bigger than your expenditure – 'happiness'. HOORAH. Apart from jumping up and down for joy, you're also relatively safe in the knowledge you can afford to save a little more or treat yourself a little better. However, that isn't a reason not to do the Money Diet or to plan. Just because you have spare cash doesn't mean you should throw it away. In one *Make Me Rich* makeover, I found a family who were 'happy'. Another £12,000 a year, by being better consumers, made them happier!

MISERY!

Your expenditure is bigger than your income – 'misery'. This tends to be a more common outcome. You're probably saying 'Wooaaah' – or maybe something more colourful – 'do I really overspend by that much?' And you're right to be shocked because it is a problem. Continued overspending isn't sustainable: you will get into debt, with more and more of your salary going to pay interest, leaving less and less to spend, making it even worse. It's time to cut your expenditure.

There are three ways:

Pain-free. This is the prime Money Diet aim. Use the cheapest and best-value products and services to mash down your spending. Do the Crash Diet (Part 2) and follow the Healthy Eating Guide (Part 3). If you're doing this exercise as part of the Financial Blitz (see page 9), great. Before you do anything else, make the product changes and then redo the table with the new figures. Hopefully, it'll reduce your personal deficit.

Pain-ful. If switching products isn't enough, then it's ouch time – you need to cut your spending. This has to be done honestly, though; don't arbitrarily cut down your paper spending unless you mean it. If you then think 'Damn it' and end up spending more than you've put aside, this whole exercise is lost.

Painless pain. There are many spending cuts that shouldn't hurt much – saving a little less, eating out a little less, taking control of your phone habit, turning the lights off as soon as you leave the room. Taking videos/DVDs back to the rental shop on time. Filling the petrol tank when it's still half-full, to give you time to shop around for the cheapest. These are the types of thing people typically laugh at when they explain to me how bad they are with money. Stop laughing. Pay attention to them. Then start smiling.

All spending reductions hurt. However, I make no apology for saying that they are necessary and you must spend within your means. This is about continually running through your expenditure until you have cut out everything you can.

THE LIST OF 101 EASY WAYS TO CUT BACK

My number-one speciality is how to cut your bills without cutting back. Yet there are times when thrift is necessary. To help, I asked scores of moneysavingexpert.com users for the things they found easiest to do to cut back and stretch their cash further.

- Use white vinegar instead of numerous cleaning products – it works and it's cheap
- Cancel unused digital/satellite television channels
- Only use half a dishwasher tablet per wash
- Grow your own fruit and veg

- Use government MOT test centres (they've no vested interest in prescribing repairs for your car so it's more likely to pass)
- Take a packed lunch to work
- Use energy-saving light bulbs
- Close the fridge door quickly to save energy
- Don't leave electrical goods on standby
- Take out a magazine subscription if you always buy a mag each month anyway – it's cheaper
- Quit smoking
- Walk/cycle instead of using the car for short distances
- Try camping for your holiday
- Invest in a slow cooker – MoneySaving/time saving rolled into one
- Use rechargeable batteries
- Use empty Coke/water bottles, filled with tap water, as dumbbells
- Keep your old perfume bottles in your undies drawer – that way the drawer will always smell fresh without using liners
- If you're cooking using pans, place your plates on top to get them heated, instead of using the lids. Be careful they don't overheat
- Start a compost heap
- Use the coach rather than the train – you can get cheap tickets
- Try for student night haircuts at top salons
- Stock up monthly at Aldi, Netto or Lidl for the staple food-stuffs
- Buy fruit and veg at your local market
- Check out local ads/eBay for gym equipment then kit out your garage – it's cheaper than joining a gym

- Use your local beauty college for cut-price beauty treatments
- Buy cheap cola to flush down the toilet to keep it sparkling clean
- Go to the cinema 241 with the Orange Wednesday deal
- Try house swapping for an alternative and different holiday
- If the oven is on, use it well – cook multiple meals/cakes and freeze them
- Don't have the heating on and the windows open
- Use a sponge/buff puff in the shower to reduce the amount of shower gel required
- Borrow rather then buy
- Use your library for internet access, books and DVDs
- When making tea or coffee, only fill the kettle with the amount of water required
- Start a car share scheme at work – MoneySaving and environmentally friendly
- Try going to the supermarket late night when they have more reduced items
- Cut out snacks between meals – healthier and you'll save a fortune
- Keep kids happy with new toys every two weeks by using a local toy lending library
- Don't 'rinse and repeat' when shampooing your hair – one application is enough
- Buy some clippers and cut your own hair or your family's/friends'
- Use vegetable cooking water to make your gravy – conserves heat and vitamins
- Organise a clothes-swapping party with your friends – one (wo)man's trash is another (wo)man's treasure…!
- Brew your own beer

- Keep the fridge/freezer free of ice if not a frost-free one
- When shopping, write a list and keep to it
- Have a shower instead of a bath – it saves heating and water
- Bulk buy milk, bread and cheese when reduced and freeze it
- Check the cistern for leaks, easily done with food colouring – you may well be losing a lot of water
- Organise fun nights in for friends and family instead of going out
- Bake your own bread – no need to buy a bread machine, by hand is good enough
- Keep your fridge only half-full – if you overfill your fridge it will take longer for the food to cool as it slows the flow of the cold air
- Use e-mail instead of the phone or texts (and text for free on the web)
- Use cotton wool and lotion/water rather than baby wipes
- Turn your central heating thermostat down by one degree – you're unlikely to notice the difference in the heat, but you'll notice the difference on the bill
- Find out about local food co-operatives where you buy in bulk and split between you
- Ensure that your current tax code is correct or you could be paying more than is necessary
- Use money-off coupons, online and offline – save the money off in a piggybank, don't spend it
- Car boot or eBay unwanted possessions
- Become a vegetarian, or at least cut down meat intake
- Never go shopping when you're hungry
- When you're hiring any kind of equipment do it over bank holidays so you'll get a free day's hire
- Don't buy anything 'new' EXCEPT food and underwear

- Turn off lights if you aren't in the room
- Recycle items like old envelopes as shopping lists
- Plan your meals in advance and stick to it
- Retain your mobile instruction book – they often give you money back if you return it!
- Make things, if you can, rather then buying them – surprise yourself and be arty!
- If using storage heaters, watch the weather forecast as you might be able to turn them off for a day or two – no point wasting electricity
- Don't use vending machines – particularly for drinks and cans – buy a flask and save a fortune
- Buy toys and children's books from car boot sales – prices start around 10p!
- On days off, cook meals and freeze them – especially for days when you're too tired to cook and would normally end up with a takeaway
- Always take into consideration the cost of fuel when you drive to the (cheaper) shops
- Use vinegar as a fabric softener and add a couple of drops of essential oil for a fresh scent
- Instead of buying special scented ironing water just use water and a few drops of essential oil in a spray bottle – shake before use
- Check if your local catering college has a restaurant attached – good food at cheap prices
- Use *www.fixtureferrets.co.uk* or *www.madabout bargains.com* to identify special offers at your local super-market
- Get a calendar to record when bills need to be paid or library books need to be returned

- Use 'economy' settings on appliances where possible
- Use free/opensource software on your PC – usually just as good as its costly equivalent
- Before you throw cleansing wipes away, use them to clean the basin
- Check out PC magazine cover disks rather than buying software
- Make your own posh perfumed body lotion by adding basic unscented lotion to the empty bottle
- Buy remanufactured ink cartridges rather than new, or even better, refill
- When buying a PC, don't buy a monitor, just reuse an old one
- Wipe over stainless steel kitchen appliances with a little baby oil on a clean rag – comes up like new
- Renew library books over the phone or online to save potential fines
- Check out charity shops, especially for vintage clothes or books
- Lay your dishcloth on top of the dirty stuff in the dishwasher and it will be cleaned at the same time
- Go to bed 30 minutes earlier than usual – get more rest and save on electricity!
- Put a water-saving device in your toilet cistern (such as a water-filled Coke bottle) if you have a meter
- When cooking slow-cook dishes, turn the oven off five minutes early – there should be enough residual heat for it to continue cooking
- Don't buy gifts, give vouchers for your time, like 'cook a meal' or 'tickle your feet!'
- Never take the children to the supermarket with you!!!!
- When you go on holiday, switch appliances off

- Always check the price by weight of products at the supermarket – you may be surprised to discover what the cheapest version is
- Use a defunct shower curtain as a garden water slide for the kids – you get a faster slide if you put a few drops of washing-up liquid in the water
- Use a shelf in your airing cupboard to dry clothes rather than putting the heating on or using the dryer
- Use baby wipes to spot-clean clothes
- Rinse milk bottles with cold water and then use the rinsings to water house plants – the milk is a mild fertiliser
- Cut old tights into strips and use as ties in the garden – much better than string
- Don't buy shaving cream/lotion for your legs – conditioner works just as well and softens up the skin too

THE CAPPUCCINO CONTRACT

To cut back, use Part C – the monthly desired spend column in the tables (pages 36–9) – to set yourself a limit for each category. Once done, that's your new limit. You need to be conscious of it. Stick it on a pinboard, and always be aware of what you're doing.

Alternatively, use the old 'spending diary' and note down everything you buy, no matter how small. When you look back, you'll be surprised at how much you spend on the tiniest of things. I call this the 'Cappuccino Contract' because you may need to agree with yourself that from now on there'll be no more cappuccinos – that £2 every day at work is £500 a year. Unfortunately, it may be necessary to cut back on a lot more than coffee – going out, new clothes or a takeaway may be too expensive. Be creative and thoughtful, but ruthless. This is one of the most important decisions you'll make. And

---

The Four Golden Numbers

When it comes to spending, the golden numbers are 12, 52, 250 and 365. When you're trying to cut back, use these numbers to see the real significance of your expenditure:

X 12 when you buy or spend once a month

X 52 when you buy or spend once a week

X 250 when you buy or spend every working day

X 365 when you buy or spend every day

For example, if you buy a £1 bottle of Coke and a 50p packet of crisps every working day then £1.50 x 250 = £375.

That's how much you'd save by cutting it out. (Never mind the weight you would lose!)

---

always remember, £10 a month mightn't sound much, but saving £120 a year is worthwhile.

Sometimes we need shouting at or scaring. So let me do it here. If you're not convinced of the need to manage your money, turn to 'Debt Crisis', page 411. Read some of the stories. It may be that getting the bus instead of a taxi could just tip the balance in your favour.

Step 4: Trust Your Piggybank

Your budget is set. Now we need to make it as easy as possible to stick to it. To do that we must turn 'It's the beginning of the month. I can go shopping, hoorah!' into 'It's the end of the month. I've got money left, I'll go shopping.'

You may laugh at the thought of ever having money left at the end of the month, yet stop spending at the beginning of it and there may be more than you think. The trick is to take temptation out of your path with a wee bit of organisation.

This is where my piggybanking comes into action. It's about putting your money into different piggybanks. In practical terms, these are different bank accounts, each designated for certain types of spending. Every month, as soon as you are paid, siphon off the right proportion of money (according to your planned budget) into each of these accounts.

The accounts you choose depend on your particular spending patterns, but let me use an example to explain. Let's assume you set up the following five accounts in addition to your normal day-to-day account.

- Bills (including mortgage)
- Family food
- Holidays
- Christmas
- Savings

When I say different accounts, I literally mean using separate current accounts at your bank. Even better, put the cash in a savings account (preferably high-interest) with easy withdrawal facilities so it will earn decent interest too (see page 215). There's usually no problem having more than one account at one bank, and there's definitely no problem having a few accounts at different banks. You could even just do it by allocating amounts on a computer or on paper, as long as you keep it up to date and stick to your plan. Do whatever you feel most comfortable with.

Once you have the new account, automate moving the budgeted amount of money there on the day (or day after, to be safe) you are paid. This can be done by direct debit, standing order or manually.

The goal here is to leave in your main account only the money available to spend, and no more. The other accounts will contain the money to meet specific demands on your cash. This may mean that now you can see you can't afford the first-class holiday you wanted, but in reality you couldn't before either. At least now you'll vacation with the peace of mind that you won't suffer the rest of the year because of it. Do this and your bank account will finally be trustworthy.

DIFFERENT PIGGYBANK BANKING ACCOUNTS

The piggybank technique should be honed to your own needs. Each account is a box separating its spending from all others. This controls the impulse to overspend. Use accounts that best fit your buying – for example, you might use a 'Major Purchases' account when you want to buy a new washing machine to see directly what you can afford to spend. To help, here are a few options – but there are as many possible accounts as ways to spend.

1. Holiday spending There's nothing wrong with going on holiday, but there is something wrong with trying to pay for it all in the month before you go. A holiday is an annual expenditure that needs planning by putting aside a little bit of money each month.

Let's say you take two holidays a year costing £1,000 each, for both travel and spending money (easily done with a family). That's £2,000 a year, the equivalent of £166 a month. If, each month, you put this aside in a special account, when it comes to buying your holiday, the money is waiting for you. You then know exactly what your holiday spending limit is, and can enjoy it without the worry of knowing you're going to be skint.

2. 'Rainy day' fund Everyone needs a rainy day fund (known in financial circles as an 'emergency cash fund'). You never know what's going to happen in your life. In truth, we should all have three to six months' income saved away, so that we're ready for any emergency. This does sound a huge amount, and it's not the type of thing you can save up in a year. But there's nothing wrong with starting to siphon money away for a rainy day. (See 'Where to Start with Savings', page 209.)

3. Shopping and big purchases account Put some money in a special account for big purchases or clothes shopping. Start to build it up and you will know what you've got available to spend. It may even allow you to make the one-off big purchase you've always dreamed of. It could be a car, a television, a DVD recorder, a designer suit, a dress for a wedding. It could be anything, but now it won't have to come out of your day-to-day funds.

You can even have two 'buying' accounts, as long as they're correctly budgeted. For example, a big purchase fund and a shopping fund for monthly spending – an especially useful replacement for those people who habitually get out the plastic and spend without thinking.

4. Christmas account This is the one that's crucial for my friend (see page 28): the Christmas fund. Make a habit of putting cash aside for Christmas each month, and you can have a good time without having to worry about debts in January or missing the sales.

5. Self-employed tax account This is crucial. If you're self-employed, as soon as you are paid, immediately siphon off a chunk of the cash to pay your tax bill. That money simply isn't yours. Failing to do this can cause a nightmare. This way the money earns you interest, there's no 'tax bill shock' and you will hopefully have cash left over. I'd suggest higher rate taxpayers put 40 per cent aside, basic rate 25 per cent.

THE TRANSITIONAL STAGE

This budgeting technique works a treat when it's up and running. However, it's important to acknowledge that moving from unplanned to planned finances can be difficult. Changing over from your old habits to new ones does take a bit more discipline.

If you've old debts to pay off from past poor planning, this can leave your finances tightly squeezed during this stage. It's worth the investment though – a couple of months of slightly less jangly pockets and in the long run your money life will be a whole lot easier. You'll know what you've got to spend, and you will have more money when you need it.

If you do it right there will be no more 'I'm always skint after Christmas' and you will be able to shop in the sales. There will also be less 'We really can't afford that holiday.' Dare I say it – I know it's a boring word – 'sensible' planning will mean you actually have more.

TAKING THE DISCIPLINE UP A LEVEL
Piggycash

For those who need it, there's an even more stringent way to enforce this discipline. It takes the main Piggybank technique and turns it into the Piggycash technique. To really enforce some self-discipline, rather than having the money sitting in

---

Cash-machine Inflation

It's a phenomenon of our age. When most of us want cash, we put our plastic in the hole in the wall, and it magically appears. Yet ... let me ask you a question: do you now withdraw more money each trip than you used to?

Personally I don't like carrying too much in my wallet, so I usually take out quite small amounts. Even so, it used to be £20, but now it's £30 a time. The interesting thing, though, is that I tend to spend the £30 in the same amount of time as I did the £20. This is cash-machine inflation.

The truth is, we often count one trip to the cash machine as an actual amount of money – let's call it a HIT (Hole In T'wall). The number of HITs in a week tends to be reasonably static, so reducing the value of a HIT can help govern your expenditure. In other words, get less cash when you go to a cash machine. If you usually take out £50, start taking £40 out.

This might all sound slightly simplistic, but it does work. We tend to use the amount of money we've got in our pocket to judge the actual amount of money readily available to spend. If there's less there, you can't spend as much, or at least you need to make the extra effort of going to the cash machine to get more out – and this hassle in itself is good as each trip is a vivid reminder that you've been spending money.

---

your current account, withdraw a set amount of cash each week, and no more. If you are going to do this, the best time is a Monday morning – that way you know 'spend now and there's nothing for the weekend'. This also means that if you've done well during the week, you can reward yourself by spending the cash you've got left once you come to the weekend.

The Double Dip

The final trick in the Money Diet cash-machine-cracking arsenal is the 'double dip'. To do this, don't ever put the cash

Martin's Money Memories: There's Nothing Wrong with Flying Concorde

One of my scariest professional memories is an appearance on ITV1's *Loose Women* – a show with four female presenter panelists, and an audience full of women. Being the sole man in a room full of women usually has an appeal. Yet when I was introduced with the words, 'Guess what? We've got a bloke joining us. He's going to be talking about shopping. And he says you're all useless at it,' it felt similar to climbing K2 with non-stick shoe soles.

The truth is I'd never actually said women were bad shoppers. My point was everyone – men and women – can be much better shoppers. But television doesn't like bland phrasing, and so the challenge was set.

It went well at first. My initial tactic was to explain that cutting the cost of the boring stuff like gas, electricity and telephone bills means more shopping cash in your pocket. The discussion whizzed along until Claire Sweeney, one of the presenter panelists, was asked, 'What's the most you've ever spent on a dress?' To the aghast faces of the audience she replied, 'I think £3,000.' They turned to me and said, 'I bet you've got something to say to her about that!', the subtext being, 'Come on Mr MoneySaving expert, we've heard you introduced as the tightest man on television so have a go at Claire.' However, MoneySaving is more subtle than that, so I asked her, 'Why did you spend that much?'

It turned out the dress was for a specific concert appearance, part of her job, and an exclusive one-off from a designer she really liked. In other words, she'd bought an item that was necessary and wasn't available anywhere else, so there was no way to get it more cheaply. It was a planned and considered expenditure from someone who could afford it. So my reply was quite simple: 'There's nowt wrong with what Claire's done. MoneySaving isn't about being tight – there's nothing wrong with flying to New York on Concorde and returning on the *QE2* providing you can afford it; there's only something wrong if you pay £7,000 for it when you could have got it for £3,000.' This is the basic Money Diet philosophy. If you budget, prepare and plan, know what you need and can afford it, there's nothing wrong with treating yourself. If it makes your life more pleasurable, go on, enjoy it.

in your purse or wallet. Instead move it around so you don't always instantly know which pocket/bag it's in. This means it'll take at least a double dip to retrieve the cash, adding valuable extra thinking time to delay the impulse to spend.

Use a Debt Buddy

While my piggybank technique is a good way to manage your money, you may find controlling your spending beyond self-regulation. Either the debts are racking up, or you find it really difficult to keep control of your cash. If this is the case, it's time to pour a bucket of cold water over your spending.

A classic technique is the 'spending diary'. Simply write down in a notebook every single thing you spend, so you know exactly where your money is going, and how much – if anything – you've got left. Unfortunately, this simply isn't a powerful enough tool for some.

I've a solution, and it's inspired by the guilt-ridden faces of my friends whenever they come to ask for money help and admit to dire spending habits. It's called 'debt buddying'.

Hopefully, you have at least one friend who is good with money, or at least quite conscientious. What you need to do is ask them if they will sit down with you, once a month, and go through the amount you've spent. If you're young, want to turn the heat up and are really, really brave, you could always make your debt buddy a parent!

I can almost hear the cries of 'way too embarrassing'. Of course you don't want anyone to see what you've spent – that's the point. The mere fact your buddy will see where your money has gone acts as an extra conscience to prevent you from spending on frivolous or unnecessary things when you are stuck for cash. You could always lie and not write things down, but that defeats the purpose – the debt buddy is there to help you help yourself.

Merrick's Money Diary

You're about to get access to a unique MoneySaving diary. 'Merrick' is a 31-year-old man who lives in the south of England and earns around £22,000 a year. As a regular contributor to the Chat Forum of www.moneysavingexpert.com, when he heard he might be made redundant, he decided to concentrate on his spending and radically reduce it.

Using the information available from the site, and the help of other Chatters for hints and tips, he started to diarise his weekly savings.

With his very kind permission here follows an edited version ...

Week 1: *Clearing up the mess*

I am deep into a relationship. My girlfriend wants to move back to England from Canada and we want to set up home next year. So today I have looked at my finances (and they are a mess) and changed a few things that I pay out monthly.

£10 union membership cancelled. I have never used it.

£2.50 clothes insurance. Never claimed and don't need it.

I have changed the following as well:

Taken a three-month payment holiday from a loan I have (11 per cent APR) and will put the money I'm not using on that into paying off a sizeable chunk of my store card (28 per cent).

Moved a credit card balance to a six-month 0 per cent interest rate. Cut up all but one card and my current account card.

Used the 'aapetrolbusters' website to find a garage I travel past regularly and estimate savings of £200 a year.

(Martin's note: Sadly the AA has now closed petrolbusters, which helped locate cheap petrol stations. The AA is now owned by venture capitalists and this useful tool has been lost to consumers.)

Looked at my daily expenses (food, mainly) and decided to take sandwiches to work as well as drinks. I estimate savings of £3 a day (food is expensive in London).

I am going to stop driving the car to the station. Will only save me 50p a day by switching to public transport, but is probably just as quick.

Noticed that pizzas are about a third of the price I pay in Asda if I cook them myself. Estimate savings of £120 a month.

Total savings per year (excluding credit cards which I cannot work out): £1,920 (estimated), and I will probably save a bit more because my priorities have changed now I must save for a house.

Week 2: A glossy cut

This week, I have looked at magazines. I buy a computer magazine monthly for its advertising. This works out at £39 a year. By subscribing, I pay just £23.97. A saving of about £15 a year. Not a fortune, I know, but every little bit helps.

Week 3: Water palaver

In my personal pursuit to find a way to keep the same lifestyle but cheaper, I have this week looked at several things, and the biggest shock to me is water. I drink a lot of bottled water during the day at work (can't trust the tap stuff) and buy one 500ml bottle going to work and one coming back at 89p a bottle (London is expensive). This equates to £8.90 a week.

But by buying a six-litre pack of water at Tesco for £3.49, I would save around £280 a year.

(Martin's note: This comment provoked a great deal of debate on the Chat Forum. One major argument concerned the cost of using water filters rather than buying the water at all – and overall that was calculated to be cheaper. Others simply recommended buying one plastic bottle of water, and once it's finished filling it up from the tap or, if available, purified water from work.)

Week 4: Ringing up the savings

Hoorah, I have changed my overseas telecom provider. I phone my girlfriend twice a week in Canada for two hours each time. I spend £100 a month phoning Canada, but by switching to Telediscount, that will come down by 75 per cent.

Brilliant or what?

(Martin's note: Telediscount is a cut-price telecom provider that can be accessed from any phone. At the time of Merrick's writing it was my recommendation as the cheapest way to call Canada. See 'Calling Overseas', page 200.)

Week 5: Electric savings

Well, Sunday was strange. I had to defrost the freezer. Being a single male, I am not too well versed in the ways of kitchen appliances. So, after defrosting, these blue marks numbered 1 to 10 appeared on the side wall of the chest freezer. 'Wonder what they are?' Looked in the manual and slap me if it's not a marker for setting the freezer – i.e. if the package says the food has to be stored at number 3, you switch the dial to number 3.

Now, I haven't a clue how much I am going to save, as it has been on setting 10 for the last three years, and I never have more than half of it full with food. So off I go to look at other things in the house. And here is what I discover:

- Video – used once a week at most, so now it's unplugged when not needed.
- Three security lights outside – changed the time they stay on from seven minutes to two minutes each.
- Television – never to be left on standby.
- I have started turning lights off when I am leaving a room. Can't quantify savings, but one evening the girlfriend phoned and we spoke for two hours and I actually turned off the light in the study (three spotlights).
- Washing machine – has an economy setting. Now using that for all my knocking-about clothes.
- Switched on 'powersaving' on my PC. Monitor now switches off if I'm away for more than five minutes.

I haven't a clue what I will save, but my goal is to save and at the same time not change my lifestyle too much.

(Martin's note: There are loads of ways to save energy, helping you and the environment. Energy-saving light bulbs and better draught insulation are two to think about. The Energy Saving Trust's website lists many more (www.energy savingtrust.org.uk). As for the money, the biggest and easiest saving all of us can make is to move to the cheapest energy supplier – check out 'Gas & Electricity Bills', page 175.)

Week 6: A view to save
I audited my Sky TV package and found the following: I don't watch Film Four and TVX (for the lads). I am paying about £13 a month for unwatched channels. I'm thinking of keeping a

diary of what I watch for a week to see whether I have all the right packages.

Looked at my DVD collection and found I spend about £50 a month on DVDs I watch once, maybe twice. The upshot of it all is that I joined Blockbuster, saving around £35 a month by renting rather than buying.

(Martin's Note: Worth checking out your local library for DVDs too.)

So this week's cost-saving is around £570 per year.

Okay, I haven't got as many nice DVDs on my shelf, but I'm a hoarder so they would be dead money anyhow.

Week 7: 'Get rid of your junk'

Last Sunday I had to go up to the loft for some suitcases. While up there, a load of boxes fell over. This prompted me to start sorting out my junk. And believe me, it is junk.

I have always done a little selling on eBay, and decided to be totally ruthless and get rid of anything I didn't need.

The sales total so far is £395 (after taking out all the various costs) and I still have a similar amount of items to list.

So this week, hopefully, I can dispose of a thousand pounds' worth of rubbish and pay off my store card (28.8 per cent). This will save me the £40 a month I currently pay on it.

I am going to tackle the shed and garage after the loft, and hopefully expand on this.

(Martin's note: Store card debt is almost invariably the most expensive form of debt on plastic, with rates up in the 30 per cents. In week 1, Merrick should have moved this debt to the 0 per cent credit card via balance transfer ahead of any other debt, as it is the most expensive.)

The final amount I made on eBay from junk in and around my house was (drum roll, please) £874.80 after all expenses.

My mum has now asked me to get rid of all my junk at her house. So there's a lot more selling coming up.

This means I'm now debt-free on store cards. I've cut them up as well. There's a store with a beautiful plasma television round the corner and I don't want to be tempted.

(Martin's note: Cancelling is even better than cutting them up, see page 380.)

Week 8: Keep the savings in the family

Had the pleasure of taking my nephew to town last Saturday. While walking through the shopping centre, he says, 'Uncle Merrick, can I have a Playstation magazine, please?'

Now he had been good and was no trouble, so I agreed. He then says, 'Let's go to the market then.' It turns out that our town market has a guy who does last month's magazines for around half the shop price.

Savings could be quite substantial for those with kids, as he also does comics and other kid-related stuff like stickers. I guess the lesson is 'spend a morning learning your town and save money'.

After clearing all the rubbish from the spare room (see eBay, last week), I was left with a nice room with a bed, double wardrobe, television and large desk in it.

Now what to do with it?

I was in the pub on Wednesday, and a friend who is constructing a rail link mentioned the lack of affordable rentable accommodation.

He has now moved into my spare room at £50 a week, and left his place that was costing him £80 a week.

He saves and I gain.

Thanks to my zeal in saving, I am now making money.

three
KNOW THYSELF

We're all different. And this is our secret weapon. Providers tend to base their decisions on the conglomerated masses, but by knowing yourself and finding your niche you can play against these averages, and win.

Finance has become 'massified' – big institutions are dealing with huge numbers of people at the same time. They usually treat people identically, making easy assumptions. One of the most common, and often correct, assumptions is that most customers are apathetic and ill-informed – and by targeting this side of people's personality they can supercharge their profits. At certain times companies even use actuarial risk tables which divide us up into easy-fit demographics, and attempt to predict our behaviour.

Yet, they're wrong: there's no such thing as one-size-fits-all. We're all different, with different life stages, family situations, incomes, likes, habits, risk profiles, spending habits and decision-making criteria. And just as in buying clothes when knowing the size, style and colour that fit and suit you means you look better, knowing who you are and how you behave gives you the edge – simply by choosing what's right for you, not them.

SELF-KNOWLEDGE

There are three steps to climb to really push home your self-knowledge advantage over providers:

Step 1: Getting to Know You

The most important question is, are you an active or passive Money Dieter? To stretch this book's analogy slightly, it's a bit like saying, do you want to exercise by walking more briskly to or from work, or are you itching to pump iron and sweat to maximise your savings?

Just like with real exercise, most of us tend towards good intentions and poor delivery. How many people do you know who have a gym membership yet never go? In itself this is a fitness and financial problem – after all, gym membership is expensive – but when it's not just the gym but all money matters you're deluding yourself over, it's a much more severe problem.

Coolly and clinically assessing your own behaviour is crucial. Good powerful resolutions are great but – look back – are you the type of person who follows your resolutions? Do you set goals and achieve them? If not, you are better off being less ambitious and choosing long-term easy solutions rather than following the cutting-edge power-playing techniques.

To help you, in this book I separate the easy and the best solutions. Easy isn't wrong. It mightn't deliver the same savings as the best solutions, but it takes less work. And it's much better to go for the easy solution if you honestly don't think you will be able to put in the effort for the best.

BE A TART OR HAVE A STABLE RELATIONSHIP?

Enough psychobabble gobbledegook, let me put this in practical terms. Take the tricky world of credit cards – as you'll see in 'Healthy Eating', page 356.

There are two different interest-cutting offers for everyday spending. The best way is to be a consistent 0 per cent player, applying for a new 0 per cent introductory offer each time the old one runs out, moving from one card company to another. This is the classic credit-card tart strategy. And I'm happy to proclaim proudly, 'I am a tart.' Frankly, if I weren't, I should-n't be writing this book.

Card companies hope that once the 0 per cent interest ends you'll continue to keep your money with them, so they can smile all the way back to the (their own?) bank. Credit-card tarts thwart this easily and simply by moving money from 0 per cent card to 0 per cent card.

The second route is for those who prefer a stable relation-ship to tarting. Here you just stick with a card that has a low standard rate, around 8 per cent, over the long term.

So what happens if you don't know yourself well enough and get it wrong? Wannabe tarts who go for 0 per cent offers but don't remember to switch will be seriously out of pocket. Take a look at the table below.

Who are you?	What do you do?	Interest charged on £1,000 debt*				
		After 6 months	After 1 year	After 18 months	After 2 years	After 5 years
The Tart	Continually rotates 0% cards	£0	£0	£0	£0	£0
Failed Tart	Starts on 0%, forgets to change, and ends up on 18%	£0	£90	£180	£280	£1,108
Stable Relationship	8% the whole time	£40	£80	£120	£170	£470

*For ease of illustration, I've assumed the debt starts at £1,000 and is never paid off. In truth that would never happen as there are minimum payments.

The real Tart wins by a mile, but the Failed Tart is the big loser. Even after just one year, someone in a Stable Relationship does better than the Failed Tart, and after five years the difference is enormous. Picking the wrong card for you can be an absolute financial disaster – and is exactly what card companies want.

Always remember – MoneySaving fervour can feel like a forgotten fad in six months' time. So be very careful to analyse yourself before choosing, and head to safety.

This pattern stretches way beyond credit cards – it hits virtually every product out there. Take savings accounts (see page 215). Here the choice is between riding the wave of top rates by switching from account to account, or settling for a good, steady, high rate which tracks the Bank of England base rate.

It even impacts personal finance's blue whale, mortgages. Either remortgage to a better rate time and time again or just stick with a low standard rate, keeping the payments consistently low.

All this boils down to asking yourself: 'Am I willing to do the work required for the very best results or am I happy to stick with good, solid, safe and easy?'

There's no right or wrong here. There's just you!

Step 2: You Know You Better than They Do

Product-providers can do all the statistical number-crunching in the world, but they'll never know as much about us as we do. This knowledge deficit can be manipulated to earn cold hard cash. Think through the things that specifically affect you in a different way from other people.

This is most effective in the world of insurance. Here prices often depend on actuarial risk tables, which predict how individuals behave so insurance can be priced accordingly. It's done by statistically looking at the standard behaviour of the masses. Yet you can predict your behaviour better than they can.

Let me introduce a moment of culture here. Purely to show off, you understand. The phrase 'Know thyself' was born as an inscription on the Oracle of Apollo at Delphi (well, the ancient Greek equivalent was, anyway). The most tangible MoneySaving benefit of 'Know thyself' is with mobile phone insurance. This provides no symmetry at all as Apollo was the god of music, and surely his wrath would have been awakened by the tin-toned faux 'tunes' mobiles play.

Yet there is an Olympian-sized gain to be made from self-awareness. If a phone's lost, stolen, cracked or crushed, insurance will cover you – but more important is the question of whether it's worth insuring in the first place. There are some whose mobile phone has been safely clipped to their waist belt for five years; it's never been damaged or stolen and no one ever gets near it.

Then there's me. On average I lose a mobile phone three times a year. Don't ask me why – I'm good with money but bad with phones. If you're a waist-belt clipper, you may be smiling smugly, but hold on a second, because if you've got mobile phone insurance, did you know you're subsidising me? In fact you're paying for my lost phones. And I'd really like to say thank you.

Let me explain. Mobile phone insurance prices are not based on any of the standard risk factors – age, gender, occupation, where you live, health or, most important, whether or not you've lost your mobile phone before. This means my insurance payments haven't risen beyond the average, even though my phone is more difficult to locate than Shergar. Waist-belt clippers pay the same as me, as the overall cost is worked out by the market's, not the individual's, average loss. This is where the cross-subsidy comes in – those who never lose partially pay for those of us who are losers.

Loser Update: In the 18 months since the first edition of The Money Diet, *I've only lost two phones, an improvement. Plus I've now got a phone I can synchronise with my computer to back up my data regularly.*

That's why it's important to ask, do you really want or need mobile phone insurance? Of course the past never predicts the future, as all financial communications rightly tell us. But if you've not lost your phone in the last five years, the chances of you losing it in the future are pretty unlikely. It's always possible, but I still suspect you're less likely to lose it than I am, so should you really pay for the insurance?

Martin's Money Memories: 'You Were Very Handsome' – Good, Fair, Unbiased Opinion

My first trial appearance on *This Morning* was a truly nerve-racking affair, not the being on telly, but the fact that if I did well, I might get a regular slot – a long-held ambition. After the show, I decided I needed an honest, unbiased critique of my performance. So I called my grandmother.

'What do you think?'

'Oh, Martin, you were very handsome,' Grandma said.

'But what about what I said, did it make sense?'

'Well, I didn't understand it, but you were very handsome. And my friend Dorothy Leverhume called and she said you were very handsome, too.'

'But, Grandma, isn't she going blind?'

'Yes, Martin, but she said you sounded very handsome.'

This means you could choose to 'self-insure'. Here, instead of paying premiums, you put money in a savings account, so in the eventuality that you lose your phone, there's ready money to pay for it and it's earning interest. After a number of years, if you've never lost the phone, you can take some cash out and enjoy it. People like me, of course, should get mobile phone insurance – as I pay substantially less in insurance than for repeated replacements. As I know my own behaviour and demands, I have a policy that gets me a new replacement phone straight away.

There is a middle ground. Cheaper mobile insurance is available with some bank accounts or by simply adding 'all-risks' cover to your household insurance (this covers objects taken outside the home). Neither of these systems provides as quick a replacement mobile, but they do offer cheap peace of mind.

This 'playing against the average' works across a range of risk-based policies. For example, adopt this tactic for private medical insurance: if you're fitter than a fiddle and healthier than humanity, why not just put money away in a bank account for potential treatments and self-insure again? For additional peace of mind, you could also hedge against any serious problems by getting a private medical insurance policy with an incredibly high excess, such as you pay the first £5,000 of any treatment. This means it's very, very cheap, but if you have serious problems, you're covered.

Step 3: Forewarned is Forearmed, So Stay One Step Ahead

Who is the first person you tell when you discover you or your partner is pregnant? Parent, friend, grandparent, cousin, aunt, uncle, work colleague, lover, secret friend you meet every day on the bus?

It may be any of these, but it certainly isn't your bank, credit-card provider or insurance company. This means you've a good few months of advance knowledge. The same's equally true of other life changes – moving house, changing or quitting work, leaving for a sabbatical all affect your finances. And at any of these crucial transitional life points you have the upper hand over the banks and building societies. You know what's likely to happen and they don't.

Sticking with the original example, pregnancy. If you or your partner is pregnant, the likelihood is that you or she will quit work for a minimum of six months. During this time you will credit score substantially lower because of decreased income. (See 'Credit Scoring', page 310.) So if you need to borrow money, apply while you are still in work. This should mean you score more highly and have better access to cheaper credit, something probably useful during maternity leave.

This means we must become educated fortune-tellers. 'Know yourself' becomes 'know your future'. And whenever you know more than the bank does, take full advantage.

THE TEST OF ARE YOU A MONEY DIETER ALREADY?

As we're moving through the Diet now, I thought a little test of your instincts would be in order. Answer the following questions by selecting the best fit. Keep a note of your answers and find out your score using the table at the end. Then you'll know whether you're a true lean, mean, Money Diet machine.

1. It's Sunday afternoon. A friend's mentioned a way to cut your gas and electricity bills by 20 per cent. It should take about 20 minutes. Would you:

a. Put it on your list of things to do and have a quick peek?
b. Know you've already tracked down the best supplier by using internet comparison tables?
c. Take a trip out for a bite to eat – a Sunday's simply too good to waste on utility bills?

2. You're buying a new wide-screen television because the old one is on its last legs. Do you:
a. Buy *Whose TV?* magazine, research the technology needed to optimise it, then go to the nearest shop that sells it and grab it?
b. Walk into Dixons or Comet and buy the cheapest one that seems to fit the bill?
c. Scan the internet using shopping robots for the cheapest price, having already done the technical research to ensure you're getting the model you want at the lowest price?
d. As c, but then take the quote to the high street and barter with every shop, playing them off against each other in order to get it cheap and instantly?

3. You're in the pub and that rather intense money-focused friend of yours intriguingly asks you what rate you're paying on your mortgage. Do you:
a. Reel it off instantly?
b. Not have a clue?
c. Not know the rate, but know where your mortgage form is and how to find out?

4. A market research company stops you in the street and asks you what an ISA is. Do you answer:
a. It's a way to invest money in the stock market?

b. It's Italian frozen water?

c. It's an Individual Savings Account that allows you to save or invest tax-free in cash or shares?

d. It's an Individual Savings Account, and while many people tout it's tax-free, they ignore the fact there is moderate tax to pay on share dividends, plus of course there's share stamp duty within a self-select ISA?

5. You are about to pay for some cinema tickets. You open up your wallet and there are your credit cards. How many?

a. Two. A Visa and a Mastercard.

b. Four. All high-street cards on which you make only the minimum monthly repayments, and the debts now stack up to £14,000.

c. Nine. All have had debts on them, but you only ever pay 0 per cent interest, continually rotating the debt via balance transfers and saving the money you're not spending in a high-interest savings account to make a profit.

d. One card. Your bank's, and you pay it off in full every month.

6. The telephone bill arrives. It's £95 for the month, a lot more than you want to spend. How would you cut it?

a. Look into switching provider, do some research and find the best plan.

b. Move nearer your friends so more of your calls are local.

c. Forget changing products, deciding instead you'll just cut down slightly.

d. Do the research, first switching the main phone-line tariff, then making a note of the 14 different call providers to find which is cheapest for each type of call.

YOUR SCORE
1. a. 3 b. 5 c. 1
2. a.1 b. 2 c. 5 d.10
3. a. 5 b. 1 c. 3
4. a. 3 b. 1 c. 5 d. 10
5. a. 2 b. 1. c. 10 d. 3
6. a. 5 b. 0 c. 2 d. 10

MONEY DIET POINTS

5–12: Obese You're obviously quite happy to throw your money away, and it seems you don't know your ISA from your elbow. If you're very rich, fine – though it won't last. If not, you need to start taking more of an interest in your finances. Then again, you've made a great start by getting hold of *The Money Diet*. Well done on making the first move.

13–25: Need exercise You try not to overspend, but you don't want budgeting to rule your life. There are lots of easy ways for you to save without too much effort, though. The one-off methods in the 'Crash Diet' will pay dividends.

26–48: Trim, lean and fit A great score. You care about how much you're spending and make sure you get value for money. There are always ways to ensure companies make less profit out of you though, and some of the more cutting-edge techniques in later chapters should teach you a few more tricks.

48–50: International money athlete You're willing to go to extremes to cut your bills, and you've knowledge levels to match. In fact, you should probably be writing this book rather than reading it! For you, money is more important than time. You're the type of person who turns their windscreen wipers off when you go under a bridge to save energy. Your bills and costs will enable you to have a better lifestyle, but will you ever manage to get off the internet in time to enjoy it? *51+: Unbelievable* Your scores are not as good as they may seem at first. The maximum possible on this questionnaire is 50. Be very careful. You're the type of person who'd go out and buy 10 colour television sets, because you only need one licence. Pay a bit more attention to your cash, seek advice and don't just jump straight in there and assume you're doing it right.

The No-Butts Guide to Smoking

Know the Cost of Your Habit

Do you smoke? Are you aware of its impact on your finances? Before you think I'm about to rant, actually smoking isn't always as bad for your wealth as it is for your health. Don't get me wrong; usually being a smoker means you pay more and your finances burn, but occasionally, lighting up is a bonus (see 'Annuities', below).

This isn't even about the more-than-four-quid-a-day (£1,500 a year) a 20-a-day smoker pays for cigarettes. Ignoring that, quit smoking and you could pay over £26,000 less for your financial products over 20 years.

Smoking impacts any product where the price depends on the likelihood of illness or death. Common medical opinion is that the benefits of exercising, eating well and losing weight combined pale into insignificance compared to the benefits of quitting smoking, as the risk from most smoking-related illnesses decreases rapidly after you give up.

What is a 'Non-Smoker'?

To qualify as a non-smoker you normally have to declare you have been smoke-free for at least a year. Cigarettes, cigars, roll-your-owns and pipes all count as smoking for most policies. Always notify providers when you quit smoking, and again after you've been smoke-free for at least a year. Most policies rely on your honesty when it comes to declaring whether you smoke. Lying is easy and results in cheaper premiums, but can be disastrous when it comes to making a claim. It's at this point that medical or other evidence of your habit is likely to be discovered. Your provider can and probably will legitimately refuse to pay out and not even refund your premiums. Even people who have almost, but not completely, stopped smoking may be detected and lose out this way.

Quit smoking and as a non-smoker you'll save money on the following:

Term Assurance: This is the cheapest type of life assurance. It pays out only if you die within a set period. (See 'Crash Diet', page 275.)

(Other life assurance policies are much less affected by smoking as, unlike term assurance, they're investment-based – it's their underlying performance, not whether you light up, that counts.)

Approximate non-smoker cost-saving: 40 per cent

Private Medical Insurance (PMI): PMI provides medical treatment and hospital accommodation. You'd think its costs would be massively upped for smokers. They're not. Providers usually make a detailed analysis of your health, even if only via a phone questionnaire. Smoking-related health issues or signs are therefore taken into account in their own right, leaving the actual fact that you smoke as a side issue, hiding the real cost.

Approximate non-smoker cost-saving: 5 per cent

Permanent Health Insurance (PHI): Often called 'income-replacement plans', these pay a proportion of your normal salary if you're incapable of working after a set amount of time. The payments stop once you return to work.

Approximate non-smoker cost-saving: 25 per cent

Critical Illness Insurance: Pays a one-off lump sum if you're diagnosed with one of a pre-defined list of critical illnesses. These policies have the biggest smoking price-differential – this indicates how much bigger the risk of serious illness is for smokers. The increased cost also reflects the fact that, unlike PHI, the payment is all in one big lump sum.
Approximate non-smoker cost-saving: 50 per cent

Annuities: Up to now it has been all bad news for smokers. However, at retirement the situation can change. I'm in no way advocating people should start smoking, but if you are a smoker and about to retire, it's worth considering the timing of when you give up. The main bright spark for nicotine lovers is that smokers get better annuity rates, and these better rates can add nearly 10 per cent a year to your retirement income.

At retirement, you're usually obliged to spend at least 75 per cent of a money purchase pension fund buying an annuity, which pays you each year until you die. The rate depends on your fund size and on how soon you're predicted to die; therefore smokers, with their reduced life expectancy, can receive substantially higher rates. For a 60-year-old woman in 2003 with a £100,000 fund, the best-paying smoker's annuity pays £800 more a year than the best non-smoker's annuity – that's 10 per cent extra, and over 20 years means a gain of £16,000.

Bizarrely enough, some smokers lie and claim they're smoke-free when they get their annuity, both out of guilt and mistakenly believing it's the 'correct' answer. This may cost them a fortune. However, there's no point in non-smokers grabbing a fag just before retirement, as you normally need to have smoked continually for 10 years to get special rates.

Annuity providers rely on your honesty, as it's difficult to detect how long someone's been smoking for – but remember, lying is fraud. On the other hand, if you are a smoker, there's nothing preventing you quitting the day after you've set up your annuity contract, as payments are fixed at this point. Therefore, if you are about to quit just before retiring, consider holding off.

four
BE A BETTER SHOPPER

Retail therapy at a price you can afford is possible. First, control your 'gotta have' impulses with the right money mantra. This control allows you time to think, so you can have more and pay less.

Martin's Money Memories: Cheap and Cheerful, Darling

Backstage at *This Morning*, I was chatting to two top television stylists (who will remain nameless) also on the programme that day. Before long my appearance was being deconstructed. Overall the verdict was 'Casual's good, but you're overly so.'

Then, item by item:

Jumper: 'It's a good shape, but the wrong colour.' (It had cost me £55.)

Trousers: 'Totally the wrong choice, wrong shape, wrong cut, wrong colour.' They cost £99 (though admittedly I bought them in a sale for £49).

Shoes: 'They're cool, and seriously funky, where d'ya get them?' They cost me £10, bought the evening before in an emergency, from a nearly empty high-street store's rack.

Do the Money Diet and you will have more in your pocket, possibly to lessen debts, but maybe also to spend and enjoy. It's about being a better shopper, so that when you spend, your cash stretches further and you can have even more.

Now I must admit, I'm quaking as I write this. You see, for many people, shopping is not money but sport – a prime recreational activity. This is only wrong if it gets out of control – then it can ruin lives and stop you shopping ever again. I promise not to ruin your enjoyment, if you don't!

Becoming a better shopper is a mix of knowledge and self-discipline.

RETAIL SNOBBERY:
MORE EXPENSIVE ISN'T BETTER!

You see two stereos, one priced at £50, the other at £150 ... which is better? Admit it, your instincts say the more expensive one must be – after all, there has to be a reason it costs more. This is retail snobbery and we've all been hypnotised into it by marketers. It's false pride we have to let go of. Judge a product on whether it suits you and your needs, not purely on how much it costs; pricey may be better, but it isn't automatically so.

FIGHT THE IMPULSE!

When you shop, it's not what you need that's the problem, but the things you don't need; it's when the 'gotta have' impulse rises from your belly and a lust for spending springs from your loins. The child inside says, 'I want, I want, I want,' and once that little voice is heard, it's virtually impossible to stop.

Impulse-cracker 1: Martin's Money Mantras

I've a couple of easy-to-remember mantras for you to chant to yourself when you are about to spend. One for those who are short of cash, and therefore need to be long on self-discipline, and one for those who can, within reason, buy pretty much whatever they want.

MARTIN'S MONEY MANTRA I – FOR THE SKINT

Do I need it?
Can I afford it?
Have I checked if it's cheaper anywhere else?
If an answer is 'No' or 'Don't know' – STOP!

Quite simply, if the answer to any of these questions is no, don't buy it. If you don't need it, don't buy it. If you can't afford it, don't buy it. If you haven't checked it's cheaper anywhere else, don't buy it. You need every penny. If it's 'yes', 'yes', 'don't know', then go and check (see 'Talk to People', page 103). Now if you make the purchase, you will know you're doing the right thing.

MARTIN'S MONEY MANTRA II – FOR EVERYONE ELSE

Will I use it?
Is it worth it?
Have I checked if it's cheaper anywhere else?
If an answer is 'No' or 'Don't know' – STOP!

This may sound just a little harsh – after all, you can afford it. But the funny thing is, sometimes we make purchases purely out of desire, yet get no real benefit apart from the pure shopping buzz. Are you really willing to shell out for that buzz? So ask: 'Will I use it?' If not, don't buy it.

'Is it worth it?' Even if you will use it, will you use it enough to justify the cash? If not, don't buy it. In economic terms, this is known as 'opportunity cost'. What else could you do with the money, and would you enjoy that more? Take a look at your wardrobe, book shelves, shoe rack and CD collection – are there clothes or shoes hardly ever or never worn, unread books and unlistened-to CDs? With this Money Mantra you may spend the cash on something else instead, and gain more fun or benefit.

Finally, have you checked if it's available cheaper anywhere else? If you haven't, spare a little time to do so, especially with a big purchase. The savings could be huge, leaving more money in your pocket for other things.

Remember the mantra that's appropriate to you, and as you are about to take 'it' to the till, repeat it to yourself.

SOMETIMES TIME IS MONEY

Now don't think I'm being a complete party-pooper here. I realise that at certain times money mantras are unrealistic, for those who aren't skint anyway. To quote the old cliché, time is money – and when you're in a rush, buying quickly can be cheaper than buying cheaply.

For example, if you're holding a party and need new music, I would of course suggest using a shopping robot on the internet to find the cheapest prices, then trying cash back sites and three or four high-street stores to ensure you're getting the best deal. Yet if the party is tonight, and you're rushing home to prepare food, getting the CDs in the first shop may be the MoneySaving move – if it means you can use public transport instead of a taxi; you have more time to cook so food isn't wasted; or you've more time to shop for a good deal on booze and snacks. All of these are valid reasons.

However, this realism isn't an excuse for never getting the best deal. Realism works both ways. I'm prepared to accept that sometimes you 'don't have time to save money' if you're prepared to accept that sometimes you 'don't have the money to save time!'

Impulse-cracker 2: Powerful Shopping Technology

Impulse-cracker 2 is a high-tech piece of communication equipment. A flat, two-dimensional optical tablet, with a specialised marking instrument to direct your shopping.

Actually it's not rocket science – it's called a shopping list. Before you leave home to be subjected to marketing ploys, clever shop layouts and tempting special offers, sit down and work out what you're going out shopping for and how much you can afford to spend. It doesn't matter whether it's clothes shopping on the high street, buying a new computer, or a supermarket session. There's an old adage – never go food shopping when you're hungry. Well, don't shop for anything unless you've defined your appetite. Make a list and stick to it. By deciding what you want before you go, and before you're enticed by all the various goodies on offer, your purchasing decisions will be more effective.

There are, of course, always exceptions to a rule. Spotting a substantial bargain while shopping, something that you were planning to buy another day, may rightfully loosen the purse strings somewhat, but not without following the Money Mantras first.

Impulse-cracker 3: Price Tag Scanning

What I'm about to say causes a physiological reaction in a few women. They arch an eyebrow and give me a look so sceptical it makes Jeremy Paxman look like a wilting violet. However, if you're willing to try, it can work.

Price tag scanning is a simple idea, and is especially good for clothes shopping, though it can be used on anything. Rather than looking at the clothes first and then the price tag (or worse, not looking at the price tag until you get to the till), check the price tag before looking at the clothes.

This may sound silly. Of course you'll see the clothes when getting to the tag, but in most clothes shops, garments are massed and squashed together. If you're buying a pair of trousers – having, of course, decided beforehand how much you can spend – run your eyes across the tags. When you spot something within your price range, pull it out and have a gander to see if you like it. Where the price is too high, don't even look at the item. Don't tease yourself. Don't let that inner voice seduce you into spending more than you can afford. As soon as you say to yourself, 'I have to have it,' you've lost. Either you're going to spend more and self-delude with the old 'I'll buy this now and spend nowt next week' or you'll leave the shop disappointed and with regrets. The price tag scanning technique will stop you putting yourself in this position in the first place.

Impulse-cracker 4: Blind Branding

This is one especially for designer doyens. It's just a simple one-off game to play with a friend. Go to a shop and get the friend to pick out a number of branded and similar but unbranded clothes. Ask your friend to show them to you in such a way you can't see what brand it is. Now pick the one you prefer. Do this five or six times. How many of your preferred choices are branded? If, as is likely, it's only about

Martin's Money Memories: Sometimes My Advice is a Load of Cobblers!

I was out shopping with one of my best friends, something she doesn't particularly enjoy, as shopping with a MoneySaving expert takes some of the fun away. Her big love is shoes. She adores them and has a large number sitting at home waiting for her. This particular day was a 'boots' day. There were two pairs she was yearning for in the shop. The decision for her wasn't how much to spend, but which of these knee-length, high-heeled black leather boots to go for. At this point I intervened and looked at the prices. The pair on the left cost £60; the pair on the right cost £130. Instantly she decided, of course, that the £130 pair were the best and the 'gotta haves'.

Putting my spend-buster hat on, I decided it was time for drastic action. I nipped to the cash machine, shoved my card in and took out £70 in crisp notes. Running back to the shop, for fear she was already at the till, I grabbed both pairs of boots. Look, I told her, this is the real decision you're making: either this pair of (£130) boots or this (£60) pair but with this £70 in cash. Her eyes widened and she said, 'I've never thought of it that way before,' leaving me sitting there smugly, thinking 'MoneySaving expert on the case! Job's a good 'un.' Ten seconds later she was off to the till with the £130 pair. Ah, well, you win some, you lose some!

half, ask yourself, 'Is branded always better?' I will admit, fashion is the one area where brand has a value because the brand itself can be fashionable even if the clothes aren't. However, well-made unbranded fashion clothing can often mean you look just as good. If money's tight, de-labelling pays.

FASHION IS FLEETING

It always amazes me that people on a budget save up to fork out for really expensive fashionable clothes, knowing they'll soon have passed their peak and will never be worn again.

Fashion is transitory, so fashionable garments tend to have a limited life; therefore buying cheap and often can be a better strategy. This is magnified when it comes to the bizarre trend of high fashion for very young children. First, kids grow! Second, they don't recognise brands. So why not wait and save your cash for when they're old enough to demand designer – which they surely will.

Impulse-cracker 5: Retail Therapy at a Price You Can Afford – the Game

Shopping is sexy, fun and enjoyable. It's also extremely dangerous when you don't have any money. So if you're on a cost-conscious budget but love to spend, and retail therapy is a hobby, here's a little challenge just for you.

Shopping is about both the activity and the acquisition of new things. Now, I can't re-create that perfectly, but there is a way to at least try to satisfy yourself at lower cost. If you feel the shopping urge, go to the shops, but take only a pound or two or maybe if we're being generous, three or even four – and challenge yourself to use that very small amount of money to buy something frivolous, useful or both.

The Game. To find the most enjoyable thing possible from all the shops.

The Aim. To provide your spending buzz fix at the cheapest possible cost.

This Money Diet game tries to do for spenders what a nicotine patch does for smokers. It won't always work, but anything's worth a try.

DANGER! SALES!

Sales are wonderful for MoneySavers, but they also hold a measure of danger. Bagging a discount doesn't automatically mean you're saving money. In the panicked, fevered rush to grab sales bargains, it's easy to buy lots of things you don't really need. A suit reduced by 50 per cent is a great deal, but a bad buy if it's never worn.

As I'm neither stupid nor brave enough to bring up shopping gender differences, I thought I would reprint a joke floating round the internet:

'A man will pay £2 for a £1 item he needs.

A woman will pay £1 for a £2 item she doesn't need.'

Things often look different outside the sales than in. And you have no right to return goods simply because you don't like them. Shops often grant us this privilege, but withhold it in the sales. That's why when sales shopping it's even more important to shop smart, because you can't change your mind.

Money Diet Quick Fact Snack: When to BOGOF!

Bogof! No, not you! BOGOF stands for 'buy one, get one free'. And in some circumstances these are a 'must buy'. This applies when the BOGOF or three-for-two or half-price deal is on consumable goods you use regularly that don't go off, like toothpaste, razors, toilet paper and batteries. If you see these offers, grab as many as you can store. To put it in stock-market terms, a three-for-two offer (on something you'd buy anyway) is a 50 per cent return risk-free. An amazing investment.

TOP FIVE TIPS FOR THE SALES

■ Decide what you want before you go.

- Set a budget of exactly how much you can spend.
- Don't buy on impulse, stick to a list. Use the Money Mantras (see page 79).
- Cheap isn't automatically a bargain. Good deals are great, but just because it's cheap doesn't mean you should buy it.
- Remember, overextending yourself in the sales and getting into costly debt can be more expensive even than paying full price.

THE LIST OF WHAT SHOPS REALLY MEAN

Two for the price of one/buy one get one free
Meaning: The goods are half price.
Why it's cunning: You're obliged to buy two, not one, so you spend more money than with a simple 'half price' offer, doubling the retailer's sales, and helping to shift their stock.

Three for the price of two
Meaning: A third off.
Why it's cunning: You need to spend double what you would have spent. Though they're discounting, they're moving more volume. Also they've sewn up all your purchasing requirements for that product for the foreseeable future. In other words, if you drink one orange juice carton a week, the offer guarantees your next three weeks' supply is bought with it. Similar offers on this theme include 'buy one get second half price' and 'buy two for £5'.

50 per cent extra free
Meaning: A third off.
Why it's cunning: This one's my favourite. It's just such a

damn clever numbers game. Add 50 per cent to a product and it actually means you're only selling the product a third cheaper. Add 30 per cent to a product and you're selling it around 25 per cent cheaper. This is simply the way the numbers work – so the store advertises an offer where the customer bonus looks much more generous than it is.

We'll match any other store's price
Meaning: Very little – it tells you nothing about whether its price is good or not.
Why it's cunning: While it says, 'We'll ensure you've got the cheapest price,' it's actually your responsibility to ensure you've got the cheapest price. The shops know you won't do the work. So you've a false sense of security that you've got the cheapest goods you possibly can (see 'Price Promises', page 148).

Up to xx per cent off
Meaning: Very little – very few goods are at the maximum discount.
Why it's cunning: 'Up to' is a retailer's favourite. The headline discount looks much bigger than it is. In the summer sales I went to four fashion clothes shops all offering 'Up to half price/50 per cent off' deals. I surveyed the average discount on 10 items in each, and almost uniformly they only discounted an average of 15 per cent. As a rough rule of thumb, therefore, divide the 'Up to' price by three to see the real average discount.

Shop with us and earn loyalty points
Meaning: Tiny discount on everything you spend.
Why it's cunning: Loyalty is a very clever phrase – obviously and simply it keeps you shopping at the store. Remember,

though, that just because you get a couple of pence in the pound's worth of loyalty points, it doesn't automatically make it a good deal. Always think of loyalty points as just a very small discount off the purchase price – and compare this to what's charged elsewhere. (See page 92.)

An extra 100 loyalty points if you buy this
Meaning: £1 off (assuming a point is worth 1p).
Why it's cunning: The shop is giving you a discount, but ensures you must return to the store to spend it. When you do that, you usually buy other things too. Plus, while you feel like you're getting a £1 discount, it has only cost the store the price it pays its supplier for the goods (the cost price). Not the retail price you pay. So this discount hits its pockets much less than the headline figure. Even better for the shop, it's likely that when you're there you'll earn bonus points again and need to return to spend them too – perpetuating this vicious circle of loyalty.

Lingerie shop sale! Knickers coming down
Meaning: It's a good pun.
Why it's cunning: Because it enabled me to smuggle a dodgy double entendre into the book.

More people choose us than anybody else
Meaning: We're the biggest brand.
Why it's cunning: Just because a company has persuaded more people than any other to buy its product doesn't mean it's cheaper, better or more reliable. It's probably just got the biggest advertising and marketing budget. Most of us make the wrong spending decisions a lot of the time, so following the

masses is no guarantee of success. These signs run a spending shiver down my spine and, maybe a little unfairly, my instinct says 'avoid'. If a brand or company's only real selling point is that it's popular, it can't be that good.

Consistently low prices

Meaning: Absolutely nothing.

Why it's cunning: It's a nice, easy, unsubstantiated claim. It has resonance, but there is no reference point as to what consistently low prices are. On whose terms are they cheap? Compared to whom? For what products? This is a big retailer's ploy to make us feel confident. Often it's backed up with specific examples of cheap prices, yet these are of course specially selected. When you see this sign, blink, ignore it and carry on.

Here's our ranking over the last five years

Meaning: You'll never know what it means until you read the small print.

Why it's cunning: It's not just shops that use these slogans. This technique is used by unit trusts and investment funds. Be very, very careful with these, and not just because past performance of shares isn't a good indicator of future performance. I spotted a billboard advert that listed in big bold capital letters one fund's position in its category over the past five years as something like 1st, 2nd, 1st, 4th and 1st*. This looked like razor-sharp performance, yet the asterisk at the bottom noted this was its 'quartile performance'. In other words 1st just meant it had been in the top 25 per cent of similar funds; 2nd meant it came somewhere between 25 and 50 per cent of funds, and 4th meant it was actually boasting about being in the bottom 25 per cent of performers!

five

FORGET LOYALTY

Fact: No one financial services product-provider is top of the table for more than one product. Therefore, by definition, having two products from one company means at least one of them isn't the best. Forget loyalty; it only pays them, not you.

BE LOYAL TO YOURSELF

Let me reiterate the fact at the top of this page. There is not one product-provider who is top of the table for more than one product. Thus, if you have two or more products from any one provider, only one of them can be the top, and the rest, at best, are second-best. And when it comes to saving money, even second-best is worst.

Loyalty is important for companies: it's an easy way to help boost their profits. Dealing with loyal customers is easy; it takes less time, less management and provides consistent income. This can be a bank's current account customers, specific trainer brand buyers, a credit card's users or Marks & Spencer's knicker-wearers – anything.

Loyalty is so important to banks that they even use it as a critical measure of profitability. They compare how many different products each customer has; the more products, the more profitable they are.

Loyal customers aren't as sensitive to price changes – firms know it takes a quantum leap to displace their custom. This means they make more money out of them, with less marketing spend, and use their continued custom to subsidise attracting newcomers.

Firms' attention, gimmicks and, most important, best offers are focused on *new* customers. The phrase 'introductory offer' is common parlance, but 'existing customer offer' is heard about as commonly as 'FA Cup Winners Northwich Victoria'. New customers get access and eligibility to services existing customers don't. So why be loyal?

Credit Card Companies Will Pay £40 to £80 for Your Custom

Credit card companies are willing to pay roughly between £40 and £80 to gain a new customer. This is paid in the form of introductory 0 per cent offers, freebies and cash to encourage you to join them, or in marketing and advertising in order to introduce the new customer to their products. Ask yourself a question:

'Do I want to be the person whose custom is paid for, or the person who gives it away?'

Remember, once they've got your loyalty, they've got you. So to be a smart and savvy consumer and save money, forget loyalty.

Who Are You Being Loyal to, Anyway?

Before becoming a journalist, I worked in the murky world of financial public relations – almost exactly the opposite of what I do these days. One day I heard the Scottish entrepreneur Sir Tom Farmer, then owner and chief executive of Kwik-Fit, being questioned by City analysts about his company's latest acquisition.

He had bought a chain of outlets very similar to Kwik-Fit yet, rather than rebranding them all as Kwik-Fits, he planned to operate them separately and keep their existing name. When asked why, to paraphrase his answer, he said, 'I believe in this world you're always going to have competition, and if there's going to be competition I may as well own it.' Everyone laughed, but below the humour is a business reality.

Money Diet Quick Fact Snack: Dis-Loyalty Cards

Any shop worth its salt (and many that aren't) has loyalty cards. Yet never, ever, ever choose where you will shop simply because it has a loyalty scheme. 'But,' some may say, 'loyalty schemes are good, they give us discounts, we enjoy them.' Hmmm.

At their hub, loyalty schemes are discount schemes. If they pay 1p in the pound, that's a 1 per cent discount. If, as with the Boots Advantage card at the time of writing, it's 4p in the pound, it's an effective 4 per cent off all your Boots shopping. Great! Yet it can mean diddlysquat.

Imagine you walk into Boots and there's a shampoo priced £2. Use your loyalty card with its 4 per cent discount, and it actually costs £1.92. Yet, in a neighbouring shop, the shampoo could be priced at £1.80.

If this is the case Boots, even with its 'Advantage', isn't cheaper. Yet loyalty cards somehow mist our clinical decision-making. Even if the shampoo was the same price after the loyalty discount, you'd still be better off shopping elsewhere as you'd have 8p extra cash rather than points, and cash is much more flexible and usable. This, of course, is a piddly sum, but over time piddly pays.

Therefore the rule is simple. When shopping in a place with a loyalty scheme, always use the card, just never base your choice of where you're going to shop on loyalty, only on value.

Money Diet Quick Fact Snack: Same Company, Twice the Price

Multiple brands are big bucks. They enable one company to target you in many different ways and push their profits to the extreme. One of the doyens of this is the Halifax Bank of Scotland Group. As well as the two big bank brands in the title, it also owns Esure, Intelligent Finance and Birmingham Midshires. Yet though it's all one big company, try getting house insurance quotes and see if one big company gives you one low price. Of course it doesn't: for one sample the range went from £125 to £242. Go to one brand and then another within the same company and the price can nearly double.

Multi-ownership is everywhere. Do you know who owns the company you're dealing with? Travel agent Going Places is owned by My Travel. Direct Line is owned by the Royal Bank of Scotland, as is NatWest. Abbey, Alliance and Leicester and Virgin credit cards are all really run by MBNA.

If you want a mobile phone, why not try Dixons or Curry's or PC World or The Link? But they're all the same company and pricing is very similar. Does trying these four really count as shopping around? Actually it means the marketplace isn't as competitive as we think. And, worse, it allows different companies to use different brands to target different customers. So even if you want to be loyal – who to?

NOT JUST WHO, BUT HOW?

To bang another nail in loyalty's coffin, remember that providers charge different people different prices. Stretching my memory back to Mr Hallis's A-level Economics class, I remember being taught the term 'price differentiation' – a holy grail for companies. In a perfectly profitable world, a company would charge each and every customer the maximum they'd willingly pay.

Way back then, this was unthinkable, but with high-tech number-crunching and internet technology it's starting to happen. The most obvious area is 'rate for risk' – where the lower credit risk at which you're assessed, the less you're charged. At least this has a certain logic to it. Yet price differentiation can be much more divisive, with pricing based on our access to information. The most stark example I remember was with Lloyds TSB's loans a few years ago.

Borrow £10,000 from it via the internet and it charged 8.7 per cent or £2,750 in interest over five years. Borrow £10,000 by walking into a branch and you'd pay 15.9 per cent or £5,140 in interest over five years. Yet worse is to come. Anyone responding to a mailshot from Lloyds subsidiary Black Horse would've been charged 19.9 per cent or £6,540. All for the same size loan, from the same company at the same time.

This means don't just think 'who' but also 'how'. Again, forget loyalty; in this case long-standing branch customers fare much less well than newcomers who happen to have a computer. The argument that 'they've given me a good deal in the past, they will do so in the future' should be consigned to history.

Loyalty's Greatest Weapon – Beware Brands

Brands are created by huge marketing spend. We pay for this spend in the form of higher prices. Yet a successful brand means the company can charge even more on top. So we pay double.

Brands are simply a way for companies to increase our spending and their profits without adding any real extra value. League tables show different brands perform differently for different products, whether it's cars, electronic goods or clothes. One brand doesn't uniformly come top of the product league. Yet people continue to think that if a brand's product is good in one area, then a different product from the same brand will be good too, despite the fact it may have been made in a different country, with different techniques and standards. After all, why should a company with a good airline be any good at making vodka, mobile phones or running savings accounts?

Brands subtly tap at our natural psyche. Purchasing decisions are neither art nor science, but instinct. When we make quick decisions, we don't usually have all the facts. We short-cut the process based on past experience, trust and guesswork.

Let's use the murky world of politics to demonstrate. You turn on the television and there's a debate amongst a group of politicians on a subject you know nothing about. If asked their opinion, even after listening for a short time, most people would echo the thoughts of the person from the party they tended to support, even if they didn't yet understand the argument.

There's nothing wrong with this – it's a perfectly rational way to behave. Essentially it's 'I usually think the way they do, so on this subject I probably will too' – after all, until we know better, what else do we have to go on?

It's this implicit instinctive loyalty that the people who manage brands try and tap into. So that when we don't have the time – or more usually the inclination – to think about our purchases, we follow brand loyalty and stick with what we know.

Stop. Don't do it. It's what they rely on, and they use huge, weighty marketing and advertising teams to back it up.

Supermarket Brands – Sheer Genius

In a modern supermarket there are usually four brand levels: 'the no-frills or basics brand', the 'supermarket own-brand', 'the mainstream brand' (e.g. McVitie's Jaffa Cakes') and 'the premium brand' – like Tesco Finest. A round of applause for the sheer marketing genius. This stratified system automatically allows supermarkets to justify huge variations in price. When we judge, often it's not based on experience but on the brand. So when Tesco says 'This is Tesco Finest' we believe that because we had a good Salmon en Croûte, the Peppered Steak will be fantastic too, even though they may have been made in factories thousands of miles apart, and that if we choose to pay the higher price, we'll get a finer feast. This means we let them tell us what 'good' is. It's any salesman's dream. Packaging and placement provide the pricing.

This isn't to say there aren't differences in produce and production quality. Yet there is no uniform guide to quality. This is something we need to judge ourselves.

The Downshift Challenge

Don't worry, I'm not about to tell you to always buy 'no-frills'. Yet I want to challenge you to try to downshift. Quality is worthwhile and can justify expense, but are you really getting it? To check, slip out of your shopping habits and occasionally try something one level cheaper. Sometimes you'll like it, sometimes you won't. For me, I don't notice the difference between no-frills and supermarket own-brand baked beans – yet I'd never dream of drinking no-frills diet cola, nor would I wipe my bottom with ultra-cheap toilet roll.

This is about finding what fits and costs less. Next time you want tinned spaghetti, get four of your normal, one supermarket own-brand and one no-frills and try them out. Downshift savings can be huge – take a look at this sample from different shops on the same day.

Bread 800g Loaf	**Tea 0.25Kg**
Kingsmill 83p each	PG Tips £1.88
Supermarket own-brand 69p	Supermarket own-brand £1.25
Supermarket no-frills brand 28p	Supermarket no-frills brand 49p
Long Grain Rice 1Kg	**Skin Lotion**
Uncle Ben's £2.15	Vaseline £2.90 (200ml)
Supermarket own-brand 82p	Nivea £2.99 (250ml)
Supermarket no-frills brand 55p	Pharmacy own-brand £1.59 (250ml)
London Hair Cut	**Sunglasses**
Vidal Sassoon £42	FCUK £56
Toni and Guy Essensuals £39	Boots Dial 45s £20
Fish £27	Boots Fixed Tint £10
Mr Toppers £6	Superdrug Fashion Tint £3.99

Take just one of the above examples. If you used one packet of rice a week, over a year Uncle Ben's would cost £112, the supermarket own-brand £42, and the no-frills brand £28. Are you really sure the extra £70 or even £80 is worth it? Try the downshifting challenge to see.

It works in practice. For an ITV programme I challenged a family to down-shift. I followed them in the supermarket, mimicking their weekly shopping, just choosing one brand level lower.

Their trolley came to £130. Mine was £85, a third cheaper, roughly what I'd expect. For the next week they lived off my trolley and, to their surprise, only noticed the difference for half the stuff. Where they didn't see a difference, they switched, and their new weekly shop became £105 – a reduction of £1,300 a year without noticing a difference.

Proof that sometimes there's no difference at all. Own-brands are often made in the same factories, with the same ingredients, as main brands. No-frills brands are sometimes identical too, the only difference being the box and brand. Of course, no company will confirm this, so I put out a request via my website called 'The Great Own-brand Hunt', asking anyone who'd worked in a factory to dish the dirt. Hundreds responded, admitting products as varied as cereals and DVD players were all the same thing. Have a look below to see a sample and you'll be surprised. There's still no way of knowing whether these are or ever were correct but it's (unbranded) food for thought

Don't be conned. Try the downshift challenge and open your mind.

Manufacturer	Product	Rumoured to be sold as
McVities'	Digestive biscuits	Tesco, Asda, Sainsbury's, M & S, Aldi, Lidl, Happy Shopper
Chanel	Make-up	Bourjois
Sony	Electrical goods	Aiwa
Papermill Direct	Printer paper	Epson, HP
Johnsons	Baby wipes	Tesco
French Connection	Clothing	House of Fraser 'Linea', Great Plains
Highland Spring	Mineral water	Tesco
Crown	Paint	Do It All
Buitoni	Pasta	Tesco, Asda
Triton	Showers	Wickes

THE TEST OF HOW LOYAL YOU ARE

Do you gorge on loyalty? Look at the list of products and services below. For each one that you have or use, write in the corresponding box how many months you estimate it's been since you last compared it to alternatives to check you're getting good value. It's not about always changing, but is about always checking. If you don't have the product or service, don't fill the box in.

☐ Digital/Satellite TV provider	☐ Pension
☐ Mortgage	☐ Mortgage insurance
☐ Gas provider	☐ Cleaner
☐ Savings accounts	☐ Home contents insurance
☐ Building insurance	☐ Car insurance
☐ Tessa-only ISA	☐ Shares investments
☐ Credit cards	☐ Mortgage payment protection insurance
☐ Life assurance	☐ ISAs
☐ Gardener	☐ Endowments
☐ Supermarket	☐ Petrol station you commonly use
☐ Clothes shop brands	☐ Cigarette seller
☐ Pub	☐ Regular fast food shop
☐ Regular Indian restaurant	☐ Regular any other restaurant
☐ Private medical insurance	☐ Internet service provider
☐ Permanent health insurance	☐ Telephone provider
☐ TV and video rental place	☐ Garden centre
☐ Pet food	☐ Toilet paper
☐ Gym fees	☐ Pet insurance
☐ Washing powder	☐ Regular mode of transport to work
☐ Coffee and tea brand	☐ Personal loan
☐ Current account	☐ Electricity bills
☐ Garage mechanic	☐ Cash ISA

YOUR SCORE

Add the total number of months in all the columns together, then divide by the number of boxes you've filled in. For example, if the total number of months is 721, and you've filled in 32 categories, then your score is 721 divided by 32, which equals 23. Then look at the list below to see how well you've done.

MONEY DIET POINTS

Over 25: Flushing it down the loo You are almost invariably paying too much across the entire range. Either that or you've had one product for such a long time it's prehistoric. Your big advantage, though, is that there's room for huge savings – doing the Money Diet should reap massive rewards for you.

15–25: Stuck in the mud Not brilliant: you've checked some things recently, but more are needed. Why not focus on the really big numbers in the list, the things you never change, and see if you can reduce the average? There's money to be saved here.

8–15: An open mind Pretty good. There are always things you need to look at more often. Credit cards and savings accounts, for example, can be changed every six months or more often. Always remember, focus on the methodology and having the best products. You can probably squeeze a few more pennies out and get a few more pounds in.

Less than 8: More churn than butter You spit in the face of customer loyalty. Congratulations! I'm assuming when you do change, you do your research and move to the very best providers all the time. If not, there's not much point in changing frequently. You're a successful Money Dieter. Keep it up.

LOYALLY PERSUADING US TO BUY MORE, MORE, MORE

'Annyulneed'

In my chequered youth, I had a good few jobs – petrol pump attendant, waiter, barman – yet the most useful for my MoneySaving education was three months spent as a salesman. Glamorously I sold caravan awnings (the tent bits to stick on the outside of a caravan). The lead salesman, James, a slick-tongued Scotsman, taught me a clever trick: suggestive selling. When someone had just made an expensive awning purchase, and was still focused on it, he would say, 'And you'll need ...,' picking another product to add on. This worked over half of the time, bagging me lots of commission. I flogged caravan kettles, floor mats and even portable televisions with 'And you'll need ...' The quicker I blurted it out, the less time customers had to question it, so *annyulneed* was born.

Insurance providers turn this consumer disaster into an art form. Get a credit card *annyulneed* card protection insurance; take a mortgage *annyulneed* life insurance, *annyulneed* buildings and contents insurance.

Sidecar Profiteering

Yet *annyulneed* is just the beginning. In the grown-up big-bucks world of flogging us money products it's developed into an even more powerful trick I call 'sidecar profiteering'. It works like this. Advertise good-value competitive products to suck customers in. Then use a quick *annyulneed* to persuade them to accept an add-on product.

However, while the main product is good value, the 'sidecar' product is nearly all profit. But as the add-on's face value is lower it attracts less scrutiny. It's brilliant, and most of the time it works.

A classic example is travel insurance on a package holiday. The holiday market is competitive, so travel agents have to keep holiday prices quite low. But buy a holiday, *annyulneed* travel insurance. Say yes and it may cost another £100 for a family on top, even though similar cover is available elsewhere for around £25. This means that although the travel insurance is much cheaper than the holiday, it's also much more profitable. Yet the customer is still considering the big purchase price, not the add-on. (See 'Crash Diet', page 266.)

'Sidecar profiteering' is a game of wits. The patter's drafted by experts, so it's unsurprising we often fall for it. It's very common with payment protection insurance on personal loans, as the cost needn't be included in the interest rate. Providers flog dirt-cheap loans, then add dirtily expensive insurance on top, costing possibly thousands over the full life of the loan, often much of it pure profit. (See 'Healthy Eating', page 400.)

This leads to one basic rule: make a unique decision each time you decide to spend. Don't follow brand loyalty. Don't follow any loyalty. Don't start buying one product and then immediately buy another.

Mix 'n' Match is the Solution

Why not get a personal loan from one company and stand-alone payment protection insurance from another? Get your mortgage from one provider and your mortgage life assurance from another? It can apply to anything – get your DVD player from one retailer but the scart lead from another. Just because you've made a big purchase, don't forget to use the same MoneySaving logic on the small ones, too.

six

TALK TO PEOPLE

We live in a time of unrivalled access to information, yet as consumers most of us simply avoid taking advantage of this. STOP! Know what you are doing and you'll be the winner. It's a question of research, evidence and simply talking about money.

I'm constantly surprised that most normal human beings don't seem to relish digging through reams of numerical data, putting it in a spreadsheet and crunching the minutiae. Yet I've decided to abstain from any talk of statistical analysis, and instead focus on quick, easy and effective ways of finding out if you're getting the best deal.

You may be wondering about the title 'Talk to People'. Originally it was 'Research, Research, Research' but I changed my mind. The most important form of all research is communication, talking to people. Whether it's face-to-face, by phone, e-mail, sign language, letter, fax, text message, internet chat room, memo, semaphore, instant messenger, morse code or Post-it note, we must make sure we converse.

REACHING OUT

To find the best information we need to reach out.

Method 1: Breaking the Last Taboo

Talk isn't cheap. If you gathered 10 of your friends together in a room, and asked them about any form of financial decision, usually at least one has a clue about the subject, probably has done it themselves, and possibly has some pointers. Yet time and time again we all try to reinvent the wheel.

Talking about money is one of the few taboos left in modern society. I don't understand it. Why is it rude or vulgar to ask: 'How much did you pay for it?' 'Did you manage to get a bargain?' 'How did you barter?' 'How much is it worth?' 'Which bank do you use?' 'What kind of accounts have you got with them?'

Many people have made decisions I've never faced, just as I've made decisions they never have. By failing to ask 'How much did you pay?' we deny ourselves incisive terms of reference for future decision-making. Knowledge is built through conversation and discussion. The reality of a friend's financial history is more lively and easy to understand than anything else.

Let me make a clarion call to change this. Don't be embarrassed. Talk, ask and be open about your money and your finances to friends and family. It's a great way to gather information and help build your knowledge, and you may also find they're able and willing to help in ways you hadn't imagined.

So, apart from reading *The Money Diet*, the first thing to do when starting any new project is talk to your friends and family about it. Shared experiences are invaluable. Of course, they're not always right, but then who is?

Martin's Money Memories: How Much Do You Earn?

'Don't ask, don't tell': that was the rule about discussing your salary in my first job after university. Of course, new and inexperienced, I obeyed, at first. After a year or so, I did start talking, though. And one day I was surprised to learn that a colleague who was asked to work under me turned out to be earning nearly twice my salary.

The bosses were right – talking about it sowed dissent and displeasure, yet the fact I knew the difference wasn't the cause, it was the catalyst. The real problem was the fact I was paid less. After all, if we worked for the fun of it, they wouldn't pay us anyway. So, armed with the knowledge, I had a valuable bartering tool to try and bump up my salary.

If a colleague asks you what you earn and you're working in the same company, don't be so shy. As with all money issues, knowledge is power.

Method 2: the Internet

The net tends either to scare people or make them salivate as they think about tapping their fingers on the magical keyboard. It offers an unparalleled wealth of immediate knowledge – the problem is knowing how to find it, filter it and trust it.

For the web-savvy, the internet is an amazing tool. However, even for complete beginners there are some easy ways to gain (see page 113). It is often said you can't trust information on the internet. Not true. Don't confuse the delivery mechanism with the source. If the info is from a reputable source, the fact that it is on the web makes no difference.

There is a range of ways to find information on the web.

1. WWW.MONEYSAVINGEXPERT.COM

Of course I would say the place to start is my own website –

which in the spirit of MoneySaving is independent, free to use, and free of ads. It is designed to complement the information in this book, includes updated articles and allows people to chat to each other (and occasionally me) about new and better ways to save money.

2. COMPANIES' OWN SITES

The great thing about the internet is there is no shortage of space, so companies can include limitless information. This can mean the terms and conditions and specifications for every single product. It's a brilliant resource.

3. SEARCH ENGINES

Search engines are the internet's 'index'. By using them carefully you can find pretty much whatever you want. The one I use, www.google.co.uk, is king. Its criteria are set up in a different way to all the others. To use it properly, take time to learn the advanced tips and tricks. Use double speech marks (" ") around a phrase to ensure it is matched exactly. This will narrow the field of your search.

4. SHOPPING ROBOTS

Sometimes called 'shopbots', these are specialised sites that trawl around web retailers for you to find the cheapest prices. They're especially good for books, games, CDs, DVDs and electrical and computer goods.

5. FINANCIAL PRICE-COMPARISON SERVICES

Similar to shopping robots, these services compare huge amounts of online info. Yet where shopping robots search many retailers for a single product, price-comparison services compare many products that do similar things to find the best rate. These could be savings accounts, cash ISAs or even airline flights.

On the whole these services will save you money, but do be careful. Though they are a great starting point for research, never rely on them completely. Don't ever think that just because a product comes top of a price-comparison engine it's automatically the best way to go. It should be seen as an information source, not an automated decision-maker. Above all, always remember price-comparison services are virtually all profit-making enterprises, and want your cash. Potential problems are as follows:

Bias! This is the most serious problem. Most financial comparison sites are actually 'best buy of those that pay us' sites. They make money by providing introductions to providers, and don't list or priortise any companies that don't pay. This is prevalent across the board, and something you have to be aware of. It's why different comparison services sometimes produce different results.

Also watch for inconsistent price comparisons. Although a site may provide a decent search for some goods, for others – often more complicated ones such as health insurance or mortgage payment protection insurance – it takes the easy route and just links to a particular affiliated company, rather than searching right across the market. If a search engine site ever simply directs you to one company, avoid it.

They don't compare like with like. Sometimes just comparing prices isn't enough. There's often a huge variance in range, specifications and terms and conditions. For example, with home contents insurance, some policies are 'unlimited sum-insured', meaning it doesn't matter what your contents are worth, they're covered. Others may limit cover to £20,000. With savings accounts, the pure rate ignores whether it's instant access or has a notice period, is accessible via the internet or the phone, has transfer penalties or limited withdrawals, is a consistent rate or an intro bonus. These factors affect your choice, so always make sure you know what you want and how to choose first.

Insufficient info. They don't always give you all the information you need. Details can be scant and out of date. Once you've gleaned the info from a price-comparison engine, always check products out directly on a provider's own website.

Exclusivity. Many price-comparison services have exclusive deals arranged with providers. So search on one service and it won't include another's exclusives. Another problem is that some direct sellers and companies sell only through their own direct agents. So you may need to look at these companies and providers separately.

Sidecar profits. They don't always rate the rate. Comparisons look at the main product price, yet often miss the 'sidecar profit' products price (see page 101). In other words, just because it comes top of the table doesn't mean all the 'extras' like insurance and accessories are good value too.

To help, on www.moneysavingexpert.com I try to link to the best comparison service for each product to cut out these problems (though for credit cards, I currently won't link to any, as none are good enough).

6. CHAT FORUMS AND BULLETIN BOARDS
This hugely powerful resource is a simple way to discuss whatever you're doing with others. Of course, you need to take whatever anonymous individuals say with a pinch of salt, but more often than not you'll find well-meaning, well-informed people willing to help. The MoneySavingExpert forums have 50,000 people discussing best buys.

Method 3: Newspapers and Magazines
This is much more familiar territory for most people. Although newspapers and magazines aren't as instantly up to date as the internet, they often do provide very useful information, both in articles and in best-buy tables.

If you want an easy way to find a good buy, then buy a Sunday paper, look through its money section and you will see lots of tables of 'Best Buys'. It's not the über-best way, but it's a good starting point. However, most newspaper best-buy tables are compiled for the papers by information and comparison services and include some of the problems noted above.

Method 4: Shanks's Pony
There's nothing wrong with physically tripping from bank to bank, shop to shop. Actually picking up and feeling what you're going to buy is a great indication of whether you really want it, though it's best used in conjunction with the other methods. As long as you follow the golden rule 'Never shop in just one shop', it's a great idea. Plus if you're there in person you can haggle (see page 116).

Method 5: Professional Advice

Undoubtedly, professional financial advice may be worthwhile if you're scared, short of time and don't feel confident doing the research yourself. Yet the cost can outweigh the benefit. If you're going to get professional advice, always check it's from an Independent Financial Adviser (IFA), as they can look across the entire range of the market, rather than a tied or multi-tied agent who can only sell you a limited product range. This is a legal distinction so ask the financial adviser, 'Are you an Independent Financial Adviser?' Don't accept any hedged answers.

WHEN TO USE AN IFA

Don't automatically flit to an IFA. It's a very common mistake to think they're experts on all money matters. They are not – their focus and training is in investments, pensions and protection products (life assurance and critical illness) and, to an extent, mortgages (though for these I would see a mortgage broker, see page 269). They are not qualified in credit cards, loans, debts, savings and bank accounts, even though they can earn commission recommending them; never pay for 'unqualified advice' on these subjects.

Even if you do go to an adviser, remember you're in charge – the decision is yours, not theirs. You don't have to do what they tell you. Read around their advice and ensure it's really right for you. When picking your IFA in the first place, always start by going to three and see who you prefer. Personal recommendations are another good way – though remember a good 'bedside manner' doesn't guarantee good advice. It's a tricky business.

If you are money savvy, my instincts would be to say avoid paying for professional advice, even on the subjects in which

IFAs are qualified. Do the research and buy via a discount broker (see 'Crash Diet', page 233) and you will be much better off. Remember, no one can predict the future and even IFAs' recommendations on what investments to go for are their best guess, not certain knowledge. However, especially with complex financial products, I understand people feel the need for help.

There are some areas where I think paying for advice is very useful. The three that immediately spring to mind are complex endowment or pension problems, and especially when getting an annuity. The reason for this is simple – when you retire, you use your pot of pension money to pay for an annuity, which then pays out to you every year until you die. Once you've got one, you can't change it. This means it's the biggest and most important financial decision you will ever make. And, if you find finance confusing, for the safety and security of knowing you're getting the very best annuity, I would suggest paying out a few hundred pounds for some good advice.

HOW TO PAY AN IFA

IFAs are paid in two ways: either a flat hourly fee for their advice (this can be as much as £200 per hour) or by commission. Remember, though: advisers paid commission may seem to be giving advice for free, but over the long run they tend to make more money this way than by charging a fee upfront.

Both payment methods have pros and cons. Pay a fee and you can be more confident the IFA doesn't bias their advice according to how much commission they make as they should then pay any commission they earn straight to you (always ask and check this is happening). Pay no fee and let them take the commission, and you may end up with a better relationship as you'll feel free to seek advice regularly, because you won't need to stump up the cash upfront – leaving you with a retained adviser looking over your finances.

OTHER ADVISERS

IFAs aren't the only ones who talk money. Tax accountants are often crucial and unavoidable if you're self-employed, have complicated tax affairs and especially for inheritance tax advice. Bank managers also talk money advice – however, this is often just a way to flog you something from their own portfolio of products, and won't encompass the entire market. Be very careful of anything your bank advises you to do. If you've serious debt problems, the free debt-counselling services are fantastic and I wholeheartedly recommend them (see 'Debt Crisis', page 411).

MOVING OUTSIDE YOUR COMFORT ZONE

'Reach out for info' and there's a massive boon – it should enable you to move outside your comfort zone, and this almost invariably results in your getting a better deal. Most people's comfort zones are familiar, omnipresent high-street shops and brands. Unfortunately, this enables those trusted patrons to price themselves higher on the grounds that they provide a sense of security.

Moving outside your comfort zone means shopping in places you've not heard of, buying on the internet and not always going for the straightforward option. It can be a little disconcerting, and occasionally you'll make the wrong decision, but more often you should benefit. And if you've done your research, comparison-shopped and are armed with information, the only real crisis is one of confidence. After all, wherever you shop in the UK you have the same statutory rights and protection (see 'Holler', page 129).

THE LIST OF TEN THINGS TO USE THE NET FOR EVEN WHEN YOU DON'T HAVE INTERNET ACCESS

The internet has re-divided society into 'haves' and 'have-nots'. Internet operators have low overheads – they've no expensive high-street premises, processes are automated and, if necessary, products can be posted or shipped cheaply. This usually makes them cheaper.

This list applies even if you don't have access to the net, specifically where the discount is for applying online, and no further internet access is needed.

For those with the time and not the money, use a local library and take a quick course in getting online. However, if there's no time then ask web-savvy friends or family to do it with you.

Do remember, though, that as there's sometimes personal information involved you need to be very careful who you choose to help, and you must be sure you can trust them not to rip you off later. And always print out the terms and conditions, and receipts.

1. Savings accounts. These are simply places for money to sit, rarely touched, earning interest. Many of the top payers are internet-access-only accounts, yet if you set up the account online initially, you can often call and operate it on the phone after that. Do check both that this is possible, and that there's no additional fee. Of course if you use a savings account to put money into and take money out of all the time, it's a no-go. (See page 215.)

2. Cash ISAs. After all, a cash ISA is just a tax-free savings account – so it's very similar. (See page 223.)

3. Flights. Whether it's long-haul through Expedia, E-Bookers or Travelocity, or a short-haul through Ryanair or EasyJet, booking is much cheaper on the internet. Once you've made your purchase that's usually it, and, if not, customer service tends to be phone-, not net-based. (See page 264.)

4. Credit-card balance transfers. Balance transfers are a long-term process. The best practice is to set up a direct debit to pay it off and put the card in a drawer without using it for anything else. So, if the best deal's online, it's worth considering. (See page 372.)

5. Personal and secured loans. The cost difference between online and traditional loans can be enormous. Yet non-net-users will usually need to just take it out online then pay off a fixed amount each month by direct debit. (See page 398.)

6. Gas and electricity. Many top tariffs are available online only. Yet some providers still send paper bills, so only the set-up needs to be online. If not, though, avoid. (See page 175.)

7. Big electrical goods. Get a friend to do a quick online search using a shopping robot to find the cheapest price for you, then either buy it, or print out the details and try for a price match in a high-street store (and put your thumb over the delivery cost when doing so).

8. Term assurance. Use an online broker to find the cheapest;

after that the actual product comes from a life assurance company and they tend to deal in paper. (See page 279.)

9. Travel insurance. Find the cheapest online, as when you make a claim it tends to be on the phone rather than on the internet. (See page 266.)

10. Car and home insurance. Using the internet to find it dramatically reduces the time it takes to get a good quote and then you can simply use the phone for further contact. (See pages 284 and 291.)

seven £

HAGGLE

There's no such thing as a fixed price. The ticket price is purely an indicator of what you need to pay. Legally they don't have to accept it, so you don't need to pay it!

CHUTZPAH
(hoot'spa) — n. effrontery, nerve [Yiddish]

Chutzpah is a powerful consumer weapon, especially when combined with talents not often evoked in the money world: 'seduction, a gentle patter and a twinkle in the eyes'. With these you can transform a twee UK high street into a stall-filled, hustling, bustling Turkish bazaar.

We British will banter and barter with the best if we're somewhere the flies need swatting. Yet on home turf we become complacent lily-livered cowards. Over the years UK shopkeepers have managed to hypnotise us into believing it's rude and impolite to haggle here and that prices are always fixed.

Haggling is neither difficult nor rude – it makes you a better consumer and the shops better retailers. And while I've used the word 'shop' so far, haggling needn't be reserved for shopping.

You can haggle for holidays, credit-card interest rates, mobile phones, new cars and hotel prices. At its most basic, haggling is just asking for a discount, yet with technique and cheek, it can become an art.

While haggling is easy in theory, doing it takes a deep breath and a conscious decision. I'll be honest, I don't always haggle – often the possible gain is outweighed by the time it'd take, or I'm just not in the right mood. However, over the years I've had many successes (just not every time).

For fun, while writing this, I tried the ultimate haggling challenge – a supermarket. In the main, I was pitiful; however, there was one triumph: I did manage to persuade the woman at the deli counter to give me a few extra ounces of cheese.

Usually, though, haggling is best reserved for bigger purchases than a pint of milk. To do it properly, strategy and timing are crucial.

BRILLIANT BARTERING IN JUST 16 STEPS (BUT FOR YOU I'LL DO IT IN 15!)

1. The beginner's haggle – 'would ya throw in the ...' If you've never haggled before it is daunting. So, to start, rather than asking for a discount, just ask them to throw something in on top. Always try to get your batteries thrown in for free on electrical goods and extra shoe polish for new shoes. If there's an add-on extra, try not to pay for it.

2. Internet prices in real stores. Use the internet to find the cheapest price available. Print the results and take them with you to the shops. Confronted with this kind of evidence, they will often price-match the net cost (though try to keep your fingers over the bit of paper that details any delivery costs).

3. *Be polite, firm, non-competitive and maybe just a touch flirtatious.* Being an aggressive or forceful haggler is usually a mistake; it often annoys the person you are dealing with – and your discount is at their discretion. If you are polite, charming yet firm and treat the whole process with humour, you'll get a bit further. In my experience this is especially true with male shopkeepers. Men tend to be extremely competitive (personally, I struggle to stop racing people up the escalator as I get off the tube), and if it becomes a battle of wills they may be prepared to lose the sale just to keep some pride.

4. *Seniority, yes. Head honcho, no.* An assistant manager or supervisor is a good person to bargain with. They have more discretion than most of the shop staff, understand the retail game a little bit better, and are used to pleasing their customers. Go to the very top, though, and the person will be short of time, and not bothered about one small sale.

5. *Reduced prices have extra flexibility.* If the price is already reduced, such as in a sale or manager's clearance, there is often more flexibility for bartering. As the boundaries have already flexed there's more room to play. Also the psychological loss for the person you are haggling with is reduced, as they have already given up the idea of getting full price.

6. *Don't commit to financing.* Don't talk about your payment method until it's necessary. Sellers prefer debit cards to credit cards, so leave this until the end of the transaction. However, if they have their own financing options, it may be worth mooting you're interested, without committing, as there's often good commission on finance, so they'll be more disposed to give a bigger discount. One final thought – if they are offering interest-free finance this is already equivalent to a discount of 5 per cent plus; see if instead of taking it you can get a discount for using a debit card.

7. *Avoid busy bartering.* Try not to haggle when the shop is crammed with other customers. The last thing salespeople are interested in is reducing their margins when they can see lots of people willing to buy. Go during times of shopping serenity, like midweek mid-mornings, when retailers are worrying about where the next penny will come from.

8. *Bulk bartering.* Discounts are often available for bulk buying. This may mean stocking up for a year, buying a combination of products, or even going with a group of friends who want to buy something similar. The advantage you have is you're going to hand over a lot more business, and you should secure a reduction because of it.

9. *Avoid seasonal products.* The worst time to barter for a scooter, convertible car or air-conditioning unit is when the sun is beating down. And it's much easier to barter for a brolly when there's not a cloud in the sky; desperation isn't a good weapon.

10. *Play them off against each other.* Take quotes and prices from other sellers, and try to play them off against each other. This has two advantages: it gives solid foundation to your request and it prods sellers' competitive instincts in your favour as they want to show they're better than the opposition.

11. End-of-month/year haggling holiday. Towards the end of their financial year, or monthly target, retailers and sales people are often much more willing to haggle. At that point it's volume, rather than profit, that really counts, so they're willing to slice their margins down to a carpaccio, just to make the sales. If in doubt when their financial month/year end is, assume it's the calendar month and the tax year.

12. Always ask for the sun and you may just get the moon. Do it with humour, do it with style, and there's no price or suggestion that's too outrageous.

13. Choose independents over chains. Bartering in independent retailers, where you can speak directly to the owner, is a better bet than a chain. There's more leeway. This doesn't mean chains won't barter (I've done it in Dixons, Comet and WH Smith to name a few). Yet with owner/retailer shops, the owner has complete discretion, so a smile and a hint that you'll become a regular shopper works wonders.

14. Closing the deal. If you are nearly ready to buy then start to use true sales negotiation language. Let them know the exact conditions they must meet in order to close the sale. But don't be afraid, even then, to walk away if they won't give you what you want – you can always try elsewhere.

15. Don't settle unnecessarily. Earlier I mentioned one of the jobs I did in my year out before university – selling caravan awnings (see page 101). As a salesman, I had full discretion to drop the price. Yet I routinely told customers I needed to check with my manager beyond a certain level.

This both put a break in the negotiations if they weren't going well for me, and allowed me to return and say, 'Sorry, it's not possible, I can only drop it so far' without looking like the bad guy.

Martin's Money Memories: Lewis v Lewis

One of the easiest and best haggles I've ever done was in the great high-street bastion, John Lewis. It's one of those stores people assume is unhagglablewith. Yet remember, its 'never knowingly undersold' price promise is effectively an open invitation. Even so, most people just walk in, get what they want, pay the set price and leave.

My purchase was a small wooden bathroom cabinet, original price £80, but on sale for £40. It was both the last one left, and the last sale item in that entire department. This, you should know by now, is a golden haggling opportunity as shops are keen to reclaim all their display space for new stock. My suspicion was if they didn't sell it that day, they'd chuck it out.

Having waited a couple of minutes, I spotted what looked like a senior departmental type walking past. Quickly I asked if I could have the cabinet for a discount. He was open to it straight away: 'How much?' My preamble was important – I wanted him to know I understood the issues, and I wanted to reinforce why he should give in. So, smiling, I said, 'Well, I'm sure you want to reclaim your display case, and I'm willing to remove this for you. So why don't I just give you a tenner for it and get out of here?' He tried to suggest £20 – already 50 per cent off! And he was half-hearted at that. 'Go on, a tenner and I'll just get it out of here.' Five minutes later I was out of the door with my £80 bathroom cabinet for £10 – and very nice it is too.

Often customers were fooled into settling at that point. Remember, even if the salesperson is telling the truth that they need a manager's permission, make them go back to the manager, or get them to bring the manager to you. All sales-people's facts are flexible when haggling.

THE LIST OF TEN HEAVENLY HIGH-STREET HAGGLES

Even for the hard-core dedicated MoneySavers on www.moneysavingexpert.com, haggling is a tough one. Only 13 per cent of them always try to barter, compared to 25 per cent who never do. Most say they'll give it a go if it feels right, but the status quo is often easier. Yet, as encouragement, here are some of their tales, hints, tips and practical successes.

1. *Finding a stitch in time saves.* 'Look for the minutest of dents or scratches on electrical appliances, and marks on clothing. I once got money off a blouse with some kid's grubby handprints on it – the marks washed out. Just point out that they'll be unlikely to sell it to anyone else unless they pay for dry cleaning.'

2. *Turning the tables.* 'I'm a sales manager in a big mobile retailer; we work on margin so get the right salesperson and you can save big pounds. Make friends with them (I don't mean ask them out or anything like that ... just ask their opinion, build an obligation). They're more likely to sell/discount to someone they feel they like. The best time is the end of the month or end of the quarter, as the shops have to meet targets and need to make sales, so they're more likely to discount.'

3. If you don't ask, you don't get. 'We wanted a washing machine from Curry's. It was in heavy demand as it had £100 off. So we nipped round the corner to a local electrical store, which had the same machine actually in stock. After a bit of chat they agreed to give us the same discount as long as we paid in cash. A new washing machine at the cheap price, there and then.'

4. Make it cheaper than interest-free. 'When 0 per cent interest-free credit is offered, I always ask what the cash price is, and usually find it's 5 per cent cheaper. Until I started this I always thought interest-free was actually free; now I realise it's just one form of discount, so I ask for another instead!'

5. Naughty but nice. 'Bought a cooker and queried why it was £75 cheaper next door. The salesman went and checked, came back and agreed to sell it at the reduced price. Then I realised that although the cookers looked identical they were different models, and I ended up with the better spec. Result!'

6. Court Tottenham Court Road. 'Big electrical shop centres like the ones in London's Tottenham Court Road are haggling heaven. We went to about three different shops to get the lowest quote, then returned to the cheapest and pushed them to do it for even less. I got the laptop I wanted £250 cheaper than Dixons' advertised price at the time.'

7. It isn't always the end of the line. 'I managed to get £50 knocked off a stereo because it was the last one in the shop and the display model. All that was wrong was that it was a bit dusty.'

8. Keen service means keen bargains. 'If you are pounced on by assistants, you know they're on commission. Tell them you will come and find them in a while – they will be begging for that sale, and may be more likely to discount or throw in freebies.'

9. Seriously prepared to save. 'I bought a dishwasher and washing machine, and was told delivery would be £25. I asked for my card back and to cancel the sale. The saleswoman didn't believe me till I took the card out of her hand, then she agreed to free delivery.'

10. Cheeky flirting in shorts. 'In a surf shop sale last year I liked a pair of shorts priced £15 from £35 and a skirt priced £20 from £40. I managed to get both for £25 through a combination of haggling and cheeky flirting!'

Mobile Haggling

Do you have a contract mobile phone? If so, one phone call can massively improve your deal. An easy haggling technique can add 300 more cross-network minutes and 30 extra texts a month, a new camera phone, and reduce your bill by £10 a month.

In a nutshell, this is all about telling your provider 'give me a better package or I'll leave'. The nearer you are to your contract renegotiation date, the better chance you have.

Rather than writing a series of techniques, I thought the easiest way to explain what to do is tell you the story of how I did it myself.

There are no hard and fast rules when it comes to negotiating, but there are many tips and techniques to try. Get it right and this is powerful MoneySaving, with many reporting savings of hundreds of pounds.

Setting the Scene

I'm an Orange contract customer and I wanted to stay that way, as it enables me to use the mobile override trick (see page 181) and the reception is very good where I live. Therefore, the focus had to be on negotiating a better package rather than actually changing network.

This also means there's no need for me to go through the month-long hassle of moving my phone over.

While my story is about Orange, it can work for many people on other phone networks. There are no guarantees here, so always think of it as a bit of a game, but if you're the winner it's worth it.

'I'M NOT HAPPY'

Tell the operator you're not happy with your package and quote a better deal you've seen elsewhere:

Martin: 'Hi, I have a package with you. Frankly I'm not happy. The mobile network "3" offers 500 cross-network minutes [means you can call mobiles too] for £25 a month and I'm paying £30 a month for just 200 minutes. This simply isn't good enough. While I want to stick with you, unless you can offer me something better, I'm going to have to leave.'

There's an interesting undercurrent here. Orange has a price promise to match other networks' tariffs. However, as I write, it doesn't include '3', unsurprising as it is much cheaper than the others.

Orange: 'Sorry Mr Lewis, let me put you through to our specialist disconnections department and see if we can find any way to improve it.'

'I'M STILL NOT HAPPY'

Repeat the same mantra to disconnections. Disconnections has much more power than normal customer service and more discretion to give you packages (within limits). In fact the real name for disconnections is the 'customer retentions' department – says it all doesn't it!

Orange disconnections: '*I think we can help, we can match that "3" tariff for the same price.*' (Note: Orange's own 400-minute package cost £50 a month.)

Martin: '*That's not part of your normal price match plan?*'

Orange disconnections: '*Nope, it's a special offer for valued customers*' (subtext: we'll pull out all the stops if we're going to lose you).

'I WANT MORE'

After quickly checking this didn't invalidate my 'override trick' potential, I proceeded to ask for more text messages and got them too, 30 more a month.

Then the man happily told me it was upgrade time: '*Pick a phone, any phone, what do you want?*' So I opted for a snazzy, tiny camera phone, with radio and tri-band – all of course for no extra charge.

WHAT IF THEY SAY NO?

Remember this is a game. If you're pushing them to the limit, and they are saying 'Okay, if you don't like the package we'll disconnect you' then be careful.

Of course moving to a cheaper provider will save you money. Do it on your terms, not theirs, though. So if you don't want to disconnect there and then, just back off. Okay, it may be a tiny bit embarrassing backtracking on your threat, but they've no idea who you really are.

TURNING 'ANNYULNEED' INTO 'ANNILLNEED'

There's a certain salacious joy to writing this bit. In 'Forget Loyalty', page 90, I detailed the *annyulneed* sales trick used to get customers to buy more goods. While I don't like that tactic, I do admire it. And by turning *annyulneed* into *annillneed* it becomes a weapon in our haggling arsenal.

It's a bonus haggle if you like. First push for the biggest discount on the main product, as that's where the biggest savings come from.

Then comes the time to use *annillneed* – once you've almost finished the haggle for the main item, but before they've closed the sale. Make it an almost instinctive reaction; act as if you're not really thinking about it and it's no big deal. Add-ons are the key: a floor mat with a tent, a scart lead with a DVD player, a better CD player in a new car. Simply say, '*Annillneed* that too.' The aim is to get them to throw it in for free, or at least try to get it for cost. Remember, if you've already been haggling, the door for discounts is open, so it's easier to swing it a bit further.

If they say no, hint it's a deal breaker or remind them how much you're about to spend: 'I'm about to pay you £12,000 for a new car and you won't throw in a nicer CD player?'

Martin's Money Memories: Use Whatever You've Got!

They sprung it on me! Three-quarters of the way through my hour-long haggling phone-in on Jeremy Vine's Radio 2 programme, JV said, 'Right Martin, let's see how good you are. We've got a car dealer on the phone. He's promised he will make the car available at whatever price you haggle him down to.'

Okay, so millions listening, my reputation on the line, no briefing on the car, its list price or real value. Well, we bartered, we bargained, we haggled. Two minutes in and over a grand off, but I wanted more so I said, 'Save my reputation with so many listening and drop it £500 more.' JV called, 'Foul, that's cheating, you can't use the fact you're on the radio,' yet of course it's not.

When haggling you use exactly what you've got, whatever the situation. It was true, so it was fair, and thankfully it worked.

eight

HOLLER

You have rights so use them! Just because you buy cheap doesn't mean you've no right to good service. And just because you've been with a company for a long time doesn't mean you should let them take you for granted. If they do, move on!

NOT JUST RIGHTS, BUT EXPECTATIONS

Knowing your rights gives you power. Consumers aren't impotent – we've rafts of legal protection. Yet Money Dieters don't just have rights, but also expectations. We live in a competitive world where many companies vie for our business. This means that even when we don't specifically have a legal right, there's nothing wrong with expecting top treatment.

Bad service, figures that don't add up, and being asked to pay for goods not received – these are all part of a consumer's year. Yet companies rely on their reputations, and even if they're not breaking the law, if their behaviour isn't what you want or expect, it's likely others wouldn't want or expect it either. So there's nothing wrong with complaining. Often it's only a matter of a simple letter or phone call to get the right result.

HOW TO HOLLER

I use the word 'holler' because it's nice and it's emotive. It evokes the all-important message – don't be downtrodden, run over or screwed by these companies. Stand up for yourself, claim your rights, and seek out what you deserve.

Yet though I want to pump you up, when it comes to making an actual complaint, cool, calm and rational is more likely to get results than an aggressive rant. It may make them want to get rid of you, but it's tough to argue coherently when your lungs are bellowing.

I'll be honest, this is a mistake I sometimes make. Those who've seen/heard me on the radio/television will realise my on-air 'name and shame' rants are common. Sadly my ire sometimes gets the better of me when complaining in person too, and there it's much less effective. The people we complain to are human too – usually it's not their personal money at issue, so get them onside, don't alienate them. Preparation and calm control work – after all, a company can deny your request even when you're right, and if they do the ultimate recourse is going to court, which massively increases the hassle factor.

Before complaining, sit down and work out exactly what your grounds are. If this is a substantive complaint, ensure you research your rights, how these rights are enforced, and what it is legitimate to ask for. Always know what you want and what you are willing to settle for. Do you want to exchange the goods? Do you want a full refund? Do you want compensation and, if so, what kind? What do you think is fair?

Run it past friends or relatives to see if they think it's reasonable or if they've had any experience of complaining in a similar way. Even better, if you know someone who works for a company similar to the one you're complaining about, ask them. All this information is useful ammunition. Once you're ready, if you're not feeling confident, try rehearsing, then holler to your heart's content and get a result.

YOUR RIGHTS

When all's said and done, though, the most powerful tool is knowing your legal strength.

While journeying towards a Radio 2 phone-in on consumer rights, I was desperately thinking of how to make it easy for people to remember all their consumer rights. Thankfully, nature came to my rescue!

The SAD FART Rules

When you buy in a shop, it must be:
Satisfactory quality; **A**s **D**escribed;
Fit for purpose; **A**nd last a **R**easonable **T**ime

Your agreement is with the retailer, not the manufacturer
If goods are faulty complain to the shop or company you bought them from. It's up to the retailer to sort it out for you. If it tries to fob you off by telling you to go to the product's manufacturer, it's wrong. Stick to your guns.

Goods should be of satisfactory quality, as described, and fit for their intended purpose
Say you buy some hi-fi speakers and they don't work, then obviously they're not fit. However, if the speakers do work, but they don't fit your existing stereo system and this was

---

Money Diet Quick Fact Snack: What is Reasonable?

Now there's a question lawyers have argued over for years. Reasonable is ...
well ... reasonable. That's the point. So whenever that word is used in a legal
context, it simply means what you or I or any normal person would consider
to be reasonable.

---

something you specifically questioned, then they still aren't
fit for the purpose specified. Of course, proving this is difficult
without written evidence.

Time is of the essence

Examine anything you've bought as soon as you get it home
and if there is a problem complain immediately. The amount
of time legally allowed to check whether goods are faulty
depends on what's reasonable for that product – it takes longer
to check a speedboat than a kettle. However, as a rule of
thumb, try and complain within a week. Do that and you are
entitled to a full refund. Leave it longer and, even if the goods
were faulty when you bought them, you may struggle to get a
full refund, though even then you're still entitled to a replacement or a reduction.

Proving goods were faulty when you bought them

Take obviously faulty goods back to the shop and, if it's within
six months of the purchase, it's up to the shop to prove they
were not faulty when you bought them. However, after six
months, the law changes, and you must prove they were faulty
when you bought them.

Yet if there is any disagreement over whether the goods are
currently faulty, it's up to you to prove they are. And, it should

be noted, if you know goods are faulty when you buy them, you don't have a right to return them.

Overall, you have up to six years to bring a complaint, but this doesn't mean whatever you buy must last six years; it's just the maximum. They must last what most people would consider to be a 'reasonable' length of time. So if there is legitimate wear and tear that damages the product, the likelihood is you have no claim.

'No refunds' signs

Some shops display signs stating 'No refunds', designed to put customers off exercising their legal rights. These are illegal, and if you see one you should report it to your local Trading Standards office. Just log on to www.tradingstandards.gov.uk, or ring your local office.

Pay on a credit card

Pay for goods costing over £100, even partially (just a £1 deposit, for example), using a credit card (not a debit card – there's no legal protection there). The credit card company is then equally liable with the retailer, giving you a second bite at the complaining cherry. This protection is known as Section 75 as it comes from that part of the 1974 Consumer Credit Act. Though of course do try and pay it off at the end of the month so there's no interest charged.

You've actually more rights on the internet or by mail order

Under special rules called the distance-selling regulations, you have seven working days to cancel after receiving goods bought on the net or by mail order (this doesn't apply to fresh food, flowers, sealed audio equipment or travel for specific dates). You also have a right to clear information, written confirmation of the order, delivery details and information about how to cancel. If it's a service you've signed up to, the seven working days is the amount of time you have, after agreeing, to cancel. However, buy goods from firms based abroad and beware: UK laws won't cover you. So stick to countries where they have well-enforced legal systems, such as the US or elsewhere in Europe – not that you'll ever prosecute, but problems are less likely.

Is there a right to return expensive stuff?

There are a number of rights commonly assumed to exist that don't. You don't have a right to return goods if you spot them cheaper elsewhere (though if I ruled the world you would), change your mind or bought them for the wrong reason. However, though you don't have rights, this doesn't mean don't ask. Many shops would rather keep customers happy than be sticklers for these rules.

Money Diet Quick Fact Snack: Settling an Old Debate

You spot a can of beans in a shop mistakenly priced at 1p. Can you force the shop to sell it to you? No, sorry. If they're mispriced the shop can refuse to sell them, as until they accept your cash, you've no contract with them. However, you can report shops that are deliberately advertising misleading prices to the Trading Standards office, who can investigate and may prosecute. This does of course get tricky if it's online and the purchase is automated; however, even then they can argue, using what's known as 'the Law of Mistake', that the transaction wasn't finalised.

Enforcing Your Rights

You know you're right and your rights. You walk in, calmly holler and they wilt. Hoorah. Unfortunately, sometimes this doesn't happen. So what then? Well, the ultimate recourse is the courts – after all, that's where rights are enforced. Yet your local Trading Standards office and Citizens' Advice Bureau are quicker and easier routes; try them first.

YOUR EXPECTATIONS

Can You Really Expect Good Service at a Cheap Price?

The Money Diet is about cutting bills and looking for low-cost services. Some may argue that you can't then realistically expect top quality or good customer service. Wrong! Cheap does not mean shoddy. Cheap does not mean poor service. The Money Diet is about value. Don't let ne'er-do-wells persuade you cheap can't be good – get it right and it just means the same product but less provider profits.

Even When You've No Rights, You're Not Wrong

There are many occasions when we don't get the service we expect or deserve yet legally don't have a leg to stand on. However, companies run on a combination of reputation, delivery and repeat business. Even though Money Dieters spit on loyalty, companies don't know that. They must consider all customers to be potentially regular consumers who will use their services or buy their products again and again. Therefore we as consumers need to twist their goodwill to get what we want.

For companies, complaining consumers are problem consumers. They may well tell other people, talk to journalists

---

Money Diet Quick Fact Snack: Cut the Cost of Complaining

There's nothing more annoying than having to pay to complain. Yet many customer service lines are sneakily charging a fortune. Many companies charge 'non-geographic' local-rate 0845, or, even worse, national-rate 0870 numbers when you call. While these don't sound expensive, they can cost up to 8p a minute for daytime calls.

So when they leave you on hold, sadly all too common, it quickly adds up. Even worse, often the company you're complaining to gets a cut of this call cost. After heavy lobbying a change is now afoot, and the regulator Ofcom is investigating. Whether it'll help is yet to be seen.

A sneaky tip to defeat them. Many companies list special numbers to call to contact them when you're overseas. These tend to be standard numbers, which are much cheaper to call. Yet these numbers put you through to the same system, so dial the number for overseas customers (leaving out the GB code) when in the UK and save. Check out www.saynoto0870.com for a list of the numbers.

---

or television programmes about their bad experience, or even stand outside with a placard. Even though, legally, a company might not have done anything wrong, most people identify with other consumers, and sympathies are usually directed towards the little guy, not the big company. Use this to get compensation, a better product or better treatment.

THE LIST OF SIX SPECIFIC RIGHTS

Every area where you face a problem tends to have specific rights. It's worth checking these out before complaining. Here's a few to start you off.

1. PACKAGE HOLIDAYS

Should be as described. The holiday should reasonably match the description you had beforehand. It is a criminal offence if descriptions aren't truthful and accurate. 'A minute from the beach' is by foot or by taxi, not supersonic jet; accommodation should not be overbooked; photos shouldn't mislead either. Plus, under package-holiday regulations, you've a right to compensation for any negatively misleading descriptions.

Changes before you go. There's an automatic right to cancel, but if they substantially change the holiday terms, you've a right to a full refund. If you still want the holiday, but aren't happy, write and tell them that you will assess the impact the changes actually have on the trip.

Problems while you're there. If things go wrong during the holiday, ask for a complaint form there and then, otherwise you may lose the right to any compensation. You must give them the opportunity to put it right. Take video or photo evidence and notes from other holiday-makers if there is a problem. Keep details of who, what, where, when, how and why things went wrong, and receipts of any extra costs incurred.

If the tour operator won't do anything, either take them to court or go to the ABTA tribunal service.

2. eBAY

As Hoover is to vacuum cleaners and Biro is for ballpoints, eBay is for online auctions. Over 10 million UK adults now use it, but very few know their rights.

The first thing to be aware of is that eBay itself takes no real responsibility. It's a marketplace: all it's really doing is putting buyers and sellers together. It does offer limited protection, but limited really means just that.

It depends on who's selling. If you are buying via a 'buy it now' (more and more common) from a 'UK-based trader' on eBay – someone who makes a living by selling goods regularly – then provided it's not an auction you have all the same statutory rights as buying from a shop.

However, as there is no strict definition of a 'trader', this is something that would be decided by the courts. Yet if it's someone obviously doing this on a regular basis as part of their living, then it's very likely they're a trader.

If, on the other hand, you're just buying from a UK private individual, then the law says 'let the buyer beware'. If your purchase arrives 'as described' you'll have little legal comeback – you may want to ask yourself 'Would I be willing to buy this off a man in the pub?'

Just because it's on eBay doesn't make it cheap. One common misperception about eBay gives me the willies. Of course there's many a bargain to be had on it, but some things are overpriced and available cheaper, new, elsewhere.

Some traders deliberately price higher on eBay, using our innate 'it's on eBay so it must be cheap' feelings against us.

There are lots of free ways to check whether you're really getting a bargain, such as Google, shopping robots and the moneysavingexpert.com chat forums.

3. DRY-CLEANING
Check the cleaners belong to the TSA. The Textiles Services Association carries out quality checks, so it's well worth checking your dry-cleaner belongs to it.

Problems with dry-cleaning. Always give them as much

information as possible about the goods. If a re-clean doesn't solve it, you are entitled to reclaim the product's value when it was cleaned (not 'as new').

4. SECOND-HAND GOODS

You still have rights. Second-hand goods and sales goods bought from shops follow the same rules: if they're faulty, you can return them. Like other goods, they must be of satisfactory quality – but after the price is taken into account. If you buy a laptop for a fiver, you can't really expect it to run normally. And if you are made aware of any faults when you buy, you can't return it later because of those.

With private sellers it's 'buyer beware'. Buy second-hand goods from private sellers, and then it's *caveat emptor* or 'let the buyer beware'. If the seller doesn't say anything and you buy it, then even if it doesn't do what you thought it might, you were not mis-sold. The only restriction is that the product should be correctly described and the owner has the right to sell it.

5. SECOND-HAND CARS FROM DEALERS

Same as all main goods, but a car should be fit to use on the road, be in a condition that reflects its age and price, and be reasonably reliable. 'Sold as seen' has no basis in law; your Sale of Goods Act rights still apply.

Note: Private sales of cars work like all second-hand private sales (see above); however, unless stated, you have a right to expect it will pass an MOT.

6. RESTAURANTS

Prices. All pubs and restaurants should clearly display their prices.

Quality. Food should be of 'satisfactory' quality; this includes being hot when it's meant to be. If it isn't, claim a full or partial refund, depending on the problem. You may want to report the restaurant to your local Environmental Health Department, as improperly cooked food or food served at the incorrect temperature may pose a health risk.

The food should be as described. If it says 'home-made' on the menu, it should be home-made – if not, it's a breach of criminal law under the Trade Description Act and a breach of contract. This means that you could fairly deduct the value of the difference between home-made and manufactured cost from the food price.

Service charges. There's no requirement to pay extra for 'service', and if the service charge is included in the price, you are legally entitled to deduct a reasonable amount if it wasn't as expected – say 10 to 15 per cent. Also, be careful not to pay a service charge twice – some restaurants encourage this by

A Long-term Complaint

During a radio phone-in about bank accounts, one caller complained, 'I've been with my bank 19 years and it's always been appalling. The service is terrible, they never do what I ask, it's one mistake after another, and they pay me virtually no interest. I want everybody to know how useless they are.'

To be honest, I laughed. 'Why on earth do you come on here complaining about your bank, telling us about its awfulness, and yet you've been with them for 19 years?' I asked. 'Have you never thought of switching, never thought of changing to someone better, never thought of trying a different option?'

While hollering is useful, rarely is the remedy better than picking a good provider in the first place.

leaving a blank space on the bill or credit-card slip or asking you to enter it in the electronic card machine, even when it is already included.

What if they say 'Pay or we'll call the police'?

If you are reducing the price as you don't think it is reasonable, always explain why. If you feel forced into paying, then pay 'under protest' and then dispute the cost and/or make a claim later; after all, it's never worth a fist in the face. If you do pay a reduced amount, give the trader your name and address, and invite them to sue you in the County Court. If you're in the right then they won't usually bother.

nine

THINK THROUGH THEIR LOGIC

Shopping around isn't enough – you may just get the best of a bad bunch. To really see through their charades ask, 'How do companies make money from me?' and 'How much do they make?'

'Shop around' is oft-quoted advice, and while it's not wrong, it's too bland for more advanced Money Dieting. More important is adding, 'How are they making money out of me?' The answer allows us to start to work out how to cut their profits and reduce our costs. I'm not pretending this is easy, and there are no fixed rules, but let me give you a couple of practical examples.

LOGICAL SAVING 1:
WHEN FREE ISN'T REALLY FREE

Though it sounds complicated, level-term life assurance is a simple issue. It pays out a fixed lump sum if you die within a set amount of time. As whether you die or not isn't open to debate, and the amount paid out is fixed, it simply boils down to 'the cheaper, the better', providing the company you get it with is reliable.

Most people buy this product straight from their bank. This is almost always a bad idea: a) it costs a fortune; b) it doesn't involve shopping around; and c) banks take every extra penny they possibly can.

Some people at least try a few providers. A few, especially following newspaper advice, find themselves at the doors of a life-assurance broker. These companies promise to shop around the entire market to find the cheapest price for you. This route usually cuts the cost by 20 to 40 per cent.

Martin's Money Memories: Utilising Logic

Thinking through the logic is a powerful weapon. After some nagging by an overly persistent press officer, I agreed to have lunch with the Chief Executive of a new small gas and electricity price comparison service (see 'Crash Diet', page 175). While eating she asked me, 'What would it take to get you to recommend us as the best service?' The obvious answer was 'Nothing!' but then I had a flippant thought: *why not try and cut its profits?* Price-comparison services make money because, if someone switches via their service, providers pay them to do the back office functions. So I said, 'If you want me to recommend you, give customers a cut of the cash.' I was a little surprised when she said she'd try, and more so when one week later she e-mailed me to say they'd crunched the numbers and could do it. And for two months, it both found customers the cheapest provider, and paid £10 per switch on top. Other companies have since followed the lead, two companies now consistently offer cashback to those 'in the know', permanently scarring the marketplace to consumers' benefit.

Sounds good? But this is only 'shop around' not 'think through the logic'. At this point ask yourself, 'Why does this broker do this for me?' The answer, of course, is commission. This then leads to, 'Will anybody else do exactly the same for less?' In the life-assurance market the answer is a definite yes.

Many brokers, often smaller firms, will rebate some or even most of their commission. As commission makes up a huge part of the life-assurance cost, this cuts another 20 per cent or 30 per cent off the price. (See 'Crash Diet', page 233.)

LOGICAL SAVING 2: THE WRONG PRODUCT FOR THE RIGHT THING

It's possible to use some products in ways other than they're designed for. This may sound slightly bizarre but, to quote an old comedy phrase, 'That's exactly what they want you to think.' Shopping around limits you to one set of products, but by looking at what else could do the same job, you widen the choice and can take advantage of a greater marketplace.

The classic example is my old favourite, personal loans, where prices range between 6 per cent and 15 per cent interest. The 'wrong product' (i.e. the one to use) is a credit card, as while there are no interest-free personal loans, there are many interest-free cards. So bend a credit card to work like a personal loan, then you've cracked it and can cut the cost. (I explain the mechanics in 'Healthy Eating', page 406.)

This works across a range of different areas. Don't think within the boxes they create for us – think around the issues. Ask, 'What would solve my problem?' and seek it out. There are no limits to this – it could be using level-term insurance to cover your mortgage, white vinegar as a household cleaner,

---

Martin's Money Memories: Taking a Different Route

Cheap flights don't necessarily mean outside toilets on the plane. My friend was tripping to Sri Lanka with her mother to visit family there. The only flights available cost around £600 per person on a scheduled airline. She gave me a quick call and asked if I could help. I checked the usual sources, and didn't come up trumps. Most annoying! I hate not to be able to beat a deal. But in a moment's inspiration I decided to check chartered package-holiday offers, and found dozens of specials to Sri Lanka at a much, much cheaper price. One self-catering holiday flying only a day apart from the scheduled flights was around £400 – so I called her back. 'We're staying with relatives, though, why get a package?' The wrong product, the right thing – just because you get a hotel room, you don't need to use it. It's the £200 saving that counts.

'all-risks' household-insurance cover to protect your mobile phone, or a chess board to play draughts on.

If It Sounds Too Good to Be True, It Probably Is

Every time something looks too good to be true, rack your brain to think it through. Could it simply be a loss-leader to envelop your custom? Could there be a cunning undercurrent to how they make money? Could it be a special trick to make you pay more in an entirely different way?

Find the answer and you will be one of the very few who know. You're then in a position of power. Think through the logic, then work out how you can turn their tactics to your advantage.

USING THE MAXIM-UM LOGIC

The following is a real example of a 'think through the logic' thought process.

Question. The magazine *Maxim* is usually £3.30 a copy or £24 a year (12 issues) for a subscription from its own website or the magazine itself. So why (on the day I'm writing) is there a special promotion of two years' subscription for £9.99 (40p an issue) from a cashback website? (See page 209.)

First check the deal. Maybe there's a catch. I've checked all the usual – there's no additional markets bumf, no extra tie-ins, no additional subscriptions needed. It's clean.

So why are they doing it? Now, sometimes we never know, but if you can't work out a plausible reason (loss-leaders, building market share or others) you need to be sceptical. In this case, after thinking it through, here is my go at it (I don't know, just suspect):

Magazines make money in two ways – sales and advertising revenue. Advertising revenue depends on circulation. Therefore at certain times of the year, building circulation is crucial. Now, if the magazine just reduced its price via its own website or in the magazine, it'd be reducing its revenue from people likely to subscribe anyway. Its aim is to bring in new subscribers at speed without cannibalising its existing custom.

So what does it do? It goes to a cashback website, where people are very responsive to top deals, and flogs subscriptions cheaply. In this way it builds its circulation to help advertising revenue without cutting the price for the people who'd buy it anyway.

Think through the logic and then, in this case, you realise it's a cracking deal, worth grabbing (providing you'd buy/read *Maxim* anyway).

THE LIST OF THREE REASONS TO USE STORE CARDS

Store cards are the devil's debt. They make me more angry than any other financial product. Specifically, these are the special cards usable in just one store or group of stores. You will know the type I'm talking about – Debenhams, Selfridges, Top Shop ... those cards.

The application forms sit near the till, and are sold based on joining inducements.

The interest rates are usurious, often 30 per cent or more; that means spend £500 on a store card without paying it off and by the end of the year, you'll owe it £650 – an extra £150 for nothing. (See also page 372.)

Yet think through the logic and there are three decent reasons for having store cards.

1. A feeling of belonging. They often provide membership rights such as special offers, storecard-holder-only evenings, privileged access to new collections. There's nothing wrong with this. *Just never, ever, ever use it for borrowing.*

2. Extra discounts for shopping with friends. Sign up for a store card and they often tempt you with discounts of 10 per cent or even 20 per cent off your first purchase. Grab them and repay in full: nothing wrong with that. Yet Money Dieters can push this further. Never sign up for, and use, a card on your own – rather, go shopping with friends, sign up and then pay for everyone's purchases on the card. This way everybody benefits from your discount. Of course, ensure your friends give you the money and be sure to pay the card off in full so there's no interest charge. Then a few weeks or months later, go back with your friends and let one of them sign up for a new card and its discount, and likewise allow all to shop on it. You can do this again and again and again. *But never, ever, ever use it for borrowing*.

3. A handy tool. If it's late at night, it's dark and you're locked out of your house, waggle the store card correctly in the lock on your door, and you might just be able to persuade it to open. But remember: *never, ever, ever use it for borrowing*.

PRICE PROMISES HAVE THEIR FINGERS CROSSED

Price promises are devious, misleading devils – whether it's 'we're never beaten on price', 'never knowingly undersold' or 'find it anywhere else and we'll refund the difference'.

All, surprisingly, favour the retailer more than the consumer. They're a clever psychological ploy. They offer reassurance that you're getting the best price, but without delivering anything of the kind.

Just because something has a price promise doesn't actually make it the cheapest. All it means is the price may be dropped if you're prepared to do the work. However, people allow themselves to feel it's a good deal just because the store has a price promise, and therefore don't bother looking to beat the price. Price promises are worth nothing unless you put them to the test.

Stores offering price promises can set prices at any level they choose, as if they're caught, the worst is they'll just have to lower them to the same level as another shop.

To put this in context I popped to Comet's website. One of its main special offers was an all-in-one printer/scanner/copier for £69.99 including delivery. Flashing at the top of the web page was the price-promising phrase: 'We always check others' prices online – then we lower ours.' Quickly I clicked across to the internet shopping robot 'pricerunner' ... the same printer was available online for less at five other retailers. The cheapest was £54.99 – £15 less.

The worst example I've ever seen was that supposed bastion of pro-consumerism, 'Nationwide'. Its price promise was 'get a car insurance quote cheaper elsewhere within two weeks of buying our policy and we'll refund the difference'.

How many people get more car insurance quotes just AFTER signing up for a policy? Double the difference and fair enough, but this was pure tosh!

(Martin's Note: Since I wrote this section, Nationwide has changed its price promise to a 'double the difference' one. Unfortunately for Nationwide this simply means that I tell people to get a quote from Nationwide and then use my car insurance cost cutting system (see page 284). If Nationwide isn't the cheapest and the terms are right, take it out, then requote from the cheapest and make it give you double the discount back. This is an effective loophole to undercut the market's cheapest. Sorry Nationwide, sometimes you can't win!)

ten
FIND THE LOOPHOLES

They make money out of you so always ask, 'Can I make money out of them?' Companies assume everyone is lazy and apathetic. If you're not, you can surf a wave of offers to make money. Go on, twist their terms and conditions. You've got everything to gain.

This is the hardcore circuit-training section of the Money Diet, beyond 'what's the best possible product?', beyond even 'how are they making money out of me?', and on to 'let's do it to them before they do it to us'. It's about how to find, activate and use legal loopholes, breaks and gaps in the system to benefit in ways product-providers haven't expected or planned for. But it is not for everyone. If you have any doubts STOP! Do not read on. It plays on the margins of finance – get it slightly wrong and it can all go pear-shaped.

The primary targets are financial service providers, simply because they complicate terms and conditions in a way nobody else does. Yet it's not exclusively them – in the past others have been my targets too, including online casinos' intro offers, gas and electricity companies, car salesrooms and shops.

IT'S CONSUMER REVENGE

Loophole-spotting isn't for everybody. Even if you have the inclination you may not have the time. It's not as easy or as straightforward as other Money Diet techniques, and takes much longer. 'Consumer Revenge' teaches companies they can't expect to take advantage of apathy any more, and if they do we will snatch their pounds and put them in our pockets.

Spotting loopholes is not an integral part of the Money Diet. It's more like the icing on the cake. It's for people who like playing games and finding a better way to do things. It can be really rewarding.

THE FIVE PENTACLE POINTS OF SCREWING THE SYSTEM

Hmmm – how to explain spotting a loophole? After mulling long and hard, I think there are five pentacle points, five thought-processes to build on. Each has a slightly different methodology and the best results come when more than one is available. Most people are apathetic; most people don't learn how products work; most people don't study the instructions; most people stick with what they've got – companies expect this. Be different and you gain.

(If you're wondering what happened to the 'four corner-stones' from the first edition, well I've added a new one, and anyway pentacle points sounds naughtier!)

Pentacle Point 1: TLC for Ts and Cs

I'll say it once, I'll say it loud and I'll say it proud: *I love terms and conditions*. Some people can see a sheet of music and hear the notes; I look at a list of terms and conditions and start dreaming loopholes. The legalese, the rigid way of working, is designed by teams of lawyers and marketeers attempting to stop us doing things they don't want. But to err is human, and they make mistakes. It's often possible to use products in ways providers have never dreamed of.

So look carefully at those terms and conditions. What is it you'd like to do? Is it possible? It's rare, but spot a gap in the Ts and Cs and the big bucks are possible.

AN EXAMPLE – THE GREAT BARCLAYCARD 0 PER CENT FOR LIFE LOOPHOLE

My guess is the most expensive loophole I've spotted (expensive for them, not us) was one that perhaps cost Barclaycard millions of pounds overall.

It was all based around a new promotion that sang '0 per cent for life on your balance transfers'. An amazing deal! Yet of course there was a catch: 'providing you spend on the card'. As I will explain in Healthy Eating (page 376), credit-card companies allocate repayments to pay off all cheap debt before touching the expensive debt – leaving it sitting there hastily and heavily accruing interest.

The clever thing about this Barclaycard deal was it forced you to spend in order to get the 0 per cent balance transfer. Digging into the Ts and Cs, though, the 'new' spending only needed to be £1 a month. This was again a clever idea; it takes into account that actually spending £1 – no less, not much more – every month for years is a difficult thing to do.

As always the solution seemed simple – after I'd found it. Set up a direct debit (on a credit card it's technically called a recurring payment) for £1 a month to go to a charity – and thereby automatically fulfil Barclaycard's terms and conditions. The charity gains, you gain, Barclaycard loses. Even at an ultra-conservative estimate, thousands of people followed the system exactly, all denying Barclaycard millions in profits over the next few years and instead pocketing it themselves.

Perhaps the most pleasing (and disappointing) moment then came when I saw Barclaycard announce it was closing the deal just a few weeks later. A couple of articles even named and shamed me and this loophole as the reason why (though, believe me, I was anything but ashamed).

The replacement scheme looked similar, except with a minimum £50 spend per month. No way round this particular offer, unfortunately, so best avoided. Still, many people still have the debt there at 0 per cent a couple of years later. Fantastic!

THE KEY QUESTIONS
- Have you read all the terms and conditions?
- Can you think of any way you can manipulate the product?
- Is there any term that they've missed or wrongly drafted that allows you to do so?
- Is it legal?

Pentacle Point 2: Riding the Waves

Introductory offers are gold dust for the loophole-spotter. Companies, especially new ones, are desperate to build their market share and suck in new customers with market-beating introductory offers.

They hope people will get the intro offer and then not be bothered to move, so gradually the companies can claw the savings back by pushing up prices. Yet milk the system, move from offer to offer, riding the waves of intro bonuses, and you will always be one step ahead.

Without doubt this is the easiest type of system playing.

AN EXAMPLE – 'SUCK, SLAP AND FLOG'

'Suck, slap and flog' is my name for a common trick played by savings-account providers. They suck you in with high interest rates, slap the rates down while you're (presumably) not looking, and then flog a new account with a very similar name so you think you're still getting the best deal. Yet monitor and repeatedly move and you flog them.

Always have an easy escape route – easy transferability is the key to riding the wave. Do this and you can consistently earn more than the base rate. Keep track of all products and surf to continually be a 'new customer'.

THE KEY QUESTIONS

■ How long does an offer last?
■ How much of it can you have?
■ When should you move?
■ Can you escape?

Pentacle Point 3: Cut the Commission

If you've ever had advice from an Independent Financial Adviser and didn't pay a fee, often part of the money you pay each month for the products pays this adviser's commission. And, scandalously, if you bought a product direct from a financial services firm that could've been bought via an adviser, this firm keeps the commission itself, so you're paying for advice you never received. This happens on a vast range of products – critical illness cover, income protection, life assurance, unit trusts, stocks and shares ISAs, pensions – right across the board.

However, there are specialist execution-only companies, 'discount brokers', whose offer is 'Get it through us and we don't give you advice, so we will rebate some of this commission, so your plan is either cheaper, grows more quickly, or you get cash back.'

Of course, the best thing to do is buy it this way in the first place, if you don't need advice. But even if you have a plan running at the moment, it's often possible to jump ship and shift your nominated adviser to become a discount broker. In many cases this means some of the commission will be rebated either to you or to your plan, so that you gain. (For a detailed example of this see 'Repensioning', page 259.) So always ask, 'Am I paying for advice I'm not getting?' If so, move.

THE KEY QUESTIONS
- Are there hidden costs for commission?
- Would these hidden costs be cheaper anywhere else?
- Is it possible to move? Are there any moving costs?
- When do you pay them?
- Is the same advice available for free?

Pentacle Point 4: Precision Products

Most product-providers like to sell us multi-use and multi-function financial products. The more things you use a product for, the more money the company makes, because more cash flows through it. This is one of the reasons offset and current account mortgages are coming on to the market – after all, if you've got a mortgage that's also a bank account, savings account and personal loan, this company now has your custom for four products for the price of marketing one. There are a whole host of these linked products: telephone, television, broadband and credit cards with reward schemes and balance transfer offers; gas bills with cheap phone packages attached. Yet multi-use is often multi-cost.

However, the loophole-spotting Money Dieter can seek revenge. To sell a product, companies advertise their strongest, sharpest and cheapest point. Maybe it's the cheapest credit card for spending abroad; it may be its rock bottom broadband costs; it may be the mortgage that allows you to overpay the most each month – anything.

As in physics, for every action there's an equal and opposite reaction. With money, for every positive element there's an equal and opposite negative one. Providers make sure that where we gain with one hand, they profit with the other, so the cheap broadband is offset by hideously expensive costs for calling mobile phones. Instead, loophole-spotting says, 'I will only use it when it's good, and use something else to fill in the gaps.'

'Precision Plastic' ('Healthy Eating', page 366), is the epitome of this. Only ever use products for their very, very best feature. This is simple, effective and works across the board. For example, many mobile phones offer free 'cross-network' minutes so you can call landlines or mobiles with your free minutes. As calls to mobiles cost more than landlines, use your mobile to make as many expensive to-mobile calls as possible, even when at home, and your landline for calling landlines as often as possible, and you skew the provider's equation, leaving you spending less.

THE KEY QUESTIONS

- How does it work?
- Who is it targeted at?
- Can you gain by using it accurately?

Pentacle Point 5: Do the Minimum to Get the Maximum

This one's especially useful when a product has a freebie or useful added extra. Check what the minimum needed is to get the full gain.

This could be simple. For example, if a games console shop is advertising £20 off a brand new game you want if you trade in an old one, nip to your local market, buy the cheapest used game you can for a couple of quid and use this as the trade-in for the discount.

AN EXAMPLE – CONSUMER TERRORISM ON FIRST DIRECT

While the Barclaycard loophole was the biggest ever saving, my repeated attacks on First Direct were the most acrimonious (so far). The loophole was simple: set up a bank account with First Direct and you get £25. Yet unlike most account-opening bribes where you need to make it your main account and pay your salary in, here you just needed to be in credit. So my technique was easy: this was a poor account not worth having so put £1 in it, let it pay you £25, then close the account. Easy money.

After I'd shouted this from the rooftops (well my website and a few national radio programmes), First Direct got miffed and changed the terms so 'you must deposit at least £100 for the bonus'. No problem! Put £100 in and it adds £25 at speed; still a fantastic deal. Again, close the account and withdraw the £125 – still free cash.

Eventually First Direct closed the offer. Tens of thousands had taken their free cash and it's rumoured the phrase 'consumer terrorism' was used to describe my actions.

If you're feeling sorry for First Direct, remember it's owned by worldwide mega-bank HSBC, which made over £9.6 billion profit that year. The aim of its incentive is to draw customers in to a poorly paying account. It leans on consumers' apathy, making them an easy target.

THE KEY QUESTIONS
- What do you gain?
- What is the minimum needed to activate the gain?
- Any downside?
- Does the gain outweigh the cost?

THE LIST OF 12 WAYS TO SCREW THE SYSTEM

1. Free cash. Credit cards give you cash back when you spend and may lend you money at 0 per cent at the same time. By making all spending on the card, you can earn cash back and save your unspent wages. This way you earn interest on money they've lent you for nothing. (See 'Healthy Eating', page 387.)

2. Flex an inflexible mortgage. Good bog-standard old-fashioned mortgages charge less interest than flexible ones. By, amongst other things, manipulating the length of your mortgage term you can re-create many of a flexible mortgage's features without paying the high rates. (See 'Healthy Eating', page 342.)

3. Less-than-no-commission life assurance. The cheapest life assurers on the market charge you a fee but don't take any commission. However, a range of other brokers who normally try and suck loads of commission out try and make themselves look competitive by offering 'price-beater' policies. So go to the cheapest life assurance company on the market, get a quote, then take it to the price-beating brokers and ask them to give you exactly the same deal without commission and without the fee. (See 'Crash Diet', page 275.)

4. Free mortgage advice. The big mortgage brokers all charge you a fee, except for London & Country. So seek three of the big brokers, get them to give you their best advice – and as you only actually pay for the advice when you complete the mortgage, process it through London & Country. You won't pay a fee but will have ensured you got the best advice possible. (See 'Crash Diet', page 269.)

5. Healthcare cashback schemes – be sure you claim. These pay cash back on your spending on dental, optical, osteopathic and similar treatments. The reason they can give you really good rates is that most people simply forget to claim small payments. If you do claim you beat their pricing policy, and can claim back up to six times what you pay. (See 'Crash Diet', page 245.)

6. Repensioning. If you are no longer receiving advice from your pension adviser, or you bought direct, then 'repensioning' is my invention to make you more money. You simply move your existing pension to a discount pension provider. This means with exactly the same pension you get more growth. (See page 259.)

Martin's Money Memories: You Always Remember Your First Time

Sorry, no salacious gossip here. Actually, I mean the first time I spotted a really big loophole. This was for the *Deal of the Day* programme, my first television job at Sky channel Simply Money. The then newly launched internet bank Cahoot was offering an incentive to join: shift a balance from another card and you'd get 5 per cent of the debt back as cash.

Hidden within its Ts and Cs was the fact it allowed two balance transfers on to this card, paying 5 per cent each time. Therefore this money could be moved to the Cahoot card, back to your original credit card, and returned to Cahoot to get 5 per cent on the same debt twice, leaving you with almost 10 per cent less debt overall (nerdy note: it's almost 10 per cent, as the second time you are only getting 5 per cent of 95 per cent of the original debt, leaving you with 90.25 per cent of the original money).

Not only that, but using a technique similar to 'Free Cash' (page 387), you didn't even need to have debts to do this. With a £5,000 credit limit, it was possible to make nearly £500 in cash at no risk in just a few weeks. Beautiful.

---

7. *Override your mobile network.* It's possible to use one of a few special providers to bypass your mobile phone network's charges. You dial a freephone number to access the service, and then make your calls on this secondary network. This means calls from your mobile cost the same as from a landline. (See 'Crash Diet', page 181.)

8. *Half-price plastic personal loans.* The best credit cards are cheaper than personal loans – manipulate your credit card into becoming a loan. Create a debt on your current credit card and transfer it to a new card using the special balance-transfer rate. (See 'Healthy Eating', page 406.)

9. Make the networks cross. Push the override provider system above a little further. Take out an Orange phone which has cross-network calls – free calls to other mobiles or land-lines – then use the override number to call landlines and only use the free minutes to call other mobiles. This leaves all your free minutes as mobile-to-mobile calls, the most expensive type, allowing you to ride roughshod over Orange's plan that the cheap mobile-to-landline calls will offset their expensive mobile-to-other-mobile costs. (See 'Crash Diet', page 181.)

10. Cash ISA fixed rate? Unlike fixed-rate savings accounts, where you really can't withdraw money early, government regulations require cash ISA providers to allow you to. This means that you can fix your rate over a long period but with a cheap get-out clause if rates change and there's better on offer elsewhere. (See 'Crash Diet', page 228.)

11. Perfect phone tariffs. Sign up for a phone provider and they expect you to make all your calls via them, but there's absolutely no need to do so. Other providers can be accessed via a special code, so you can connect to their services at no cost, and so pick the cheapest tariff for each type of call. (See 'Crash Diet', page 183.)

12. Christmas presents at January sales prices. RBS and HSBC have price-beater policies – find anything cheaper afterwards and they will refund you the difference. When you're shopping at Christmas, use this credit card. Then, when prices are reduced in the January sales, you can simply send off and get a refund on the difference in price. And hey presto! Christmas presents at January sales prices! Ho! Ho! Ho!

THE ADVERSARIAL CONSUMER SOCIETY

We spend our lives being screwed by companies for profit.
Our job is to stop them or (legally) screw them back!

THIS ALL BOILS DOWN TO 'WE NEED TO GET ACTIVE!'

We live in an adversarial consumer society. A company's job is to make money – nowt wrong with that. Yet a consumer's job should be to maximise their cash too – nowt wrong with that either.

I'm purely, unapologetically, a consumer lobbyist. Billions are spent on marketing and advertising to help businesses profit, while consumers are left to fend for themselves.

Sales staff get training to close deals, so why shouldn't consumers have buying training? Let me reiterate: I don't blame companies for trying to make money, yet equally I want to enthuse consumers into doing the same. My personal mission is plain – to turn as many poor consumers as possible into the equal of the companies,

It's about redressing a balance. Let's return to the core, the *'they screw us, so we should screw them'*. This doesn't worry me; it is our system. The danger is they're really good at screwing us and we're really bad at screwing them. Companies' profitability is often based on consumer inertia, apathy and confusion. We accept this situation and rarely use targeted consuming methods to take them on. They invest the time and we don't.

For Those who Think I'm Talking Rubbish!

As you read through this in more detail, you may disagree; this is my philosophy after all and there's certainly a political element to this chapter. You may believe that companies have a duty to put something back into society, and that's fair enough.

Yet don't let this cloud your view of the Diet itself. If consumers perceive companies as friends, we make irrational, emotive decisions that take cash out of our pockets and put it into theirs. Whatever your beliefs let me caution you: the adversarial nature of society means you get a better deal via healthy and wealthy scepticism.

LET'S GET INTO IT: LOOKING AT COMPANIES
All Companies are the Enemy!

People often balk when I say that. Yet, I don't mean companies are bad. They're not. There's nothing wrong with them aiming to make profit and take money out of consumers' pockets. After all, that's their job!

Of course, there's a level of hyperbole here. I suppose in truth it's less the *'enemy'* and more the *'opposition'*.

I tend to think of it a bit like a football match. I'm a

Manchester City supporter and when they play Man. United, I want City to score all the goals. However, this doesn't mean I think United are wrong to try and score, or to attempt (all too often successfully) to try and stop us scoring. That's the nature of the game.

It's the same with companies and consumers. They're in opposition, but neither is doing anything wrong. Chief Executives are rewarded based on their company's profitability. Consumers improve their lifestyle by making better choices, paying less and having more.

We All Play for Both Sides

Just as there's an active football transfer market, in a consumer society people switch sides too. Most people work for companies, have a salary and income. Me too! This book is a commercial entity with an international conglomerate as publisher. Many of the newspaper columns I write and television programmes I present make their money from selling advertising space alongside.

Again, none of this is about blame. It's about 'how it works' and 'how to think accordingly'.

I'm regularly e-mailed something along the lines of 'Thanks, you've saved me loads of money in the past, but I'm a travel agent/mortgage broker/market stall holder [etc.] and I think what you're telling people about travel/mortgages/haggling is completely unfair and damaging to my business.'

Yet it's impossible to have it both ways. Companies have had their own way for too long. Better-informed consumers make for a freer market and a more competitive society. No one is forced to sell unprofitable products. It mightn't make companies' lives easy, but it isn't wrong.

Martin's Money Memories: 'Commercial Double Think'

A speaker invite came via my agent: 'Would you like to give a talk at the big annual financial services industry conference – the keynote speech?' I jumped at the chance. 'What's the title?' they asked. 'You're the enemy and I'm going to screw you!' I replied. 'But don't put it on the programme, I want to surprise them.'

Staggeringly, the invitation wasn't withdrawn. I started with a constructive opening: 'Which phone provider do you use?' and explained to the majority how they were paying ridiculously over the odds with BT. Then on to gas and electricity bills, again detailing the huge savings possible. My 'disgraceful isn't it?' was greeted by keen nodding heads. Then ...

'You're worse. You pay pitiful interest rates, suck customers into debt, disguise salespeople as advisers, target apathy and profit from inertia. You leave 80-year-olds in savings accounts where they're losing money.'

The nodding audience became a slightly stunned huddle. We all wear different clothing; with our 'consumer' hats on, an activist approach is champion, yet at work for many the idea of consumers fighting back is terrifying.

Hold on, Companies aren't the Enemy, They Look after Us?

Of course some companies provide good customer service; they look after us, go beyond the call of duty. On Radio 2, whilst proselytising about changing bank accounts, a woman in her early 80s called to berate me: 'I love my bank, I popped in there the other day when I was feeling faint and they gave me a glass of water and told me to sit down.'

Now of course I wasn't brave enough to chastise her, tell her she still had a pitiful account and was possibly losing hundreds a year with it. Yet is this a good way to choose a bank? Why did they give her the water? Most probably it was nothing to do with the bank but because there were some genuinely nice people amongst the staff, helping out someone in distress.

However, even if we assign it to good customer service, then it's believable. For me customer service is a function of profitability. The company that treats its customers well will probably retain them. More importantly most people are a much better judge of customer service than they are of product price and value, so it's quite an easy way to build market share.

Of course, good customer service can be expensive or time consuming or possibly both. It's no coincidence the no-frills flight or phone operators have the cheapest prices. After all, they have rigid terms and poor levels of service. More often than not there's a trade-off between customer service and pricing.

So let's not say 'company X is very nice so it's not the opposition'. No, company X has great customer service, thereby retaining customers and generating referrals, both of which push up profits. It's still about driving shareholder value. It worries me that people believe any commercial company is altruistic and simply helps for the good of it. Don't confuse the practical outcome with the actual motivation.

There's nothing wrong with valuing customer service, but I mean exactly that – value it. Work out how much you could save by going to the very cheapest provider, and then make a rational decision as to whether you are willing to pay that much of a premium for the service.

But Some Companies are Charitable – They Aid Society?

Of course they do, and bravo for doing so. Adversarial consumerism isn't 'anti-corporate'. There's no blame or malice attached.

Yet companies are rarely altruistic in the true sense. When they give money, it's generally done to help, but also because it's great PR, good marketing and helps motivate their staff.

However, it goes further. 'Corporate social responsibility' is often discussed, the role of a company and how it should behave in society. For me this concept is nonsensical: generating income for shareholders conflicts with social responsibility, so it is only done where reputational damage and ensuing lost profits would occur.

Now this doesn't mean companies should be able to behave willy-nilly and be unconstrained. It just means I don't think it's a company's job to regulate itself. Society should restrict companies as it believes they should behave, whether that's environmentally, ethically, or simply on product terms.

Let me use an example. I was presenting a *Tonight with Trevor McDonald* programme called 'Rich Bankers' about the money that banks unnecessarily squeeze from our pockets. The producers wanted me to rant about the unfairness of rural bank branch closures, automatically assuming it'd push my buttons.

Yet it doesn't. Why shouldn't a bank close an unprofitable branch? Its job is to make money, not provide a societal benefit.

If we want rural branches then we, as a society, have two choices. Either we regulate so they must remain open, or we choose to fund a non-profit-driven banking system to do it. Either way, we pay, through higher bank charges or taxation. Yet let's not rely on the banks to do it for us – it isn't their job!

What about Building Societies and Co-operatives?

Hmmmm, while it should be better ... sadly the products on offer often aren't an improvement on the banks.

Whilst I wouldn't expect building societies to compete in the rate tart market, they often fail on the 'consistent long-term good value' test. The maxim 'forget loyalty' applies to these organisations too. If they're not giving you the best product, and there's no additional service benefits, why use them?

Even non-profit institutions have problems that may lead to poor results for consumers.

Let me give you a couple of examples ...

Building savings at all costs. A senior building society staff member once lectured me on how valuable his job was: 'Unlike the banks, I have a genuine belief in encouraging people to save,' said he.

So I asked him how he was remunerated? And unsurprisingly, it was salary plus a performance bonus related to the amount of savings he could generate.

Sounds fine, but as discussed elsewhere in the Diet, most people with debts should pay them off before saving. This is a golden rule. However, did his building society make it a policy to benefit their customers by telling them this each time? Of course not. That might just have hurt his bonus, instead it simply focused on bringing in more cash.

Is the customer more important than the society? After invectively deriding their product ranges in a speech to the Building Societies Association, I was questioned by one chief executive: 'It's all very well for you to say "never have any bad product" but we have to have some savings accounts that pay poor amounts. If we didn't, we wouldn't survive.'

Yet, building societies are there for the members, not to protect the jobs of their management. My answer was plain: 'If you can't afford to run a decent savings account, if you want to help your members, why not tell them who else they can get the best rates with?' If the argument is 'we can't give customers decent, never mind market-leading products and survive', is it worth surviving?

THAT'S COMPANIES, NOW WHAT SHOULD WE DO?
This is about Accepting Responsibility

Society's adversarial nature is the root of real MoneySaving. When you look at a product, you must assume it's been set up to benefit the provider, not you. Even the best products are only there as loss-leaders to build market share or due to a lower cost base or service levels.

Once you accept a company is the opposition, it then becomes very difficult to blame a shop for selling you something at twice the price of the shop next door. Nor can you blame a bank for lending you money at a high interest rate. Why shouldn't it?

Surely it is our responsibility to ensure we're getting, if not the ultimate best product, at least a good deal. Our role is always to be sceptical, to think as a member of the opposing team; to ask 'why are they doing that?', 'how will they gain?', 'is this really the best for me?', 'are they just saying that because it's beneficial?'. When someone tells you 'yes, we're best value', don't believe them.

This isn't about Simplicity

For too long, the quick-fix solution of the media when it comes to money has been 'cut back', 'stop spending' and 'don't do

Don't Believe All You See on the Telly

Phflup – the noise my sock made when hitting the television. The cause of my rather frustrated throw was a 'money makeover programme'. From memory, a family with a credit and store card debt of £12,000 were instructed by the friendly but rather simplistic 'expert' to cut up their credit cards immediately.

Yet doing the sums as I watched, their current interest cost was £2,500 a year. If they had a decent credit score, with very little effort that was cutable to £500 a year, in perpetuity. Even if they were now credit-stymied, doing the credit card shuffle (page 391) could definitely have saved them over £1,000 a year.

Lower interest means more money repays the actual debts and an earlier debt-free date. Yet the trite financial simplicity of 'cut up your cards' trapped the family into overpaying expensive interest in the long run.

The expert's answer was the credit card companies' dream – their pockets continually lined for years. Now don't think for a second this means that stopping people from over-borrowing is bad. I'm not saying that, after lowering the interest, they shouldn't cut the cards up (or lock them in a safe). Just don't accede to the clarity of simplicity. That's the way we as consumers all lose!

anything'. Yet this plays into the hands of retailers and financial services companies.

Finance is complex, well at least it is until you try and understand it. You don't have to be a genius; just willing to spend a little time. This approach gives us a more competitive system.

It's no coincidence this book is the Money *Diet*. Part of my inspiration stems from the revolution in health. Had you told people 20 years ago they'd need to understand carbohydrates, fats and proteins, they'd have scoffed at the possibility. Now these concepts are commonplace.

The same must and should become true in the world of money. 'Repayment schedules', 'commoditisation', 'pensions as a wrapper not a product' should all become common knowledge. If not, then we all lose.

Our society is in schism between the money-savvy few and the large, stagnant money illiterate. The first are reaping the rewards of applying knowledge to the most competitive market we've ever seen, driven by overly rich information sources. The latter, meanwhile, are being screwed.

The question for us as individuals is 'who do you want to be?' and how much effort are you prepared to put into it?

PART 2
THE CRASH DIET

Want to save money quickly? Simply look down the Money Diet Calorie Counter on page xiv to the products you have or need. Turn to the page indicated and make the saving. This section is not an exhaustive list of every possible product, but a wide selection of ways to save money. If something you're looking for isn't included, read 'Financial Fitness for Life' on how to get the best deals on anything and everything, as well as MoneySaving hints, tips and tricks.

CRASH DIET TOPICS

Each topic is divided up into the following:

THE MENU
The hoped-for result and how and why you can save.

CHOOSING YOUR DISH
How to find the cheapest and best.

CALORIE COUNT
The scale of savings. Examples are taken from real-life situations at the time of writing. They are for guidance only and, of course, the scale of savings will vary vastly with personal circumstances.

SUGGESTED INGREDIENTS
Where to find the cheapest and the best.

(News) means Sunday papers, which carry best-buy tables for the product, but always check for traps pointed out. Also for most dishes there is a direct link to the relevant regularly updated articles and best buys of www.moneysavingexpert.com

This is followed by a list of providers. These have been picked as they are traditionally good payers and players. Do remember, though, things change quickly in the money world, so they may not remain the best; newcomers may be better. See the ingredients as the first port of call to set a benchmark standard, but don't be shy of checking others. Always follow the logic of the main article to establish their worth, though.

ADDED SPICE

Special hints and tips to customise the recipe to your special tastes.

GAS & ELECTRICITY BILLS

NUTRITIONAL INFORMATION
Typical Saving: £150 per year.
Time Taken: 10 minutes.
Difficulty Level: Easy.

THE MENU

Perhaps the easiest dish on the Money Diet menu. If you've never changed supplier you could be paying up to 25 per cent too much. Even if you have switched, saving up to 15 per cent is possible.

Shifting supplier is not a big deal: you keep the same pipes, circuits and wires; the only difference is the customer service and billing. The new supplier will perform the switch – all you need do is sign the right forms and take a meter reading.

CHOOSING YOUR DISH

Unless you're a slide-rule Jedi, forget doing the comparisons yourself. A range of phone and internet comparison services do the work for you. Simply plug in your details. It's best to compare using the kilowatt-hours amount detailed on your bill. If you haven't got your bill cost, an educated guess will do. Some comparison companies will even estimate your energy usage for you, based on house size and heating supply, etc. Even with these services there are a number of things to watch for:

- **Dual fuel isn't always cheaper.** It's a marketing myth that getting gas and electricity from the same supplier automatically makes it cheaper. While it's usually true, it isn't always, so always check the prices of the best stand-alone suppliers.
- **Direct debit is cheaper.** Save up to 10 per cent through paying by fixed monthly direct debit from your bank account. If you've overpaid you will be refunded at the end of the year. If you've underpaid extra will be due. The reason it's cheaper is suppliers are sure you won't default, plus they can earn extra interest on your money where there are overpayments.
- **Missed providers.** Due to some technicalities, some price-comparison companies omit certain tariffs. If you have time, do the same comparison on a couple, to be doubly sure of the best deal.

Whichever supplier you choose, remember to take regular meter readings so you don't overpay. As tariffs change regularly, it's worth redoing a price comparison once a year to check you're still with the best. Also, the government's Energy Saving Trust has some great booklets on how to cut energy use and therefore reduce bills.

CALORIE COUNT

A family spending £700 a year using their regional electricity company and British Gas's standard policy could save around 15 per cent by switching to the cheapest providers, or 25 per cent by using direct debit.

Switch to save Manchester family spending £700				
	Gas	Electricity	Total	Saving
Current (bills)	£250	£450	£700	–
Switch to cheapest				
Dual fuels (bills)	–	–	£586	£114
Stand-alone (bills)	£191	£371	£562	£138
Dual fuels (direct debit)	–	–	£549	£151
Stand-alone (direct debit)	£175	£360	£535	£165

SUGGESTED INGREDIENTS

Price comparison companies: www.buy.co.uk; www.saveon yourbills.co.uk, 0870 005 2095; www.simplyswitch.com, 0800 781 1212; www.ukpower.co.uk; www.uswitch.co.uk, 0845 601 2856; www.switchandgive.com, 0800 074 0743; www.energy helpline.co.uk; www.energylinx.co.uk

Other: www.staywarm.co.uk, 0800 1694 694; Energy Saving Trust, www.est.org.uk, 0845 727 7200

Updated info: www.moneysavingexpert.com/energy

ADDED SPICE

■ *Over 60s special.* If there is someone over 60 living in your house, one energy supplier, StayWarm, provides a special flat-fee service. You must get both gas and electricity from it, and then, rather than paying a charge depending on energy usage, you simply pay depending on the number of people and rooms in your house. The big advantage is the security of knowing how much you'll pay, and it's great for anyone who wants to turn the heat up but is worried about cost. It's not always cheap, though, so compare it to the best result from the price-comparison services. As a rule of thumb, unless StayWarm is more than 5 per cent costlier, choose it.

■ *Green energy.* Some companies offer special tariffs, which promote environmentally friendly energy sources. It is more expensive, but you can still use the price comparison engines to find the cheapest greens for you.

Martin's Money Memories: How to Knock Knockers

I always remember one chap who mistakenly arrived on my doorstep touting gas and electricity and promising, 'Did you know you can save a fortune if you switch to us?'

'No,' I say. 'I didn't know.'

'Oh yes,' says he. 'Move to us and you can save up to 15 per cent.'

'No,' I say again. His 'I've found another punter' smile was short-lived. I didn't know he could save me money, because he couldn't. His offer was 5 per cent more expensive than my current provider.

As I pointed this out, his lips turned down. So I thought I'd try and cheer him up.

'Where do you live?' I say.

'Eh?' says he.

'Where do you live?'

'Round the corner.'

'Who do you use for your utilities?' I asked.

Within 10 minutes I'd written on his clipboard which suppliers he should switch to, and I added his cheapest phone company to boot. Better than commission any day, surely? Then again, he was lucky. Most of the time I feel confident saying, 'I'm fine thanks,' and closing the door.

■ *Cashback.* As you'll have read on page 143, one comparison service once gave cash back to anyone who switched via it. Similar incentives are becoming commonplace – it's worth trying a few comparison services to see what current offers they have. There is a regularly updated list on www.moneysavingexpert.com/energy

WATER BILLS

NUTRITIONAL INFORMATION
Typical Saving: £100.
Time Taken: 10 minutes (internet) or 25 minutes (otherwise).
Difficulty Level: Easy (internet), Mid (otherwise).

THE MENU
The choice is simple. As the market isn't open to competition, either fit a water meter or stick to the old-style bills.

It's all about choosing the right way to be charged. The traditional bill depends on the 'rateable value' of your home, regardless of how much water you use. This very roughly means the more your home can be rented out for, the more you pay for water.

The alternative is a meter, which measures water usage. Many product-providers have accused me of talking excrement in the past. This time it's true, as what comes in usually goes out, so water meters also calculate your sewerage bill. Meters must be fitted free of charge, unless it's justifiably impractical. If you switch to a water meter you have a right to switch back within either 12 months, or a month of getting your second measured bill, whichever is later. However, move into a home which already has a meter and you can't switch back.

the money diet

CHOOSING YOUR DISH

Whether to fit a meter or not depends on the water company's area and your usage. Those with access to the internet can use www.buy.co.uk, which asks questions about your water usage, and quickly calculates whether a meter will cut the cost.

For those without internet access, as a very rough rule of thumb, if there are the same number or fewer people living in your house than there are bedrooms, check out fitting a meter. Just contact your water company, which should send a table to work it out. If the saving looks to be minimal, don't fit a meter, as the security of knowing exactly what you will pay regardless of usage is worthwhile.

CALORIE COUNT

The table below shows the savings in three water areas in early 2005. It's for a four-bedroom home for residents with average water use. The savings from switching to a meter can be over £200.

Waste not, want not: traditional bill £360 per year								
	1 person		2 people		3 people		4 people	
	Cost	Saving	Cost	Saving	Cost	Saving	Cost	Saving
United Utilities	£143	£217	£198	£162	£252	£108	£316	£44
Thames Water	£105	£255	£145	£215	£184	£176	£230	£130
Northumbrian Water	£114	£246	£156	£204	£199	£161	£248	£112

SUGGESTED INGREDIENTS

www.buy.co.uk or your water company.
Updated info: www.moneysavingexpert.com/water

MOBILE CALLS AT LANDLINE PRICES

NUTRITIONAL INFORMATION

Typical Gain: £350 per year.

Time Taken: 45 minutes.

Difficulty Level: Mid/Hard.

THE MENU

If you don't want to invest in a 10-mile-long cable, there's another way to sneakily make mobile calls at landline prices. Some override providers work by utilising freephone numbers from home phones to access their networks (see 'Calling Overseas', page 200 for a full explanation). Mobile networks usually kibosh this working on their phones, but there are a limited number of override providers who work round the system.

CHOOSING YOUR DISH

- *Orange contract customers (must be on an Orange tariff).* Calls to freephone numbers are usually free (always check) and don't use up your free minutes. Therefore you should be able to dial the override number and connect to it at no charge. However, usually Orange simply detect it and add a charge.

  There are a few companies, however, who play a cat-and-mouse game. They launch freephone numbers, which really are free on Orange, until at some stage Orange catches them and issues a charge. When this happens, you will hear the dulcet female tones that characterise such messages announce, 'All calls to this calling card service are now at a standard rate.' At this point the override

181

providers slap back by issuing a new freephone access number that is still free – all customers need do is call them to find this new number out. This cycle normally takes about 10 weeks.

The whole thing is a legal grey area: override providers aren't breaking any rules by issuing freephone numbers; equally, the network may legitimately block them to protect its investment. There is a chance that calling an override may breach your mobile contract, so do check, but the network's usual reaction is to target numbers, not customers.

To really push these savings see 'Make the networks cross', page 161.

■ *Other networks' customers.* Other networks do charge for calls to freephones, usually at the same rate as normal calls to landlines. However, this still means savings are possible on calls to mobiles and overseas, as even the normal call charge to access the service plus the override provider's cost of calling a mobile together should be cheaper than the network's cost. As there's no cat-and-mouse game here, most override providers can be used (see 'Calling Overseas', page 200).

CALORIE COUNT

The possible savings here are really huge, with mobile calls to landlines sometimes less than 2p/minute or calls to the USA on your mobile for just 3p/minute. The size of saving varies hugely depending on which network you are on, which package, and which override provider. Yet it is possible to cut a mobile bill by over 80 per cent with this system.

SUGGESTED INGREDIENTS

Swiftnet, www.swiftnet.co.uk, 0208 446 9494; Connaught
telecom, www.ctelecom.co.uk, 0800 074 0111; Telco*,
www.telcoglobal.com, 0870 996 1111; Onetel*, www.onetel.
co.uk, 0845 818 8000

*Tend to limit overrides only to those who use their other services.

Updated info: www.moneysavingexpert.com/override

HOME PHONES

NUTRITIONAL INFORMATION

Typical Gain: £350 per year.
Time Taken: 60 minutes.
Difficulty Level: Easy/Mid.

THE MENU

The big problem with the phone is it's in your home, very
convenient and doesn't have a price meter. Five minutes on
the phone to Bolton feels the same as five minutes to Bogota.
Plus, get in a heated conversation and the last thing you think
about is the cost.

That means the only thing to do is sort out the right
providers before you make call:

■ *Your line provider and call provider needn't be the
same.* There are only three major UK line providers: BT,
NTL and Telewest, but hundreds of call providers. Most
people use a BT line, and BT is obliged to allow other call
providers to operate via its lines. (A growing number of
companies such as One-Tel and TalkTalk also offer 'line
rental'; actually this is just a disguised BT line that they
provide the customer service for.)

The big difference comes if you're using an NTL or Telewest line. These providers are not obliged to allow other call providers to operate through them, so you tend to be locked down. While these providers can be competitive for mixing television and phone packages, there are often hidden high call costs, such as for phoning mobiles, which can actually make them more expensive even than BT.

■ *Carrier pre-selection (CPS)* is fast becoming standard practice. This means that while using a BT line, all the calls are automatically routed through your chosen call provider without you needing to do anything. If you use it, make sure you pay BT only its very basic line rental.

■ *Phone and internet together.* Unless there's an exceptionally good promotion on, it's best not to wrap up your phone and internet provider with one company. You tend not to get the best deals, and may find yourself locked in.

CHOOSING YOUR DISH

The first thing to do is take a look at your bill. What are you spending the most on – is it landlines, mobiles or international? To really make the hard-core savings these need to be considered separately.

■ *Calling landlines.* It's cheap to call a landline from home, so providers focus their ads this way as it makes them look cheap. Yet actually, as I'll explain in a minute, mobiles are where the real rollercoaster savings are to be made.

This doesn't mean you can't cut the price for calling landlines and make savings there too.

There are two main ways to go here, either a 'free calls included' package or a 'pay per minute package'.

1. 'Free calls included'. The free calls packages are heavily pushed by all the main players – BT, One-Tel, TalkTalk, Toucan, etc. – where for an additional monthly fee you get 'free' calls for 'evenings and weekends' or 'at all times'. The correct term is actually 'unlimited' (not free, as you're paying extra to get these calls), as the length and number of calls isn't monitored.

For most providers even this is a lie, since calls are only 'unlimited' for the first hour and are then charged by the minute. To get round this, just put the phone down before that time is up and redial, and it's 'unlimited' all over again.

There are big price differences between operators though. For example 'all calls' varies from £8 to £15 a month, so picking a cheaper provider can result in savings of nearly £100 on this alone.

2. Pay per call. While this may look the old-fashioned route, for most people this is cheaper, but only via special providers. Let me be straight with you, one of the difficulties writing this book is future-proofing it, so that when you read it, the info's still relevant.

As I write, the two providers I'm about to mention have been top of the tree for the last 18 months. Their prices may change, yet my suspicion is they'll remain competitive. And as this pay-per-call method only really works with these two, I don't have a choice but to mention them.

Money Diet Quick Fact Snack: Real Friends and Family Savings

It's cheaper to call a landline from a mobile than it is to call a mobile from a landline. Therefore make a pact with friends and family that when one of you calls a mobile from home, the other should immediately hang up and call back. This means a lot less money in phone companies' pockets.

They are www.call18866.co.uk and www.call1899.co.uk. You set up an account via the internet (they're not available for non-net users) with a debit or credit card.

They're accessed by dialling a prefix (18866 and 1899 on a BT line) followed by the number you're calling. It's not greatly convenient, but the cost saving is huge. To make it easier, set up the prefix as one of the programmable buttons on your phone.

Both of these have an interesting pricing structure for calling landlines. There's no per-minute charge, just a flat fee of (as I write) 2p and 3p respectively. In other words, you pay nothing per month and then just 2p or 3p per call for as long as you talk. They also have the advantage of being very competitively priced for most other call types too. Many people are currently using them for all calls.

Which to choose? It's pretty simple. If you're being offered unlimited calls for £10 a month compared to a 2p flat rate per call, then you'd have to make over 500 calls a month (£10 divided by 2p) to make it worth while. That's a hefty 115 calls a week or 16 a day.

This means unless you're a heavy caller then you'll be much better off on pay per call.

■ *Calling mobiles.* While we usually call mobiles less than landlines, the per-minute cost is massively more. So calls to mobiles make up an increasing proportion of our bill. This price is rarely mentioned in home phone providers' advertising, yet it is often the most important factor, as there can be huge discrepancies.

The solution? Use a specialist provider just for your mobile calls – there are a range that can be accessed by dialling a prefix code before you make the call (see 'Calling

> **Money Diet Quick Fact Snack: Call a Mobile from a Mobile**
>
> The best answer for many people is to call a mobile using a mobile, as many mobile contracts are 'cross-network' meaning calls to any mobile are included in the free minutes. If you have these minutes, use your mobile to call mobiles even while at home, and your landline only to call landlines. By focusing this way, it defeats all costing assumptions and shifts the odds and savings in your favour.

Overseas', page 200 for an explanation). This can massively cut the cost of calling mobiles.

The best tend to offer a fixed tariff of between 4p and 10p to call any UK mobile any time. Normal providers charge roughly 17p for days, 10p for evenings and 5p for weekends. These override providers are therefore much cheaper during the day and evening, and possibly (though not always) at weekends too.

> **Example Price Differences for Calling a Mobile**
>
> Cost of a 10-minute daytime call to a T-mobile phone (July 05)
>
> | | |
> |---|---|
> | NTL | £2.50 |
> | BT Together | £1.49 |
> | Tele2 Standard | £1.34 |
> | 1899 | £1.03 |

■ *International calls.* It's almost never worth considering your main provider's prices. Inevitably they will be much, much more expensive than the best override providers', so just turn to page 200 to save.

CALORIE COUNT

The savings available from using the correct solution are simply enormous. Many people using just one provider are overpaying by as much as 80 per cent. Most people's phone bill will simply disappear in comparison if the right phone choice is made. Someone currently spending £60 a month on the wrong mainstream option could easily cut their bill to £15–£20, a saving of £500 a year.

SUGGESTED INGREDIENTS

Free-calls-included providers: Carphone Warehouse, www.talktalk.co.uk, 0845 4565599; www.onetel.co.uk., 0800 9570700; www.powergen.co.uk; www.tiscali.co.uk/smarttalk, 0800 954 2223; www.tesco.com; www.tele2uk.com, 0800 279 5333; www.toucan.com, 0800 0613 613

Override providers: For calling mobiles and overseas, see 'Calling Overseas', page 200, for a full list

Updated info: www.moneysavingexpert.com/homephone

ADDED SPICE

Two things I spit at:

■ *Spit number 1 is for 0870 numbers.* Call a number starting with 0870, a so-called National Rate number, and actually you pay a vast call charge, much higher than a normal call – up to 8p a minute. These are rarely flagged up and often the company you're calling gets a share of the call revenue.

   It's a disgrace – these are just disguised premium rates. There is a way to cut the cost of these calls, though (see 'Cut the Cost of Complaining', page 136).

■ *Spit number 2 is for voicemail – do the five-ring slam.*

Free voicemail means engaged tones are history. When you call, you're connected. This mightn't sound much, but it means each call generates your provider a guaranteed minimum revenue, usually around 5p.

If every UK adult unnecessarily hit one voicemail a day, it's an annual half a billion pounds! Of course if you want to leave a message this is fine, but if not, why not do what I call the five-ring slam – the average voicemail answers after roughly six rings, so slam down after five.

HOW TO ROAM – USE YOUR MOBILE ABROAD

■ NUTRITIONAL INFORMATION
Typical Gain: £200.
Time Taken: 30 minutes.
Difficulty Level: Mid.

■ THE MENU
Use a mobile overseas and your mobile phone provider will jump for joy. When overseas, calls and text costs magnify, plus you pay possibly £1/minute just to receive calls and voicemails.

Of course, the cheapest solution is to leave the phone at home, but many would find leaving their left lung behind easier. Therefore the real MoneySaving option is switching your phone's SIM card, so your calls will go through a different provider, effectively an overseas pay-as-you-go.

There are some things to check to see if this solution can work for you.

■ *Will your phone work in the country visited?* Different countries use different frequencies; most UK phones will

189

> **Money Diet Quick Fact Snack: What's a SIM Card and How Do I Switch it?**
>
> It's the small (roughly 2cm by 1cm) microchip card you insert into a phone when it's first set up. It provides the identity of a phone for the mobile network, so it can recognise, bill and send calls to individual customers.
>
> Switching SIM is a bit fiddly, but the potential savings are huge, providing you receive and make more than an hour's worth of calls annually while abroad. Otherwise the cost of buying a new SIM outweighs the call cost saving, so don't bother.
>
> It's worth remembering that changing your SIM will mean people have to dial a new phone number for you when you trip abroad, although there is a way round this (see 'Added Spice').

work everywhere within Europe, but only 'tri-band' phones work in the USA and much of the Americas. Call your mobile provider and ask. If the answer is yes, then it should still work, even with a different SIM.

■ *Is the phone 'unlocked'?* Some phones are locked to a network, meaning switch SIM and they won't work. To unlock the phone you can take it to an independent high-street mobile shop that'll do it for £20–£30. Yet for those on the internet it's relatively simple to do yourself for free.

Use unlocking websites such as www.trycktil.com and www.unlockme.co.uk where you enter the details of your phone and are given an unlock code. For most people it's relatively straightforward and takes about five minutes.

Don't confuse *unlocking* with *unblocking*. Unlocking is legal, though some networks do make it that, 'it'll invalidate your warranty', to prevent it. However, *unblocking* means illegally tampering with a phone blocked for all usage, usually because it's stolen.

CHOOSING YOUR DISH

This depends whether you want to buy a new SIM per country visited, or prefer one roaming SIM for all overseas trips.

- *A different SIM per country – local SIMs.* This is best for those who make a lot of calls when overseas, as buying a new SIM each time is then offset by the much cheaper calls, plus call quality is generally better.

   The Sim can be bought before you go from UK suppliers (they don't stock all countries) for £15 to £30; or more cheaply, but less conveniently, from local mobile retailers once you are there. Local SIMs usually have some call credit already on them.

   As you're using a local SIM, calls are cheaper and you won't pay to receive them. However, the people calling you will be calling an international number, though this should only cost pennies per minute, providing they use specialist cheap dial providers. (See 'Calling Overseas', page 200.)

- *One SIM for everywhere.* This offers the convenience of the same number every time you go away, and you only need to buy one SIM, one time. Making calls isn't as cheap as a local SIM, but is much cheaper than using a normal mobile, plus it's still free to receive calls.

   For this service, we must say thanks to Liechtenstein! Its mobile phone companies don't charge when you receive calls wherever you are, so an entire industry is developing utilising its SIMs. To buy a UK-based Liechtenstein SIM (sounds bizarre, doesn't it) will set you back around £30.

   The only complication here is that you dial out via a 'call-back' system – you call, are immediately disconnected, and then 10 seconds later your phone rings to connect you. This is done so Sim4Travel can route the call via a landline cutting the cost.

When people call you they'll be dialling a Liechtenstein mobile phone number, which if they follow the section on page 200 shouldn't set them back by more than 10p/minute – roughly the same price as calling a UK mobile.

CALORIE COUNT

Someone spending a fortnight in Australia and a week in Spain during a year, receiving a total 4 hours of calls and making 1 hour would spend over £250 using a standard contract mobile. By switching SIMs either to a local SIM or Sim4Travel, they'd save over £200.

Abroad Saving				
	SIM Cost	Receiving Calls	Calling UK	Total
0044 Local SIMs	£55 [1]	-	Included [1]	£55
One Roaming SIM	£30	-	£27	£57
Standard mobile[2]	-	£200	£70	£270

Call Breakdown. Spain 90 mins received, 30 mins made; Australia 180 mins received, 30 mins made. (1) SIMs purchased for both Australia and Spain, these include some call credit, which is used to make up the calls (the cost of the calls made separately is £17) (2) Vodafone 60-400 min tariff: 75p/min to receive, 79p/min to make in Aus, 75p/min to make in Spain

SUGGESTED INGREDIENTS

Unlocking: www.trycktil.com, www.unlockme.co.uk
UK-based overseas SIM sellers: www.0044.co.uk, www.uk2abroad.com
One roaming SIM: www.sim4travel.co.uk

ADDED SPICE

www.uk2abroad.com offers an add-on service which autoroutes all calls (though not texts) made to your normal mobile number through to the SIM you're using overseas, either local or all destinations, whether its own or someone else's.

Of course it charges for this, roughly 20p/min depending on country, but that's still cheaper than some normal mobiles. It also rather generously offers a rebate service, so if you top the phone up, but don't use the credit, you can have all barring the first £10 refunded.

UK2Abroad also offers the ability to call back through its service – but this is much more expensive than either of the two options above and should be avoided. If you're using it, simply do so for receiving calls.

It may be possible for you to do this by diverting your current mobile phone to an overseas number. Most networks don't allow this, but some O2 users are able to do it.

Vodafone passport: Users of Vodafone contract mobiles get much cheaper roaming if they join its passport system. This is totally free, but if you don't ask for it you don't get it – so ask!

DIAL-UP INTERNET ACCESS

■NUTRITIONAL INFORMATION

Typical Gain: £150 per year.
Time Taken: 45 minutes.
Difficulty Level: Mid.
(Also see 'Broadband', page 196.)

■THE MENU

While superfast broadband is rapidly catching on, the majority of people still access the internet on a computer that dials up via the home phone. The word most commonly used in internet service provider (ISP) adverts is 'free', yet the one thing it never means is 'no cost'. It can be 'free access, but calls cost', 'free calls, but access costs' and 'free calls and access, but for a fee'.

CHOOSING YOUR DISH

Whatever the price, the quality of the connection is crucial. It's worth asking what the 'contention ratio' – the number of users per line – is. This is a useful though not infallible guide. An average ratio is between 10:1 and 15:1. Business users paying for high quality will want around 5:1. Low-quality connections go up to 40:1.

When it comes to cost, before you even start, watch for technical support phone-line charges, especially for net newcomers, as a £1 per minute charge soon eats up any cheap service benefits.

The other main sales ploy is advertising unique content and child protection software – yet inevitably similar stuff is available elsewhere on the net, usually for free. However, if you are a complete newcomer, it may be wise to start with one of the bigger providers until you get used to the internet, then start the money-saving shopping around.

■ *Heavy use.* Unmetered internet access means you pay a fixed monthly amount for unlimited net access with no call or other costs. The big three providers, AOL, BT and Freeserve, tend to dominate this market, and all offer similar prices. Yet many smaller ISPs offer the same thing for around half the price (see suggested ingredients).

Admittedly, cheap, unmetered access is hit and miss. Because of this, always ensure no notice is needed to cancel if the service deteriorates. However, if you're spending this much anyway, you'll find very little increase if you switch to broadband (see page 196).

■ *Low to medium use.* For anyone using the net for less than roughly 15 hours a month, there's no point signing up for 'unmetered access'. The alternatives are 'free' internet service providers, where accessing the service is free but the calls you need to make aren't (providers get a cut of the phone call cost). Most make you dial via 0845 local call rates, which cost a lot more than you'd think – usually 3p/minute daytime, 1p evenings and weekends, meaning an hour during the day costs £2.40.

Yet some providers do exactly the same thing, but at just 1p a minute at all times. Plus there's also a new range of 'pre-paid internet access cards', with a start price of 0.5p a minute –a much better deal for low users.

CALORIE COUNT

Using the wrong service provider can cost a fortune. Even someone using just eight hours a week can pay nearly £1,000 a year using the wrong provider.

Use: Per week:	Monthly Cost				Annual Cost
	Very Low 1hr	Low 3hr	Mid 8hr	Heavy 20hr	Mid
Local calls access (1)	£2.60 to £10.40	£7.80 to £31.20	£20.80 to £83.20	£52 to £208	£250 to £998
Mainstream unmetered	£16	£16	£16	£16	£192
0.5p/min calls access	**£1.30**	**£3.90**	£10.40	£26	£125
Cheapest unmetered	£8	£8	**£8**	**£8**	**£96**

Cheapest in bold (1) 0845 calls. The range of prices reflects when calls are charged – daytime is most expensive, weekends and evenings cheaper.

SUGGESTED INGREDIENTS

www.myinternetpass.co.uk; www.onetel.net, 0800 957 0000;

www.fast4.net, 0870 225 1055; www.free24-7.net, 0870 220 3506; www.fireflyuk.net

More info: www.moneysavingexpert.com/ISP

ADDED SPICE

■ *E-mail lock-in.* One final weapon in ISPs' arsenal is allocating you one of their own e-mail addresses. It mightn't sound bad, but it means that switching ISP requires losing this, which can be such a hassle it substantially disincentives a move. Using universal addresses like Hotmail, Gmail or Yahoo or auto-forwarding services solves the problem, and provides flexibility.

BROADBAND

NUTRITIONAL INFORMATION

Typical Gain: £100.

Time Taken: 45 minutes.

Difficulty: Mid.

THE MENU

Broadband internet means a speedy connection to the web and the end of the world-wide-wait. For most people it involves an upgraded home telephone line called ADSL (Asymmetrical Digital Subscriber Line).

Apart from speed, the other big pluses with ADSL is it's always connected, so you don't need to dial it up every time, and you can still use the normal phone line while surfing the web. To access broadband is easy. Your broadband provider will request that BT upgrades your line. It takes around a week and you shouldn't notice any difference to your phone line.

Money Diet Quick Fact Snack: How Can ADSL be so Much Quicker on the Same Line?

With dial-up internet, the computer's modem converts data into a noise (you know, that urrrrr, duhhh, urrrrr, grrrrr sound), the phone converts this into electrical signals and they're returned to noise at the other end for another computer to interpret.

With ADSL the data is more efficiently converted into electrical signals, bypassing the sound, and transmitted over a much wider frequency range so more is carried.

Then just plug your computer into the phone line via a special 'broadband modem', and bish-bash-bosh you should be online.

Many telephone providers try and get you to use their broadband service as well, as a 'dual offer', yet there is absolutely nothing requiring you to use this. You can change broadband without changing your phone provider. Best practice is to have the two services unlinked; that way you are free to shift to cheaper providers as prices change.

CHOOSING YOUR DISH

This depends very much on your requirements.

■ *Are you new to broadband?* New broadband users have an extra couple of costs to pay.

1. The modem cost. Buying a special broadband modem costs around £30–£50. It can be done cheaper through discount stores or eBay, but you need to be a reasonable technophile if you're doing that.

2. Upgrading the phone line. This is usually around £40–£70.

This hefty £100ish set-up fee suddenly makes broadband a little less affordable. Yet there's a way round this. Focus on 'all-inclusive' packages, where the modem and line installation are supplied by the provider.

This invariably means signing a contract, usually for a year, though overall it should be cheaper.

■ *It's different for existing customers.* If you've got broadband, you should already have a broadband modem and an activated phone line. Providing you're outside your contract period with your current provider, switching should produce savings.

Often you will need to pay a 'migration' fee to move, usually £15–£30, but it's likely this will be eaten up by the savings.

■ *How fast do you want it?* Internet speed is measured in Kbps, the amount of information transferred per second. A phone dial-up connection is 56Kbps. When broadband first launched, 512Kbps – nearly 10 times faster – was the standard. Now the speeds are creeping up and many people have 1Mbps (around 1,000Kbps) or faster lines.

There's a massive difference between broadband and dial-up but the difference between 512Kbps and faster broadband has less of an impact as it doesn't automatically speed up web surfing – this is often dictated by the speed of the website's servers.

Faster broadband's real impact is when downloading music, streaming video or online gaming, or if different family members connect on one line with different computers.

■ *How much will you use it?* Many providers now base their charges on the volume of data used. This is measured in megabytes, MB, or gigabytes, GB (1,000 MB). It's easy to get confused about this. It has nothing to do with the 'time spent online', and leaving the internet connected doesn't cost anything. It's only 'doing things' that uses up the bytes.

As an idea of the scale, viewing 25 web pages takes very roughly 1MB – so a 1GB monthly limit means roughly 25,000 pages. For those just doing a little web-surfing or downloading e-mails, the limits will be no problem.

Downloading music software or videos eats up the data much faster, although even then only real musos or online gaming gurus will feel the impact. For most people a 2GB limit will suffice. Though if you're going for a limited service, do check what'll happen when you reach the limit. Will you be charged more? If so, is the additional cost cheap (around £1.50 per GB) or more, and worst still, will you be cut off?

CALORIE COUNT

Some providers will charge newbies moving to their service a £50 activation fee, £34.99 for a modem and £19.99 a month. That's £325 over the first year. Yet an all-inclusive package with no set-up costs is easy to find for less than £200, 40 per cent cheaper.

UK's Cheapest Broadband Provider	Set-up cost		Monthly cost	Annual cost		
	Newcomers	Migration fee		Newcomers	Existing users	Saving
Bog-standard provider	£85 (includes modem cost)	£50	£20	£325	£290	–
Top newbie provider	Free	Free	£16	£190	£190	£100
Top existing customer provider	£80	£35	£11.75	£260	£175	£115

Existing customers can find even better bargains, with providers often charging £10 to £12 a month.

SUGGESTED INGREDIENTS

www.tiscali.co.uk, www.v21.co.uk, www.btopenworld.co.uk, www.ukonline.net, www.lixxus.co.uk, www.adsl4less.com, www.aol.co.uk, www.metronet.co.uk, www.madasafish.com, www.efhbroadband.com, www.bulldog.co.uk

Updated best buys: www.moneysavingexpert.com/broadband

ADDED SPICE

- *Techie talk:* If you're getting broadband, service also matters. It's worth noting some broadband services have technological limitations that may impact exactly what you want to do. For that I'd suggest Adslguide.org.uk, a cracking site for those wanting the techie viewpoint.

CALLING OVERSEAS

NUTRITIONAL INFORMATION

Typical Gain: £300.
Time Taken: 45 minutes.
Difficulty Level: Easy.
(Also see 'Completely Free Calls Worldwide via Your PC', page 203.)

THE MENU

Cunning calls can mean it's cheaper to call Alaska than Altrincham, Singapore than Swindon, Argentina than Aberdeen.

To do this, use one of the specialist 'override' providers – so-called because after dialling a number on your home phone, you're connected to another network, thus 'overriding' the normal provider. There are two different types.

■ *Account Needed (AN) providers.* Dial a freephone number or a short four- or five-digit prefix number to access its system. Then simply dial the number you want to call. As calling to access its network is free, the only cost is the override provider's own charge. Some providers are prepay; others set up accounts and bill by direct debit at the end of each month.

■ *Simply Dial (SD) providers.* Dial a special number to connect to its network rather than a freephone number. These numbers are usually 'non-geographic numbers' such as an 0845 local-rate or 09XX premium-rate number. The more expensive the destination, the higher this charge. Thus the access call is billed via your home phone provider's bill. That's the only cost. The override provider never bills you itself. It makes its money by receiving a proportion of the income from the initial access calls.

In other words:

■ With ANs you pay nothing to access the network, and are then billed per call.

■ With SDs you pay for the call to access their network, but aren't billed by them.

SDs' advantage is that they're much easier to use, especially for one-off calls, as there's no need to set up an account. However, with SDs you are billed as soon as you dial, whether the final call is connected or not.

CHOOSING YOUR DISH

If calling overseas is a substantial part of your expenditure, it's likely you call just one or two destinations. This means it's worth spending the time to locate the ultimate cheapest provider for those specific locations. One warning: don't assume because a company is the cheapest for calling a specific country, it's necessarily cheapest for calling that country's mobile phones. Always consider calling a country's mobile as a second destination.

Override providers' line quality and connection ability vary, as they often underbuy capacity to keep costs low. Bigger providers can't risk it, so they must overbuy. Differences in routeing technology can also diminish call quality with override providers, but for most non-business calls, they should be fine.

CALORIE COUNT

Calling China on BT standard can cost over £1 a minute, and it isn't that much cheaper on BT's discount tariff. However, it is possible to make the call for as little as a penny a minute. A huge saving.

Cost savings on a 15 minute call each week over a year						
	Standard line		Cheapest override		Saving over BT	% saving
Destination	Per min	Year	Per min	Year	Year	Year
USA	22p	£170	1p	£8	£162	95%
India	60p	£465	10p	£80	£385	83%
China	103p	£800	1p	£8	£792	99%
Venezuelan mobile	131p	£1,020	15p	£120	£900	88%
TOTAL	–	£2,665	–	£216	£2,450	92%

SUGGESTED INGREDIENTS

To help find the cheapest there's a non-commercial comparison service at www.moneysavingexpert.com/callchecker which updates prices daily to every country.

If you're not on the internet, then by checking the prices of the providers above to your destination you should still save a fortune over mainstream providers. The providers below are the place to start. For the simply dial providers, call the number listed, then dial the overseas number you're calling. Often it'll give you another number to call (if the tariff's more expensive), and you'll find out the cost when calling that second number.

Simply dial providers: www.Just-Dial.com, 0870 794 0000; www.telediscount.co.uk; www.telestunt.co.uk; www.tele-savers.co.uk; www.liquidtelecom.com; www.dialaround.co.uk; www.simply-fone.com; www.cheapestcalls.co.uk; www.penny-phone.co.uk; www.ratebuster.co.uk; www.budgetcom.co.uk; www.abroadtel.co.uk; www.dialwise.co.uk

Account needed providers: www.18866.com; www.onetel.net, 0800 957 0000; www.call1899.co.uk; www.alphatel.com; www.liquidtelecom.com

COMPLETELY FREE CALLS WORLDWIDE VIA YOUR PC

NUTRITIONAL INFORMATION
Typical Gain: £300.
Time Taken: 20 minutes.
Difficulty Level: Mid.

THE MENU
Call anywhere in the world completely for free. No, it's not some naff 'free calls' competition. You can call anyone, anywhere, provided you're both connected to the internet. In some circumstances, cheap computer to normal phone calls are possible too.

Any PC made within the last five years with an internet connection should easily cope. A microphone and headset/speakers are needed, though those who prefer can actually buy phone handsets to attach to the computer.

As for the internet connection, broadband is preferable (see page 196) and provides better quality, but it's still workable if you're on a dial-up internet connection.

Of course when I say free, you need to incorporate the cost of your internet usage. If you're on a metered broadband or dial-up service (i.e. you don't pay a flat monthly fee for using it, but are charged per minute for internet usage) then you are paying for your time online too and need to compare the cost of this to normal phone calls. If it's unmetered then there's no additional cost so this is a bonanza.

CHOOSING YOUR DISH

- *Making PC to PC calls.* There's lots of free software available. All you need do is download it yourself and get the other person to download it as well, then after that you can talk on it whenever you want.

  You should never pay any charge whatsoever for PC to PC calls. Let me stress, this applies wherever you are calling from and to, meaning international calls are completely free too.

  1. Pure internet telephony v. messenger services. The most widely known internet communication devices are instant messaging services such as those provided by AOL, MSN and Yahoo. These are designed for instant online typed communications, but the latest versions also include voice and video communication options.

  While this works, often the quality isn't quite up to the

standard of pure internet telephony operators, and if it's pure phone you want, stick with them. A company called Skype (pronounced to rhyme with tripe) is quickly becoming the Microsoft of internet telephony and, like Microsoft, is sometimes derided by techies.

However, it's very easy to use and the quality is good: simply download it, create a user name, find the username of the person you're calling, and within seconds you can talk to them. It also allows free conference calling, so you can talk to two or three people all at the same time. The one big advantage of its wide-ranging use is it's the software other people are likely to have already.

2. Video-chat. Those with web cams may also video-chat across the world. This technology is gradually getting more sophisticated, and most people use it through the messenger services above.

However, if you use phone services through the computer while video is transmitting, the quality is often poor. It's easier to use the text-based messaging services alongside the video.

Is the call quality any good? If you're on broadband with good software, it's similar to using a mobile phone about four years ago, although sometimes it does lack a crisp, clean noise.

Having said that, it's easy and you can talk to someone wherever in the world they are, providing they have an internet connection. Best of all, as it's free, you can try it, and if you don't like it, don't continue to use it.

■ **Making PC to phone calls.** Many of the bigger providers such as Skype, Net2phone and Go2Call also allow calls to be made from your PC to a normal phone. To do this, simply enter the number to be dialled into their onscreen dialpad.

Yet these calls aren't free. Even the cheapest, again Skype, is 1.7 Euro cents (about 1.2p) a minute for calls to landlines in the UK and most European and North American countries, and much more for calls elsewhere.

Generally speaking, this simply isn't competitive compared to the cheapest normal international calls (see page 200), although it's unlikely to get cheaper quickly.

Yet it is useful for those who travel abroad. If you have access to the internet, you can use this software to call back to normal phones in the UK at just 1.2p/minute.

SUGGESTED INGREDIENTS
Internet telephony: Skype, www.skype.com; BT Communicator, www.bt.com/btcommunicator; Siphone, www.siphone.co.uk; Stanaphone, www.stanaphone.com/whatsstana; Net2phone, www.net2phone.com; Dialpad, www.dialpad.com; Go2call, www.go2call.com; www.google.co.uk

Messenger/video messaging services: MSN Messenger, http://messenger.msn.com; AOL Instant Messenger, www.aol.com/aim; Yahoo Messenger, http://messenger.yahoo.com; ICQ Messenger, www.ICQ.com

ONLINE SHOPPING

NUTRITIONAL INFORMATION
Typical Saving: £250 per year.
Time Taken: 10 minutes a time.
Difficulty Level: Easy.

THE MENU
Internet shopping robots (shopbots) scan internet retailers to

find the cheapest price. Simply enter what you want, press compare and the results are displayed in order of cost, including extras like delivery, which should also be broken out and listed separately.

This is a MoneySaver no-brainer. Don't go to Amazon and put in your book/DVD player name – instead go to a shopbot, do the same thing and you get prices from a host of shops (including Amazon) in the same amount of time.

CHOOSING YOUR DISH

Each shopbot searches a slightly different range of retailers, so for more expensive purchases it's always worth trying two or three. For more specialised goods, such as computer parts or fridges, you'll find some dedicated shopbots.

These sites make cash via advertising, or retailers' commission for sales links. There's nothing wrong with this providing there are no unfair promotions for higher-commission goods and the price is unaffected. Always keep an eye out for this. (See 'Financial price-comparison services', page 106.)

Martin's Money Memories: How Not to Make Friends when You've Got a Book Out

The following note is from the *The Bookseller*'s Christmas edition. It's the industry magazine for the book trade, and was part of its '12 days of a bookshop owner' Christmas feature.

'Twelve customers telling me they'd heard that nice Martin Lewis on the radio advising people on how to do their Christmas shopping. "Never buy books from a bookshop," he advised the nation. Thanks Martin. Well, seeing as his fans won't be visiting us anymore, I'm sure he won't mind me sending back our copies of *The Money Diet*.'

Also remember that price-comparison services note the delivery costs of an individual product. However, buy three or four goods at a time, and the delivery costs per product may change, in which case compare using the main product price not delivery price.

CALORIE COUNT

By just using two price-comparison services for a range of goods, I saved 35 per cent over using an individual online retailer – and that was already cheaper than most high-street shops. Over a year this makes a massive difference, especially if you buy big goods such as a fridge or television.

Shopbot savings	Chart CD	New Chart Hardback Book	New Chart DVD	New Playstation 2 Game	Delivery	Total	Saving
Standard online retailer	£11	£17	£20	£40	£4	£92	N/A
Shopbots (includes delivery)	£8	£10	£15	£33	Inc.	£66	£26

SUGGESTED INGREDIENTS

www.kelkoo.co.uk; www.pricerunner.co.uk; www.easyvalue.com; www.onlinepriceguide.co.uk; www.checkaprice.com; www.priceguideuk.com; www.dealtime.co.uk; www.comparisonmagic.co.uk; www.froogle.co.uk

Updated info: www.moneysavingexpert.com/shopbots

ADDED SPICE

- **_Cashback sites cut the cost further._** Once you've found the cheapest retailer for your product, it's possible to cut the cost even further by then buying it via a cashback website.

  These are effectively advertising sites, which split the revenue they earn with you. This means buy via them and you can get around 2 per cent more off the price. Each time you earn the cashback (or cashback points) it's added to your account and the payout usually comes once it hits £25.

  If you use these in conjunction with shopbots you should be able to finagle the price down to the raw best. Then why not pay with a cashback credit card on top (see page 387).

SUGGESTED INGREDIENTS

www.Rpoints.co.uk, www.greasypalm.co.uk, www.mutual-points.co.uk

Updated info: www.moneysavingexpert.com/shopbots

WHERE TO START WITH SAVINGS: THE SAVINGS FOUNTAIN

Okay, so I can tell you how to get the best deal on your savings, yet for many people the question is 'Which type of savings?' Should this be the stockmarket, a savings account or ISA?

So to help you decide where to begin when you want to start putting some money aside, I've come up with the 'Savings Fountain'.

Yet there are a couple of other things to consider first.

Q. Are You Ready to Start Saving?

Sounds stupid, doesn't it. You've decided to save, and here's me questioning it. However, many people decide to start saving when they're still in debt, and this ain't good.

The reason is simple. It's likely what you're earning on your savings is much less, after tax, than debts are costing you, so use your savings to pay off your debts and you're quids in. I mention 'the two-sided money coin' elsewhere in this book, but it's so important I make no apology for repetition.

> **The Two-sided Money Coin**
>
> Debts and savings are very similar, two sides of the same coin (hence the name). Both involve paying a set amount out of your salary each month.
>
> Debt simply pays for something you've already had, whereas savings pay for something you're going to have. The big difference is with savings they pay you a little interest and with debt you pay them a huge amount of interest. Make sure you're on the right side of the coin.

Look at the numbers. On a typical high street credit card £1,000 debt would cost you around £170 in interest over a year. In even the best savings account £1,000 would pay you around £40 interest after tax. So if you used this £1,000 of savings to pay off the debts, you'd be £130 a year better off.

Of course, for advanced MoneySavers, who effectively, carefully and conscientiously manage to move debts to be constantly free of interest, the logic changes. If you're one of the rare people doing this, save the cash (see page 387).

What about Mortgage Debt?

Funnily enough people don't often consider their mortgage as debt, yet it is. However, rates are typically much lower.

For example, when mortgages are around 6 per cent interest, the best savings accounts pay only around 4 per cent after basic rate tax. Yet this still means, pay off £1,000 of your mortgage with savings and you're £20 a year better off, or more for basic-rate taxpayers.

Take this further, and consider 'paying off your mortgage' as a form of saving. To earn 6 per cent annually on £1,000 of savings you'd need to earn 7.5 per cent interest before tax – gobsmackingly more than the best normal savings account. Therefore paying off your mortgage is a very effective use of cash.

Sadly, though, it's not that simple. Put the savings into your mortgage and it's gone – you're effectively locking it away and losing the ability to use it in the future (except those with flexible mortgages, see page 339, which have over-pay and borrow-back facilities, who can thus withdraw the cash willy-nilly).

Thus the financial gain has to be balanced against the loss of flexibility. Yet providing some funds are held back for an emergency, it's still a good idea.

Savings versus Investing

Now assuming you're ready to put money away for your future, you've one more choice to make: to save or to invest.

■ *Saving.* Putting money away in complete safety, so you'll get it all back plus interest.

■ *Investing.* Risking losing some or all your interest and/or original investment for the chance it'll grow more quickly.

Conventional wisdom states the longer you're willing to put your cash away the more you should consider investing in the stockmarket to get bigger growth, but it's always a personal choice.

There is no right answer. (Surprisingly, most people find this tough to grasp, but only hindsight will tell you which is the correct choice.) The choice is down to your priorities; are you willing to risk this money shrinking in order to chance it growing more quickly?

Now, let me be straight here. Investments aren't my expertise. You'll find Crash Diet pieces on the cheapest way to buy shares (page 236) and the cheapest way to buy funds (page 256), but not on what to invest in.

The reason for that is simple: no one knows what will happen in investing; it's an art, not a science. Investment experts are just taking a guess; it really is an attempt to predict the future. There is no guarantee their guess will be any better than your own. No one knows the 'right answer'.

So I have to say for those looking at investment options, this isn't the book. However, a couple of good reads I'd recommend are the *Which? Guide to being your own Independent Financial Adviser* and *How to Read the Financial Pages* (FT). For me, savings are my bag.

THE SAVINGS FOUNTAIN

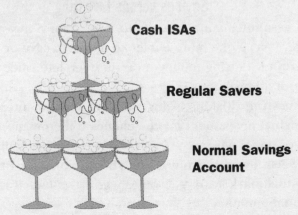

Cash ISAs

Regular Savers

Normal Savings
Account

Why the Fountain is Necessary

This is all about prioritising where you put your cash in order to maximise your interest because different savings products work in different ways, with different rates and tax treatment.

The fountain is simple. Pour as much cash as possible into the best-paying savings vehicle possible, then, when it's full and overflowing, fill up the next best and so on.

POOL 1: CASH ISAS

All taxpayers should first pour money into a mini cash ISA (Instant Savings Accounts). These are just like a normal savings account, but tax-free. Each tax year every UK adult gets a new ISA allowance for cash, shares or life assurance investments. Up to £3,000 a year is allowed in cash savings, and if you don't use it you lose it.

The tax advantage is an important one. On all other savings you pay tax on the interest earned. Basic-rate taxpayers pay it at 20 per cent and higher rate taxpayers pay it at 40 per cent. Therefore for every £100 interest earned, you'd receive £100 in a cash ISA, but only £80 in a normal savings account (or just £60 for higher-rate taxpayers).

For full details on cash ISAs, see page 223, and for fixed-rate cash ISAs, see page 228.

POOL 2: REGULAR SAVINGS ACCOUNTS

Once the cash ISA overflows, use special Regular Saver accounts as they consistently outpay standard savings accounts, without locking your money away harshly (like fixed-rate savings accounts). As the name suggests, they require a monthly payment into the account.

The drawback with Regular Savers is you can't just dunk cash straight in there – instead you drip-feed it with a standing order from a normal savings account.

For full details on regular savings see page 217.

POOL 3: STANDARD SAVINGS ACCOUNTS

Once the money splashes over the edge of a Regular Saver, or for instant-access flexibility, it's on to the best-paying standard account.

For full details on instant access savings see page 215.

Non-taxpayers' Note

The non-taxpayers' fountain differs slightly as there's no cash ISA tax gain. Yet potential future taxpayers should still consider them as, if you open one now and don't withdraw the money, the interest should still be tax-free once you start paying tax.

It's a good preventative measure. If you won't ever pay tax, the fountain starts with a Regular Saver as the interest is highest. After that, pick a cash ISA or savings account depending on which pays more interest.

Remember the rates on all these accounts can change. It's worth checking every six months or so to see if there's a higher-paying equivalent.

Married Couples Can Save Tax on Savings

If you're married and one of you pays tax at a higher rate than the other, then do make sure all the savings (providing you trust each other) are in the name of the lower-rate taxpayer. This way you'll pay much less tax on the interest, saving you money.

SAVINGS ACCOUNTS

(Please read 'Where to Start with Savings', see page 209, first)

NUTRITIONAL INFORMATION

Typical Gain: £100 a year.

Time Taken: 20 minutes.

Difficulty Level: Easy.

THE MENU

Savings accounts are bank accounts that pay more interest but have less functionality than normal day-to-day current accounts (see page 238).

CHOOSING YOUR DISH

The prime consideration is the interest rate, yet even with this simple product there are a few things to watch out for.

- *Access. How quickly do you need the money?* Notice accounts mean you must wait to withdraw your cash, yet these days, the best 'instant access' and 'no-notice' don't pay much less than the best notice accounts so they're often a better pick. If you're wondering what the difference is between instant access and no-notice: with instant access you can just go to a branch and withdraw cash; with no-notice the money is available immediately but, as it's via electronic transfer or post, it takes about 3 days to receive.

- *Short-term interest rate bonuses.* These temporary rate hikes mean providers can advertise higher rates to attract custom, but the rates soon shrink. There's nothing wrong with going for these if they pay the best rate, providing you're prepared to switch account as soon as the rate drops. If not, stick to non-bonus accounts.

215

■ *Tax.* The interest on savings accounts is automatically taxed at the basic savings tax rate, currently 20 per cent. This means basic-rate taxpayers needn't do anything, but higher-rate taxpayers must declare the interest on the self-assessment form and will pay a total of 40 per cent of it. Non-taxpayers can get an R85 form so that all interest will be paid tax-free.

■ *Rates are variable.* Savings accounts interest rates are variable and move both when the Bank of England base rate moves (see page 333) and when the product-provider changes the rate for its own competitive reasons. This means it's important to monitor the interest rate you receive. If it drops, just withdraw the money and put it in a better account. If that's too much of a hassle then look for a tracker, where the rate follows the Bank of England base rate. (Also see the 'Suck, slap and flog' technique, page 154.)

CALORIE COUNT

Many people leave their savings languishing in accounts paying pitiful rates. In real terms you're losing money as the after-tax interest is often lower than inflation.

Interest on £5,000 in a Savings Account before Tax				
		1 year	3 years	Gain over 3 years
Pitiful Bank	0.5%	£25	£75	–
Top Payer	5%	£250	£790	£715

SUGGESTED INGREDIENTS (NEWS)

www.INGDirect.com, 0800 376 8844; www.egg.com, 08451 233 233; Birmingham Midshires, www.askbm.co.uk, 0845 300 2627; Abbey National, www.abbey.com, 0845 765 4321; Nationwide, www.nationwide.co.uk, 0800 302010; Alliance

and Leicester, www.alliance-leicester.co.uk (08459 26 26 26);
Northern Rock, 0845 600 4466; www.if.com; www.halifax.co.uk;
Coventry Building Society, 0845 766 5522; www.cahoot.com;
www.icici.co.uk; your local building society (some have
special rates for local people)
Updated info: www.moneysavingexpert.com/savingsaccounts

REGULAR SAVINGS ACCOUNTS

■NUTRITIONAL INFORMATION
Typical Gain: £120.
Time Taken: 30 minutes.
Difficulty Level: Mid.

■THE MENU
Regular savings accounts are an oft-unused breed, yet usually
they beat even the market-leading standard savings. They are
marketed as enforcing saving discipline as they require a
payment to be made every month, but there's a sneaky trick
to enable lump-sum investments too.

■CHOOSING YOUR DISH
The interest rate is crucial, but also check the following:
■ *Monthly payment required.* Different minimums and
   maximums apply – usually £20 to £250. Some accounts
   require a fixed payment each month, but it's preferable if
   they just require you to deposit 'at least' the minimum.
■ *Qualifying for a bonus.* These accounts work by paying a
   bonus, which boosts the interest each year, providing
   you've made all the required payments. The qualifying
   rules vary. Some limit withdrawals; others accept one
   missed payment. Pick one that suits your habits.

- *Variable rates.* Just like ordinary savings accounts, these rates are variable. If they drop the rate below competitive levels, wait until you've been paid the bonus, then withdraw your money immediately and open an account elsewhere.
- *Short-term fixed rate accounts.* Some accounts, often by big banks, tend to promote high rates of interest, but only allow small contributions, on accounts which last just a year. The benefit here, though, is that rate is usually fixed.

CALORIE COUNT

Regular Savings Accounts beat Standard Savers			
Save £200 per month for three years	Interest rate	Interest earned (basic-rate taxpayer)	Increase in interest
Poor Savings Account	0.2%	£20	–
Top Savings Account	4.3%	£370	£350
Top Regular Savings Account	6%	£530	£510

SUGGESTED INGREDIENTS

Ipswich Building Society, 0845 230 8686; Derbyshire Building Society, 0845 004 005, www.thederbyshire.co.uk; Leeds & Holbeck BS, 08450 50 50 75; Abbey, 0800 389 9875; Furness BS, 0800 781 4311; Birmingham Midshires, 0845 300 2627; Halifax, 0845 7263646; Monmouthshire BS, 01633 844444; your local building society (some have special rates for local people).

ADDED SPICE

- *How to invest a lump sum.* To invest a lump sum using these schemes, put the money first in the highest-paying standard savings account. Then set up monthly payments from it to the regular savings account, at the maximum level in the first months to get the cash in quickly. However, always ensure there's enough left to keep up the minimum payments over the year. This way your money trickles across and you always meet the terms and conditions. You'll be earning maximum interest both on the money in the regular saver and the cash that will eventually move over.

BEST CHILD SAVINGS (AND USE YOUR CHILD FOR A SNEAKY TAX-FREE ALLOWANCE)

■ NUTRITIONAL INFORMATION

Typical Gain: £40 (and some good education).
Time Taken: 20 minutes.
Difficulty Level: Easy/Mid.

■ THE MENU

This is a triple-bonus saving. At its simplest level, it's ensuring your children are maximising the interest earned on their accounts. The secondary benefit is it's a great opportunity to explain to them how interest works, how to monitor a bank account, and to understand that while a bank is a custodian of our money, its job is to make the money for itself and not you.

Yet there's a third benefit. It's possible to use your children as a hidden secret weapon against tax. Used correctly, each child is a way to save around £2,000 in a higher-interest account without paying tax on it (though you'll have to wait for 'Added Spice' for that).

■ *Children's savings are not tax-free* This is commonly misunderstood. Children are in fact taxed in exactly the same way as adults. This means, just like each adult, each child has an annual personal allowance (just under £5,000)

219

that can be earned from salary, savings or investment income before it is eligible for income tax.

The reason for the confusion is that, unlike most adults, most children don't fill their allowance up with earnings, so their savings are in practice tax-free.

If, like the vast majority, your child isn't paying tax on their savings, it's important to ensure any interest is paid without the tax being automatically deducted. Fill out the Inland Revenue R85 form, available from whoever you're setting up the account with.

CHOOSING YOUR DISH

■ *A great lesson, teach your children to bag freebies.* Sadly, many people are still with the same bank now that they were with in childhood. The banks ain't stupid; they know this, and, gleefully aware, buy perhaps 40 years of loyal custom for the cost of doling out a free piggy bank or calculator.

However, you can turn this around, and at the same time will teach children a disloyalty towards banks (there aren't that many greater gifts a parent can give!) The first thing to note is if your child has only a small amount of money to invest, then choosing on the basis of the freebies isn't that bad. The freebie's value more than outweighs any interest earned.

Yet there's nothing stopping a child opening a range of accounts with the minimum deposit, usually £1, and grabbing all the freebies. I still remember the very cool (well, I couldn't have been more than seven) free T-shirt courtesy of a pound from Bradford & Bingley (thanks Mum and Dad).

■ *For real savings, grab the highest interest rate.* If there is any real money going into an account, the focus must be interest rates. Many children's accounts pay better rates than the 'adult' equivalents, though some still try to sucker in the nation's little'uns with poor-paying accounts.

Don't be fooled though; their rates aren't fixed. They can change both with Bank of England base rate moves and as banks decide to be more or less competitive.

In one notable case, the Alliance & Leicester, having previously been a market leader, disgustingly decided to dump on the nation's children by cutting the interest it was paying by a third. It's really not wise to assume providers will behave nicely just because they're dealing with children. So monitor your accounts regularly; it's a good lesson for children to learn.

CALORIE COUNT

If a child saved £1,500 (see below for why the amount could be so large) in a poor-paying children's account over three years, it'd pay only around £120 interest, but by picking the best you could boost the returns to £240.

£1,500 in a Child's Instant-access Savings Account over 3 Years		
	Rate	Interest earnt
Poor Children's Account	2.55%	£120
Top Children's Account	5.05%	£240

SUGGESTED INGREDIENTS

www.nationwide.co.uk, 0800 302010; Saffron Walden, 0800 072 1100, www.swhebs.co.uk; www.halifax.co.uk, 08457 263646; www.thechelsea.co.uk, 08457 446622; www.furnessbs.co.uk, 0800 781 4311; www.britannia.co.uk, 08000 134860; your local building society.

Updated best buys: www.moneysavingexpert.com/child accounts

ADDED SPICE

Now on to the sexy bit. Using your children 'tax-efficiently' may sound a little nasty, but if it puts more cash in your pockets, then it should benefit them too.

Saving money in a child's name means it's likely to be tax-free, and possibly at a higher rate of interest than you can get on your own savings. Now if you're worried about mixing the cash up, It's perfectly possible to have one account for your child to put their pocket money in, and another for any larger amounts.

■ *The rules.* Don't assume you can dunk fortunes in your kid's name. If a child generates interest of more than £100 in the course of the year from money specifically given by *each* parent, this income is taxed at that parent's tax rate.

In practical terms this currently means you could put a little less than £2,000 in the top-paying children's account, and it wouldn't be taxed, as that would generate around £100 interest. Sadly, this isn't an annual tax-free allocation; it's the interest generated from all cash given in this and previous years.

Yet these rules apply only to parents, not grandparents, aunties, uncles or friends – they may all give your children as much as they like and, providing it's a genuine gift (it's often worth them coupling it with a letter to confirm this), then it counts as the child's money without a £100 limit.

The only other tax implications of making cash gifts is the possible spectre of inheritance tax if the donor dies within seven years of making it.

And a quick warning, for any clever devils thinking, 'If I gave my sister's kids £10,000 and she gave mine the same...', well good thought, but no cigar. If the Inland Revenue spots you, you're in trouble.

■ **Whose money is it anyway?** If you're going to do this, remember that if the money is in your child's name it is your child's cash. Though don't worry too much about them spending your hard-earned cash on a Playstation 2, Anastasia CD, two dozen packs of football stickers and enough sweets to give a junior school a sugar rush. Many accounts allow you to stay in control of the cash.

To open an account themselves, a child will usually need to be at least seven. Under-sevens require a parent, guardian or grandparent to set up an account and act as signatory. This method can also be selected for older children, and if it is, then usually until they're 16 the signatory can still manage and withdraw the cash without the child's approval.

Do note many accounts have terms and conditions stating withdrawn money must be used 'for the benefit of the child', but this of course encompasses a wide variety of definitions.

MINI CASH ISAS

■ NUTRITIONAL INFORMATION

Typical Gain: £80 per year.

Time Taken: 20 minutes.

Difficulty Level: Easy/Mid.

(For a full, easy guide to how ISAs work, read page 230. If you already have money in a cash ISA also see page 225.)

■ THE MENU

Mini cash Individual Savings Accounts (ISAs) are simply savings accounts you don't pay income tax on. This means there's effectively an extra 25 per cent interest for basic-rate and 66 per cent for higher-rate taxpayers. Each tax year (6 April to 5 April) everyone aged 16 or older gets a new ISA allowance.

If you've got savings, and don't need to utilise an ISA for shares, then you should get a mini cash ISA. Even non-taxpayers often benefit as the best cash ISA rates usually beat the best savings account rates.

Each tax year you can currently save another £3,000 of cash in an ISA. Money can be withdrawn at any time without losing tax benefits, but it can't then be returned to the cash ISA. (See page 230 for full explanation.)

CHOOSING YOUR DISH

The higher the interest rate the better, though watch for the following:

■ *Short-term interest rate bonuses.* These temporary rate hikes allow providers to advertise higher rates to attract your custom, but they soon disappear. There's nothing wrong with going for them if they pay the best rate, providing you're prepared to transfer the cash ISA as soon as the rates drop. Otherwise, stick to non-bonus accounts.

■ *Transfer penalties.* You are allowed to change ISA provider – always a good thing, as if your cash ISA rate drops, it means you can move to a better-paying provider (see page 225). Yet some providers levy a fine when you leave them, which can outweigh any gain made by moving. These may effectively trap you if they drop their rate. Try to avoid!

■ *Fixed rates.* The only way to guarantee the rate won't drop is using a fixed-rate mini cash ISA (see page 228). Yet this means your money is partially locked away.

CALORIE COUNT

Interest on £3,000 Saved over 3 Years			
	Rate	Basic-rate taxpayer	Higher-rate taxpayer
Pitiful Savings Account (sadly there are many)	0.1%	£7	£5
Top Savings Account	5%	£380	£280
Worst-Paying Cash ISA	3.5%	£380	£330
Top Cash ISA	5%	£470	£470

SUGGESTED INGREDIENTS (NEWS)

Kent Reliance Building Society, 08451 220022; www.first direct.co.uk; Portman BS, 0845 6090 600; Northern Rock, 0845 587 2764; Abbey, 0800 587 2764; Nationwide, 0870 606 6461; Halifax, 01904 611110; your local building society (some have special rates for local people).

Updated info: www.moneysavingexpert.com/cashISA

EXISTING CASH ISAS: IMPROVING THE RETURNS

NUTRITIONAL INFORMATION

Typical Saving: £100 per year.
Time Taken: 20 minutes.
Difficulty Level: Mid.
(First read 'Mini Cash ISAs', page 223, and 'How an ISA Works', page 230.)

THE MENU

Cash ISA providers smile smugly when you open an account,

as they assume they have your business for life, regardless of whether they pay decent interest. Prove them wrong.

There are three reasons to consider switching a cash ISA – to up the interest; fix the interest; or to link the returns to the stock market.

ISA transfers must be like for like, so a mini cash ISA must stay a mini cash ISA. If you're moving the current year's ISA, it must be moved whole, but a previous year's ISA can be moved and split between different providers.

However, don't withdraw the cash to switch your account or you'll immediately lose the ISA tax benefits. Instead, talk to the new provider and ask about their transfer process.

Before moving, check if your current provider has any transfer penalties – roughly one in three do. Small penalties, like 30 days' interest, aren't a problem. Yet the few with higher fines (up to about £50) may scupper the gains.

CHOOSING YOUR DISH

Follow 'Mini Cash ISAs' (page 223) for the basics. There are a couple of additional transfer factors too.

Not all cash ISA providers accept transfers, but it's easy to find out – just ask. Also, with some providers you could get paid more if you transfer the combined value of a number of years' cash ISAs.

One further option to up the risk of your cash ISA is to use Guaranteed Equity Bond mini cash ISAs. Offered by many banks, these usually last for around five years, and your money is locked away during that time. The returns are linked to the performance of one or a combination of, stock markets. For example, you may receive approximately 70 per cent of the growth of a stock market index such as the FTSE-100. If the market does well, these will outperform standard cash

ISAs; if it does badly you will just get your original cash back. This means that the worst-case scenario is you miss out on the interest from a normal cash ISA. Not a bad deal.

CALORIE COUNT

Upping cash ISA interest alone can make a big difference. It's easily possible to have a combined £15,000 in cash ISAs from this and past years. By shifting this amount, you could gain over £200 a year.

Possible transfer benefits					
	Rate	Interest			Gain
		1 year	2 years	3 years	3 years
Poor Cash ISA	3%	£450	£915	£1,390	–
Top Cash ISA	5%	£750	£1,530	£2,360	£970

SUGGESTED INGREDIENTS

Main providers: see 'Mini cash ISAs', page 223.

Guaranteed Equity Bond ISA providers: Bristol & West, 0800 1811111; Birmingham Midshires, 0845 602 2828; Norwich Union, 0800 092 7872; Britannia BS, 0800 013 4860; National Savings & Investments, 0845 9645000; Northern Rock, 0845 601 5151.

Updated info: www.moneysavingexpert.com/cashISA

ADDED SPICE

■ *TOISAS.* If you had a Tessa (the pre-runner to cash ISAs) it's likely that when it matured you put the money in a TOISA (a Tessa-only ISA) so it stayed tax-free. If you did you can transfer your TOISA, just like a cash ISA, to a provider paying better interest.

FIXED-RATE CASH ISAS

NUTRITIONAL INFORMATION
Typical Gain: £100 per year.
Time Taken: 30 minutes.
Difficulty Level: Mid/Hard.
(First read 'Mini Cash ISAs', page 223, or 'Existing Cash ISAs: Improving the Returns', page 225.)

THE MENU
There's a loophole in the mini cash ISA regulations that benefits savers. Like normal savings accounts, it's possible to fix a high rate on your tax-free cash ISA, protecting it from interest rate cuts, but, unlike savings accounts, with Cash ISAs you needn't lock the money away.

This is because years after ISAs were launched, the Inland Revenue told providers who mandated a lock-in that even though the rate was fixed, they had to give people reasonable access to their cash. Of course it isn't quite that simple – providers may still snatch back some interest via early withdrawal penalties, but it works to our advantage.

CHOOSING YOUR DISH
Most cash ISAs are variable-rate, yet the few that are fixed tend to be very competitive – not a bad start. All in all, this means you can take advantage of guaranteed earnings if interest rates are dropping, yet have a way out if they start to rise and better deals are therefore available elsewhere.

Incidentally, those whose fixed-rate mini cash ISAs were taken out before the rule change are now able to withdraw money under these conditions too.

There are three elements to consider:
■ *The rate.* As always, the higher the better.

■ *The length of the fix.* They usually last one to five years. It'll always be better to stick to the full term of the fix, rather than withdrawing early and taking the penalty. Therefore a shorter fix is safer, as it's less likely rates will vary too much, so you won't miss potential rate boons.

■ *The withdrawal penalty.* Penalties are usually measured by a set number of days' worth of interest, such as 45, 90 or 180 days. The shorter the penalty, the more escapable the ISA.

These three elements can't be looked at in isolation – a long-term fix isn't so bad with a short withdrawal penalty, as you can escape. A long withdrawal penalty isn't so bad with a short-term fix, as it's likely you'll stick to the full term anyway.

CALORIE COUNT

The table below indicates the impact of withdrawal penalties on the interest rate. Now I know it looks complicated, but hopefully an example will help. Take a two-year fixed rate at 5 per cent, decide to withdraw the cash after a year and a half and you're charged a penalty, yet you'd still have earned the equivalent interest of 4.15 per cent over that time.

Fixed-rate mini cash ISAs	Full rate	Interest penalty on withdrawal	Equivalent interest rate if money withdrawn after							
			1yr	1½yrs	2yrs	3yrs	3½yrs	4yrs	4½yrs	5yrs
Two-year fix	5%	90 days	3.7%	4.15%	5%	–	–	–	–	–
Five-year fix	5.35%	180 days	2.6%	3.5%	4%	4.25%	4.4%	4.6%	4.7%	5.35%

SUGGESTED INGREDIENTS

Portman Building Society, 0845 6090 600; Abbey, 0800 587 2764; Halifax, 01904 611 110; Julian Hodge Bank, 0800 0283746; Kent Reliance BS, 08451 220022; your local building society (some have special rates for local people).

Money Diet Quick Fact Snack: How an ISA Works

What is an ISA? An Individual Savings Account isn't a financial product in its own right – it's just a tax-free wrapper in which you can place either cash or shares-based investments.

I've always used the same analogy to explain it, so I don't see why I should stop now!

Imagine a couple of cakes, one chocolate (cash) and one strawberry (shares). The tax man comes along every year, picks up a slice and takes a bite from it, but each year you're given a tax-free wrapper, like clingfilm, which you can put around some cake as you choose.

Once inside the clingfilm, the nature of the cake hasn't changed; the chocolate's still chocolate (cash is still cash) and the strawberry still strawberry (shares still shares). But as it's wrapped up in clingfilm the tax man can no longer take a bite.

How much can be invested? Each tax year (starts 6 April) everyone over the age of 16 receives an ISA allowance with a limit of £7,000. Any savings or investments must be opened and made by the next 5 April.

Investments stay within the ISA wrapper after the end of the tax year, but nothing more can then be put in as you'll then have a new year's allowance. However, this still means it's possible to have substantial amounts invested within ISA wrappers – a maximum £7,000 plus gains for each tax year since they started in 1999.

What can be put inside an ISA?

■ *Cash:* Cash ISAs are simply savings accounts where the interest isn't taxed (see page 223).

■ *Shares:* Share-based investments in various forms are ISA-able. Self-select ISAs allow you to pick your own shares. However, a more common use is for collective investment vehicles like unit or investment trusts, where fund managers pick a basket of shares and returns depend on the average performance (see 'Discount Brokers', page 233). Placing these investments inside an ISA wrapper provides two tax advantages. First, any profits made from share price increases aren't eligible for capital gains tax (a tax on profits made when you sell), and second, it enables all the tax on bonds to be reclaimed.

There used to be a third category, life assurance-type investments, yet it was hardly ever used and is now subsumed into shares.

What's all this Mini and Maxi stuff? Unfortunately the ISA rules are unnecessarily complicated. Each year anyone opening an ISA must pick whether to go for one of two types of ISA container, either mini or a maxi.

▓ *To MAXIMISE your share-based investments go for a MAXI:* A maxi is a suitcase-type container, as everything has to be bundled together and bought from just one provider. You can have up to £3,000 in cash, and whatever you don't use up in shares. This means it's possible to have up to the full £7,000 in share-based investments. Usually maxi ISAs are therefore bought from investment companies, who pay relatively poor cash returns, so maxis are best used for shares ISAs.

▓ *For the best CASH returns MINIMISE your share-based investments with a MINI:* If maxis are suitcases, minis are like two handbags. Each can be bought from a different company and must carry something different. The limits are £3,000 in the cash bag, but only £4,000 in the shares bag. As cash ISAs can therefore be bought from specialists, minis provide the best cash returns.

The rules strictly prevent the opening of a mini and a maxi ISA in the same tax year. Do this and you are potentially invalidating any tax gains. Therefore think before opening any ISA: even if you open a mini cash ISA with just a pound at the start of the tax year, there's no going back – you're on the mini route. And if you later decide you want to invest the maximum £7,000 in shares that year, you'll find £3,000 of the allowance is lost. This is very important if you have a direct debit paying into a current ISA. If that automatically carries over into the next tax year, the choice is then made for you. Be careful.

How can money be withdrawn? ISAs don't need to be held for a set length of time. Money can be withdrawn at any time without losing any tax benefits – providing the rules of that individual product allow it. The confusing thing is the limits only apply on the way into the ISA. Some examples should clarify this:

■ *Mr Rich Devil invests £7,000 in a shares ISA at the beginning of the tax year.* Options: he may sell the investment at any time without tax implications, but no more may be put inside that year's ISA wrapper. However, he can still buy and sell shares within the wrapper based on the proceeds of the original investment.

■ *Ms Irma Indecisive invests £2,000 in a mini cash ISA at the start of the tax year.* Options: she may invest a further £1,000 in the mini cash ISA plus £4,000 in a mini shares ISA with another different provider before the end of the tax year.

■ *Irma then decides she needs to withdraw £1,000 of this cash.* Options: the fact that she has withdrawn the cash doesn't impact her allowance at all – she can still only put £1,000 more in the mini cash ISA and £4,000 in the mini shares ISA.

Can I switch provider once I've set up an ISA? There's nothing stopping you switching provider for cash or shares. However, don't simply withdraw the cash or investment as you'll lose the tax benefits. Instead, ask the new provider about its procedures for moving the money.

DISCOUNT BROKERS:
HOW TO BUY INVESTMENTS FOR LESS

■NUTRITIONAL INFORMATION

Typical Gain: £250.
Time Taken: 15 minutes.
Difficulty Level: Easy.

■THE MENU

How many fund-management companies does it take to screw
in a light bulb? None – fund-management companies only
screw us. Okay, maybe not funny but, hopefully, illuminating.
Never buy a fund unit trust or shares-based ISA direct from a
fund manager – do that and up to 6 per cent of your investment pays for advice you haven't been given.

Unit trusts/open-ended investment trusts are collective
investment funds, where the price depends on the value of a
group of shares or bonds picked by a professional manager
following a theme (like the investment type or industry) such as
smaller Japanese companies. As the combined value of these
shares rises or falls, the funds move proportionately. It is possible
to invest in a unit trust within an ISA wrapper (see page 230).

Performance is often eaten away by two types of charges.

- ■ *Initial charge.* An upfront chomp off the investment of up
  to 6 per cent, mostly used to pay commission.
- ■ *Annual charge.* A smaller snack taken every year of up to
  1.5 per cent, of which 0.5 per cent may be commission.

The commission is designated to pay Independent Financial
Advisers for their advice. No problem if you use one, but make

your decision and buy direct from the fund manager, and – outrageously – you pay without getting the advice.

The charges are clever: you never see them directly, you just receive proportionately less investment. For example, invest £5,000 in a fund with a 5 per cent upfront charge and only £4,750 buys the investment. This means you don't feel the cost, but it's still there.

If you're buying without advice, use a discount broker. They're bulk-buy fund specialists, and as you just tell them what you want, they can rebate most of their commission so you receive more.

CHOOSING YOUR DISH

■ *It's the charge not the commission rebate that counts.* Not all discount brokers are equal. To start with, some charge fees. More confusingly, though, many advertise zero initial commission, yet this doesn't mean the initial charge is zero, as each broker may have different commission arrangements with fund managers. Therefore, it's important to compare exactly what the actual initial charge you will pay on the fund is.

■ *Look for annual charge discounts too.* A few discounters also rebate a small proportion of the annual commission as well as the initial commission. This helps your plan grow even faster and is well worth going for. The only time not to pick this is if it's possible to get a much lower initial charge elsewhere.

CALORIE COUNT

Take a selection of four funds and invest £7,000. Pay full commission and if the funds all grow by, for example, 7 per cent a year, the ISA would grow by £1,690. However, buy them via the top discounter rebating both initial and annual commission, and you'd have total returns of £2,215 for the same thing. It's important to note that you may lose money investing in shares, but even if the markets drop you'll lose less buying via a discounter rather than direct, due to lower charges.

£7,000 invested in 4 identical funds (assumes 7% annual growth over 5 years)					
Discount broker	Ave. initial charge	Return	Annual rebate	Total return	Increase
Full commission	5.1%	£1,690	None	£1,690	–
Top discounter	0.6%	£2,110	£105	£2,215	£525

SUGGESTED INGREDIENTS

www.wiseup.com, 0870 8708558; www.chartwell-investment.co.uk, 01225 446 556; www.hargreaveslansdown.co.uk, 0117 9009000; www.chelseafs.co.uk, 0800 071 3333; www.money world-ifa.co.uk, 0808 118 1400; www.cavendishonline.co.uk, 08456 442544.

ADDED SPICE

Buy a unit trust inside a tax-free ISA wrapper and there's another advantage to using a discounter. Most operate fund supermarkets, which bypass the ISA rules dictating only one provider's funds are allowed in any ISA, as the fund super-market itself counts as the provider, allowing investors to pick 'n' mix fund managers. (See page 230 for ISA rules.)

SHARES

NUTRITIONAL INFORMATION
Typical Gain: £130.
Time Taken: 30 minutes.
Difficulty: Easy/Mid.

THE MENU

Instant-access execution-only stockbrokers don't give you advice but simply process your requested transactions. This reduction in admin charges translates into much cheaper dealing.

Most are 'nominee' brokers, where the shares are held electronically. Technically this means the broker owns the shares, but you have 'beneficial rights', meaning all the gains and losses are yours.

This isn't an issue, except they don't automatically confer qualification for shareholder perks (discounts the company gives its shareholders) or voting rights in company shareholder meetings, though some will if asked.

■ *What are the charges?* There are two main types of fee.
1. Commission. Simply a fee for buying or selling shares. The traditional method was to charge a fixed percentage of the transaction amount. However, there is a growing number of 'flat fee' brokers who charge a set amount regardless of deal size, a huge bonus for those dealing in larger values of shares.
2. Subscription/annual fee. Here you pay the company for holding the shares for you. Not every company charges this. With those that do, check out whether it's a fee per share or per account, incorporating all shares.

> **Money Diet Quick Fact Snack: What's the Difference between Stocks and Shares?**
>
> The easiest definition is using the sentence 'I own 1,000 shares of Glaxo Stock'. A share is an individual share in a company, indicating your ownership of that company; a stock is the collective name for all a company's shares.

CHOOSING YOUR DISH

Who is cheapest depends on whether you're a new buyer, or have existing paper or electronic shares.

- *New buyers.* The aim is to find the cheapest broker over the life of the transaction – the total transaction cost for buying, holding and selling your shares. Switching brokers is expensive, so often there's little alternative but to plan to stick with one for the long term. For most people this means going for the lowest flat-fee dealing broker, which should be less than £10 per trade.

  It's important to note that just because these are electronic brokers it doesn't mean you must do it via the internet. Some also allow 'electronic dealing' via the phone.

- *For those with paper shares.* While you may like the idea of pieces of paper for your portfolio, when it comes to selling them, the prices hurt. Paper shares trading usually costs around £25 per deal.

  Transferring them to an electronic account will save you cash. Luckily with paper shares almost all electronic brokers let you transfer them in for free.

  Therefore, it's actually again a question of who's cheapest to hold and sell the shares, so a cheap flat-fee electronic broker will win.

- *For those already with electronic shares.* It's likely your existing broker will charge you to transfer the shares to a new broker, usually more than wiping out the gain from moving. So here you need to find a new broker who will offer to compensate you for the cost of moving.

This isn't unheard of – quite a few brokers offer 'intro packages' aimed at shifting customers over to them. It's worth looking at, though the ultra-cheapest brokers tend not to do this.

CALORIE COUNT

The scale of savings can make a real difference to your returns from share dealing. For someone trading infrequently – just one buy and sell every few months – the annual dealing cost with the cheapest broker will be around £50 compared to £180 with some more mainstream providers.

SUGGESTED INGREDIENTS

www.hoodlessbrennan.com; www.comdirect.co.uk; www.halifax.co.uk/sharedealing/sharebuilder; www.share.com; www.jarvisim.co.uk, 01892 510 515.

CURRENT ACCOUNTS

NUTRITIONAL INFORMATION

Typical Gain: £175 per year.
Time Taken: 30 minutes.
Difficulty Level: Easy/Mid.
(See 'Healthy Eating', page 308, for more info on overdraft cost cutting.)

THE MENU

Current accounts are the standard day-to-day bank accounts we all use. Most people are still with the big four high-street banking mafia – Barclays, HSBC, Lloyds TSB and NatWest. These four tend to pay a pitiful 0.1 per cent standard interest in credit. Worse still, their overdrafts cost between 14 per cent and 18 per cent.

Admittedly, pay at least a £50 a year fee for a premier account, or bank on the internet with them internet only, and the big four may provide better rates, but usually better is available elsewhere for free.

Switching accounts is substantially easier than it used to be. New banks now automatically move standing orders and direct debits for you, but you must always notify your employer and others who regularly pay money in yourself. Plus, for safety, keep a sum of money in the old account until you're happy the transfer is completed.

CHOOSING YOUR DISH

Look at your account first, and determine whether you are usually in credit or overdrawn. Depending on the result focus either on the highest interest in credit (usually 2 per cent to 5 per cent), or the lowest cost overdraft (usually 7 per cent to 10 per cent). There are other things to watch for, though.

■ *Minimum monthly funding.* Most banks require you to pay in a set amount each month. In practice it's a way of setting a minimum salary requirement to qualify for better accounts. For example, the requirement to deposit £1,000 a month is the same as saying someone who earns £15,000 a year (roughly £1,000 a month after tax) must pay their salary in. This doesn't mean you can't spend the money or be overdrawn, just that a regular payment must be deposited each month.

- ***Introductory overdraft offers.*** A new trend is for 0 per cent overdrafts when you switch accounts. These are especially useful if, as some promise, they'll match your existing overdraft. If you're regularly overdrawn, forget in-credit interest rates and look at overdraft rates.

- ***Overdraft charges.*** Never go beyond your overdraft limit. Do this and fines, charges and increased interest cost a fortune. Always call the lender and try and arrange a temporary extension first.

- ***Branch, phone or internet.*** Branch banking is expensive to provide, which is why phone and especially internet-only accounts usually have more competitive rates. To bank online, it's very important that you can access the internet whenever you want, though most 'internet-only' bank accounts also offer a phone service once the account is set up; a useful backup. If internet banking does tempt you, it's actually often easier and more convenient than going to a branch: you manage your balance on-screen and move money electronically. To pay cash and cheques in, simply post it, or do it at a post office for added security using a specially receipted envelope; and to withdraw money, just do it via any bank's cash machine.

- ***Fees are evil, ditch them immediately.*** There's a persuasive piece of profiteering that depresses me. Banks call up and say 'Want better terms? For a small monthly fee you can have better interest and a cheaper overdraft.' This is a nightmare. If you've signed up, watch out, and ditch.

   The fee is usually £5–10 a month, £60–120 a year, yet simply by switching to another bank you can usually get better terms fee-free.

- ***Bribes and bonuses:*** The latest ruse is sign-up bribes – open an account and some'll give you £25–50 to start you off. This needs factoring in. Even high-interest payers only tend to pay on a limited amount of cash, e.g. 5 per cent on up to £2,500. So a big bribe is often worth more than the interest, although both is better.

Other products such as free annual travel insurance are also often included. These can be worthwhile but always check what you're actually being offered. For example, is the travel insurance European only or worldwide? Does it cover just you or your family? And don't believe their valuations. They often claim these things are worth hundreds yet compare it to best deals available elsewhere.

CALORIE COUNT

Switching pays. Someone with a £25,000 salary starting in credit could earn just £8 over three years with a Big Four bank account, but up to £310 with the best payer. For someone starting £2,000 overdrawn it'd cost £780 with the Big Four, but just £170 moving to the cheapest overdraft.

Banking interest and costs for someone on £25,000 salary over 3 years						
	In Credit			Authorised Overdraft		
	Rate	Interest after tax [1]	Extra interest	Rate	Interest cost [2]	Saving
Standard Big Four bank	0.1%	£8	–	17.8%	£780	–
Best Overdraft bank [2]	2.1%	£210	£202	0%/ 6.9%	£170	£610
Best In-Credit [1]	3.15%	£310	£302	7%	£280	£500
(1) & (2) salary paid in monthly after tax, but spent in full over the month, no interest spent or repaid (1) initial £2,500 credit (2) initial authorised overdraft £2,000						

SUGGESTED INGREDIENTS

www.cahoot.com; Abbey, www.abbey.co.uk, 0800 587 2758; Alliance & Leicester, www.alliance-leicester.co.uk, 0500 959595; www.smile.co.uk, 0870 843 2265; Intelligent Finance, www.if.com, 0845 605 8585; Halifax, www.halifax.co.uk, 08457 203040; Bank of Scotland, www.bankofscotland.co.uk, 08457 213141; Lloyds TSB (for internet-using higher earners only) www.lloydstsb.co.uk

Updated info: www.moneysavingexpert.com/currentaccounts

STUDENT BANK ACCOUNTS

NUTRITIONAL INFORMATION

Typical Gain: £150 over the course.
Time Taken: 20 minutes.
Difficulty Level: Easy.

THE MENU

Students get the best bank accounts in the business, though each bank's definition of 'student' varies. Even so, whether you're on a BTEC, three-year degree or post-grad, you should be able to find one.

CHOOSING YOUR DISH

All banks' customers have access to all other banks' cash machines to withdraw money, so differences of proximity and service aren't too relevant. Students are offered freebies to open accounts, but the big gift is the interest-free overdraft. This is the decision-making bedrock: quite simply pick the bank offering the biggest 0 per cent borrowing.

Interest-free debt is crucial as most students graduate over

£13,500 in the red. Those in credit should also opt for the biggest 0 per cent debt, and use a budgeting trick I call 'deficit banking'. To do this keep as big a negative balance as possible, but always stay within your interest-free overdraft limit. Put most of the money in an easy-access high-interest savings account (which for most students should be tax-free) – and gradually move it back into the bank account as it's needed. This means you earn interest on the money the bank is lending for free. And, remember, if you are currently a student there's nothing stopping you switching from your existing student account to a new one.

To compare interest-free overdrafts, factor in the limits for each year, not just the first year. An easy way to do this is simply to add up the limits over the course length and compare – the bigger the better. For example, on a three-year course, £1,000 year one, £1,200 year two, £1,400 year three is a £3,600 total.

CALORIE COUNT

Student accounts massively outrank even the best normal accounts. However, even within the 'student account world' there's a big variance: choosing the right one could easily save a student more than £160 over the course length.

Student bank account: Cost of an approved overdraft[1]								
Bank	Year 1 debt is £1,400 (2)		Year 2 debt is £1,600 (2)		Year 3 debt is £1,800 (2)		Total cost	Saving
	Rate	Cost	Rate	Cost	Rate	Cost		
Top normal account	6.7%	£95	6.7%	£105	6.7%	£120	£320	–
Poor student account	0% to £1k, 14.6% above £1k	£60	0% to £1,250, 14.6% above	£50	0% to £1,500, 14.6% above	£45	£155	£165
Top student account	All authorised debt interest-free	£0	All authorised debt interest-free	£0	All authorised debt interest-free	£0	£0	£320
(1) All debt is assumed to be pre-approved and therefore at the authorised overdraft rate. (2) Debt is assumed to be fixed at this level. For ease of illustration, the interest isn't compounded.								

SUGGESTED INGREDIENTS

NatWest, www.natwest.co.uk; Co-Op, www.cooperativebank.
co.uk; HSBC, www.hsbc.co.uk; RBS www.rbs.co.uk; Halifax,
www.halifax.co.uk; Lloyds, www.lloydstsb.co.uk; Barclays,
www.barclays.co.uk

Bizarrely, for once the big banks are the top players. The
reason? As an old statistic quotes, 'You're more likely to get
divorced than change your bank account.' Students are young,
potential high earners, so the banks should get many years'
custom if they can attract you early. The Money Diet counter-
move is to grab the best benefits you can as a student and
graduate, but as soon as you're switched to its standard
account then shift. (See page 238 for current accounts.)

Updated info: www.moneysavingexpert.com/studentaccounts

GRADUATE BANK ACCOUNTS

NUTRITIONAL INFORMATION

Typical Gain: £200 over a three-year account.
Time Taken: 20 minutes.
Difficulty Level: Easy.

THE MENU

There's a special prize awaiting every recent graduate, yet
many don't take it – but anyone who's left university in the last
three years can still benefit by getting the top graduate
account.

CHOOSING YOUR DISH

Most students simply allow their banks to shift them out of a
student account when they leave university. This can be a big

mistake for graduates using one of the banks that doesn't offer special terms, as it means missing out on the free money available.

Even a year or more after graduation you can move to another bank to get its graduate account. Only those who didn't complete or pass their course shouldn't switch, as banks automatically transfer students to graduate accounts on the expected date of course completion, whereas a new bank will check if you have graduated.

For the rest of 'choosing your dish', and 'suggested ingredients', follow the logic of 'Student Bank Accounts' on page 242.

HEALTHCARE CASHBACK PLANS

NUTRITIONAL INFORMATION
Typical Gain: £350 per year.
Time Taken: 30 minutes.
Difficulty Level: Mid.

THE MENU
These clever little policies can pay back over six times their cost, tax-free, every year, and cover a family's NHS and private medical bills. They're very different to and much cheaper than private medical insurance. The best-known example is HSA, though smaller providers normally offer much better returns.

Each month you pay a fixed amount, from £3 to £150. Cashback plans don't provide treatment; instead when you go to the dentists, opticians, have a specialist consultation or the like (either NHS or privately), simply submit the receipt to claim the cash back. Most plans repay only a proportion of the costs and the maximum amounts differ with each treatment, e.g. 75 per cent of optical bills up to £100. The higher your monthly contribution, the higher the maximum cashback limit.

Commonly covered treatments:
- Dental treatments and check ups
- Optical treatments and check ups
- Complementary health – osteopathy, chiropractic, acupuncture, etc.
- NHS prescriptions
- Maternity payments
- Chiropody
- Physiotherapy
- Hospital in-patient cash payment
- Special consultation fee

CHOOSING YOUR DISH

Plans are available for individuals or couples; and children are often covered for free. As well as the payout level, look for:
- ***The percentage return.*** The percentage payback is often more important than the maximum cashback. For example, 100 per cent of costs up to £90 makes it easier to get your money back than 50 per cent of costs up to £100.
- ***Guaranteed costs.*** If you always go to the dentist twice a year, and wear glasses or contact lenses, then these are guaranteed costs. Look at how much each plan pays for these specific treatments. This provides the security of knowing how much you can claim back before other treatments.
- ***Likely treatments.*** If you think you're likely to use the osteopath a lot, focus on plans with the highest limit for that.
- ***Pre-existing conditions.*** Most plans don't require a medical, but may exclude claims on pre-existing conditions for the first year or so.

- **_Immediate claims._** No plans allow immediate claims. There's always a delay of a few months to stop people signing up to claim for a current problem. And you must be a member for over nine months for maternity benefits. (I'll let you work out why yourself ...)

- **_Age, gender._** One big benefit is that age and gender are usually irrelevant to the cost of plans. This is a big bonus for those over 50 compared to private medical insurance. Some plans do have maximum age limits for new members (usually 65). However, if you're an existing member you should be allowed to continue beyond that age.

As payouts here can be huge, the obvious question is how can they afford it? The answer is simple. Just because people can claim doesn't mean they do. Many people forget to send in claim forms after the first year, yet the direct debits still drip from their bank accounts. To test yourself, sign up at a low level to start with, to see if it suits. If you're not claiming, cancel; though better still, remember and be quids in.

CALORIE COUNT

Using cash-back plans can make you money. Just look at the table below. If you had a wide range of treatments, the 'Return' indicates how many times you get your money back – the best is seven times what you pay in. Most people won't be claiming this much, but anyone with dental or optical costs should get back at least what they paid in and have the security of knowing that if anything goes wrong there's help available.

Healthcare Cashback Returns (for a Heavy Range of Treatments) (A)						
	Single Adult			Family		
	Cost/ month	Payout/ year	Return (B)	Cost/ month	Payout	Return
Worst Choice	£15.50	£325	1.8	£27	£850	2.7
Best Choice	£9	£500	4.6	£17.50	£600	5.8

(A) Each adult's bills are £120 dental, £120 optical, £150 consultation with a specialist, £350 osteopathy and 1 night in hospital for a year; each child is 1 night in hospital and £150 consultation. (B) The annual payout divided by the annual cost (the number of times you get your money back).

SUGGESTED INGREDIENTS

Over the past few years, the most consistent top payers have been Foresters and Westfield, though others are listed as they can win in certain situations.

Foresters, www.foresters.co.uk, 08457 990099; Westfield Health, www.westfield-health.org.uk, 0845 602 1629; Health-shield, www.healthshieldmembership.co.uk, 01270 588 555; Bolton & District, www.hospital-saturday.org.uk, 01204 522775; Saga, www.saga.co.uk/finance/healthcashplan, 0800 096 4085; Pinnacle, www.pinnacle.co.uk, 020 8207 9000.

Updated info: www.moneysavingexpert.com/healthcare cashplans

CONTACT LENSES

NUTRITIONAL INFORMATION

Typical Gain: £100 per year.
Time Taken: 30 minutes.
Difficulty Level: Easy.

THE MENU

Now here's a sight for sore eyes. There is a range of specialist phone and internet contact lens delivery firms. You send them the prescription and they provide the lenses the optician has recommended. The cheapness isn't due to the fact the lenses are substandard – it's because these companies bulk-buy direct from the manufacturers, sell from warehouses, not retail premises, and have limited staff. They're purely fulfilment operations – so they're not paying expensive opticians.

CHOOSING YOUR DISH

In truth, there are only a few lens manufacturers. Opticians' 'own brand' lenses are usually identical to the big name lenses but with different packaging. The discounters will tell you who makes which brand. As the lenses are identical, it's simply a case of the cheaper, the better.

Money Diet Quick Fact Snack: Are Daily Lenses Secretly the Same as Monthly?

Some moot that daily lenses are simply monthly lenses in disguise, so to save money you can use them like this for a month. To get a definitive answer, I asked the College of Optometrists.

'They're not the same design of lenses, even if in one or two rare cases they are the same material. Daily disposables tend to be thinner as if they break on removal it is not a problem and thinner is better in terms of the physiological impact on the eye.

'To rewear contacts, it's essential to clean and disinfect them, and daily lenses are not designed to be handled, cleaned or disinfected. Some may disintegrate or tear very easily and may not then disinfect efficiently, leading to possibly serious eye infections and even blindness. If someone did attempt to wear them longer than a day it'd be essential to clean them, so the patient would need to pay for solutions on top.'

In other words, play safe and don't try it!

For daily disposables, the bigger supply you buy, the cheaper they are. If you've got spare cash, it's worth shelling out for a year's lenses all in one go. With monthly disposables, factor in the cost of solutions. However, you can buy these cheaply with the lenses too.

It's easy to be sceptical – after all, it's your eyes we're talking about – but reputable discounters will supply lenses only if your optician's confirmed you've had an eye test and aftercare within the last year. And, by law, if you have already been fitted with contact lenses, the optician is obliged to issue you with your prescription and information without further charge. Of course it's still important to make sure you keep up the proper aftercare.

CALORIE COUNT

For daily disposables, you can save up to £125. It should be pointed out that this does not include an eye test and aftercare, but the cost of those is substantially less than the price difference.

Daily disposables 1 year	Lenses	Solutions	Total (inc. delivery)	Saving
High-street optician*	£30 x 12 months	N/A	£360	–
Cheapest discounter	£235	N/A	£235	£125
Monthly disposables 1 year				
High-street optician*	£15 x 12 months	Included	£180	–
Cheapest discounter	£59	£55	£99 **	£80

*Includes eye test and aftercare

**Includes £15 discount for buying solution and lenses together

SUGGESTED INGREDIENTS

www.getlenses.com, 0800 652 55 69; www.postoptics.co.uk, 0800 038 3333; www.simplylenses.com, 0870 900 1001; www.contactsuniverse.co.uk; www.bargainoptics.co.uk, 0870 1999 666; www.contactforlenses.com; www.tescoopticians.com, 0845 601 3479; www.visiondirect.co.uk, 0870 125 6240.
Updated info: www.moneysavingexpert.com/lenses

ADDED SPICE

Reclaim the cost of lenses – healthcare cash plans allow you to reclaim the cost of dental, optical and other forms of healthcare, whether it's via the NHS or not (see page 245).

CHEAPER PRESCRIPTIONS

NUTRITIONAL INFORMATION

Typical Gain: £100 for those getting regular prescriptions.
Time Taken: 10 minutes.
Difficulty Level: Easy.

THE MENU

The prescription system has a simple aim in a worthy cause. Its flat fee means people can afford any medicine regardless of its real cost, although at around £6.50 a time, the cost can soon add up.

The first thing to say is many people are exempt from charges. Those who needn't pay include children, pregnant women, the over 60s, students in full-time education aged under 19 and people on a range of benefits and tax credits – therefore always make sure you're only paying if it's necessary.

CHOOSING YOUR DISH

■ *Buy a season ticket.* Anyone who pays for regular prescriptions should consider buying a prescription prepayment certificate, which covers all your prescription fees for a set period. Though don't try and be dodgy – it may only be used for your *own* NHS prescriptions.

There are two certificates: a short one lasting four months for around £35 and a year-long certificate for under £100. The first is worthwhile if you use five or more prescriptions during the four months; the second if you use 14 or more in the year.

Therefore as a rough rule of thumb, pay for more than one prescription a month and certificates are good value; and if you have a long-term condition, the longer certificate is the better value of the two.

The easiest way to get a certificate is to call up and pay by debit or credit card, though forms are also available in main Post Offices, some pharmacies and can also be down-loaded from the internet.

■ *Prescription versus over the counter.* Many commonly prescribed medications, including painkillers, allergy tablets and dermatology creams, are also available over the counter without prescription. Often it's much cheaper just to buy them this way, rather than paying the £6.50-ish flat prescription charge. For example, a tube of hydrocortisone ointment, a common prescription, can usually be bought for under £3.

Some pharmacies, including all Boots stores, have policies to always tell you if you're better off doing it this way. However, if you're taking out a prescription for a regularly used medication, it's always worth asking.

The maths does change though if you're getting a multiple prescription from a doctor. For example, while a one-off prescription for non-drowsy allergy tablets will be cheaper direct from the pharmacist, a three-month prescription should easily work out cheapest.

CALORIE COUNTER

The possible savings from a prepayment certificate are substantial. Simply switching to a certificate could save over a hundred pounds.

Prescription Costs	Prepay Certificate	Without Prepay Certificate		
		1 prescription a month	2 prescriptions a month	3 prescriptions a month
4 months	£33	£26	£52	£78
12 months	£92	£78	£156	£234

SUGGESTED INGREDIENTS

Prescription prepayment certificate, 0845 8500038.

ADDED SPICE

It's worth noting that if you become eligible for free prescriptions after buying a certificate, you can reclaim the proportional cost of the certificate for that time.

Plus the certificate can be backdated for up to a month. Normally it starts on the day the application is received, but you can request that it counts as starting up to a month earlier. This is very useful if you've just laid out for a load of prescriptions as you can claim back the cost.

CHEAPER MEDICATIONS

NUTRITIONAL INFORMATION
Typical Gain: £75 a year.
Time Taken: 5 minutes.
Difficulty Level: Easy.

THE MENU

Brand-busting is a great favourite of mine, and there's no better place to do it than in the world of medication. What I'm about to say probably won't be huge news to most people, yet hopefully it'll push you out of your comfort zone. While intuitively most of us know 'all drugs are the same', we still buy brands due to misplaced feelings of security.

Drug companies spend millions promoting this comfort factor, the 'only use the name you know' message. This seems eminently sensible – after all, health isn't something we take short cuts with. Yet, quite simply, it's a load of marketing baloney.

When a company develops a drug it is given unique rights to sell it for a number of years. Once that ends, any company can make it, providing they meet the regulations. Therefore, most over-the-counter drugs have identical medical properties, regardless of brand, and avoiding big names means the cost is slashed.

CHOOSING YOUR DISH

The key is the 'active' ingredient – the stuff that actually does the business. And there are many generic products – unbranded or own brand – that have the same stuff but cost much less. Protections and quality control apply equally to all branded and generic products.

As a money not a medicine man, of course you may worry about taking my word on this, so I asked Dr Chris from ITV's *This Morning*: '*Look at the brand you know, note the active ingredient and then check it's the same one at the same dose as the generic brand. If you're not sure, the safest option is always to check with the pharmacist.*'

In other words, Nurofen's active ingredient is ibuprofen, so find an alternative ibuprofen with the same dose for less cost.

■ *The real difference.* It's not the medicine but the packaging and design that usually differs substantially. Branded drugs are often better packaged, with nicer-coloured tablets and better-tasting coating.

However, swallow a pill with orange juice and you shouldn't notice the difference (though medics do warn against grapefruit juice as that can counteract some medications).

If you have any allergies, always check the other non-active ingredients too. Don't automatically assume they're the same in a generic product as a branded one.

■ *Try generic products.* The biggest saving is in switching to generic from branded products, regardless of where you shop, though the big supermarkets are becoming especially competitive at this.

Also there's a chain of around 300 Savers shops, which tends to undercut even the supermarkets. It's worth checking out if there's one in your area.

Do remember, though, if the price difference isn't too great, buying generic at your local independent pharmacy may help it remain open in the face of stiff competition, something you'll value on an ill day when you don't want to travel far.

CALORIE COUNT

On the day I'm writing this, a pack of 12 Nurofen tablets costs around £1.39 in the shops, while a generic equivalent is available for a third of the cost. Even this difference is dwarfed in other product categories. For a selection of three pharmaceutical products, the total cost of the branded goods is £6.37, whereas the generic ones cost almost a fiver less at £1.48 – a saving of 77 per cent.

Branded Products				
	Active Ingredient(s)	Cheapest Branded	Cheapest Generic	Saving
Nurofen 12 tablets	Ibuprofen 200mg	£1.39	37p	£1.02
Panadol 16 tablets	Paracetamol 500mg	£1.49	16p	£1.33
Clarityn 7 tablets	Loratadine 10mg	£3.49	95p	£2.54
Total	–	£6.37	£1.48	£4.89

SUGGESTED INGREDIENTS
Tesco; Asda; Savers and your local pharmacy.

GETTING A PENSION

NUTRITIONAL INFORMATION
Typical Gain: £6,000 on pension fund.
Time Taken: 60 minutes.
Difficulty Level: Mid/Hard.

THE MENU

Stakeholder pensions are marketed as the low-charge pension solution. Even so, you can take a further slice off the charges, increasing the fund performance, just by buying it a different way.

A pension isn't an investment; it's just a tax-free wrapper where the cash is locked away until retirement. People often misunderstand this, but it's important, as its performance depends on what you choose to invest in (from shares for higher risk to cash funds for safety), not the pension itself.

The big advantage is all contributions go in before income tax is paid, meaning that for a basic-rate taxpayer to invest £100 it costs them only £78 off their take-home salary.

Stakeholder pension charges are capped, currently at 1.5 per cent of the fund each year. This includes the cost of paying commission to Independent Financial Advisers for their guidance. There's nothing wrong with this, as hopefully it pays for good advice. Ridiculously, however, buy direct from a pension provider, as many people do with stakeholders, and the charges are identical even though there's no IFA advice.

There is a way to beat the system. A limited number of specialist discounters sell pensions without advice, and rebate some of the commission earned back into your fund. While this is only fractions of a percentage point, with the effect of compounding over the years it can add up to thousands.

To go it alone with a stakeholder, it's necessary to choose your contribution level, provider and funds. As a rule of thumb, to retire on two-thirds of final salary, invest half your age as a percentage when starting a pension and continue this until the age of 65 (i.e. if you start at 30 you need to put in 15 per cent of your salary each year). This obviously means the earlier you start the better.

257

There aren't actually that many providers so the choice isn't too difficult – look at the range of funds offered and read the brochures. When it comes to choosing funds, a very general rule of thumb is the younger you are, the higher risk fund you should be in.

CHOOSING YOUR DISH

When choosing a discounter, simply ask for an illustration. The most important thing is how much commission it rebates. Some also charge fees and this needs keeping to a minimum too – however, the sheer scale of the savings over the long run means you should concentrate on the commission rebate first.

CALORIE COUNT

Using a discounter isn't for everyone; advice is sometimes crucial, especially with complicated affairs. However, buy without advice and discounters will increase the amount in your pension fund whether it grows or shrinks.

The table below shows the impact. Put £150 a month into a Norwich Union stakeholder pension (for example) over 30 years, and if there was growth of 5 per cent, it'd grow by £6,000 more if it were bought via a discounter.

Invest £150/month with *Norwich Union* for 30 years at 5% growth			
Bought via	Fee	Fund final value	Increase in fund
Direct	None	£105,000	–
Cheapest discounter	£25	£111,000	£6,000
Based on an illustration in summer 2005			

SUGGESTED INGREDIENTS

www.cavendishonline.co.uk, 0845 6442544; Torquil Clarke, www.tqonline.co.uk, 0800 0723186; www.bestinvest.co.uk, 020 7189 9988.

Updated info: www.moneysavingexpert.com/pensions

REPENSIONING: IMPROVING THE RETURNS ON STAKEHOLDER PENSIONS

NUTRITIONAL INFORMATION

Typical Gain: £4,500 on final fund.
Time Taken: 2 hours.
Difficulty Level: Hard/Very hard.

THE MENU

While remortgaging is common, repensioning doesn't exist – or didn't until the first edition of *The Money Diet*. It's my invention to increase the returns on existing personal or stakeholder pensions by over 4 per cent. This could mean an extra £4,700 on your fund over 25 years without changing plans.

It sounds impossible, but the concept behind it is quite simple. If you bought a pension via an Independent Financial Adviser, he or she reaps the commission over many years. Alternatively, buy direct and the pension company keeps this cash itself. There's nothing wrong with continually paying for advice, providing you continue to receive it – but otherwise you're doling out cash for nothing.

Unfortunately, tell the pension company 'Stop paying my former adviser commission' and it just keeps the money itself. Yet using a special discount broker who rebates some of their commission back into the plan (see 'Getting a Pension', page 256) can reduce the pension's annual charge to about 0.7 per cent from 1 per cent. Repensioning takes advantage of this – simply move your existing pension to a discounter.

The discounter should manage the process, but remember 'repensioning' isn't something advertised, it's my idea, so you may need to explain, check and monitor it. Also a few providers have started to get annoyed with it, and banned it happening, Standard Life being the main example.

■ *Stakeholder pensions.* As stakeholder pension providers aren't allowed to impose transfer penalties, just transfer your current plan to an absolutely identical one set up by the discounter, effectively keeping your existing plan but at a new lower charge.

■ *Personal pensions.* It's much trickier with personal pensions as there are transfer penalties, so it's only for those who understand their finances in detail. The gain is greatest if you are substantially increasing your pension payments, something especially common in the years leading up to retirement – for instance, you were paying £50 per month and now it's £100 per month.

This is because it's likely the existing advisor has already received commission for your planned contribution – so it's only the commission on the new amount that's up for grabs. The easiest method is to ask the discounter to become your 'adviser' so it 're-assigns' the plan and any commission to itself, rebating some to you. Still, be careful.

CHOOSING YOUR DISH

Follow 'Getting a Pension', page 256. (It's also worth comparing the discounter's illustration with an illustration based on staying with your existing set-up.)

CALORIE COUNT

Repensioning can improve your position, whether the market rises or falls, at little or no cost. The table below illustrates the gains for a 35-year-old who started a £100 per month stakeholder pension three years ago, and is increasing the contributions by 5 per cent annually until the age of 60. At 5 per cent annual growth, the fund would end up at £114,000 – repension, however, and it'd grow by a further £4,700, even though it's exactly the same pension as before.

Stakeholder fund size assuming 5% annual growth paying £100/month increased by 5% a year		
	Fund size	Extra growth
Full commission/Direct	£114,000	(–)
Repension after 3 years via top discounter	£118,700	£4,700
Investment starts age 32, continues to age 60, in managed fund		

SUGGESTED INGREDIENTS

www.cavendishonline.co.uk, 0845 6442544; Torquil Clarke, www.tqonline.co.uk, 0800 0723186.

PACKAGE HOLIDAYS

NUTRITIONAL INFORMATION

Typical Gain: £150 off bargain price, £600 off brochure price.
Time Taken: 2 hours.
Difficulty Level: Mid.

THE MENU

Travel agents make you think their prices are as fixed as their smiles, but this simply isn't true. I've a special technique to cut holiday costs.

To start, it's very important to understand the difference between travel agents and tour operators. Travel agents sell holidays and tour operators make them. This means one tour operator's holidays may be stocked by a range of travel agents, and this is crucial. It means you can find the identical holiday cheaper elsewhere.

Martin's Money Memories: Travel Agents are Revolting!

No I'm not being rude. I caused a near revolt amongst travel agents after presenting a *Tonight with Trevor McDonald* on this 'haggling for a holiday' technique.

The travel agents' trade magazine's letters page read like I had the horns of Beelzebub, accusing me of immoral information.

Yet perhaps this is the greatest testament to how powerful this technique is. My favourite tale was one outraged agent who said (I paraphrase) 'One man came in my shop, got a price from me, then called a discounter on his mobile in front of me to beat it!'

This technique works. The big chains' staff's ire is caused by the worry that the comfortable days of overinflated prices may be about to end.

---

the crash diet

CHOOSING YOUR DISH

When it comes to booking a package holiday, the later the cheaper. Yet if you need a specific destination or defined services, like children's facilities, then there's a risk that what you need mightn't be available. In that case forget late – early booking discounts aren't as big, but they're still a saving, so book at least nine months ahead and compare a number of travel agents' prices for the trip.

For those who can wait, the best bargains come from picking the right holiday and bartering for a better price.

■ *Picking the holiday.* Location and timing are crucial. Take a holiday when others can't, such as outside the school holidays in May and June, especially to family destinations like Florida, and you'll find prices are cheaper. Alternatively, venture to once in-vogue destinations, now off the boil, where there are lots of empty hotels and value's available.

■ *Martin's bartering technique.* Once you've a basic idea of what you want, immediately go to Teletext, simply because it has a big list of late-bargain travel agents in one place. If not Teletext, use the ads in the travel section of a Sunday newspaper.

1. Search. Scan the pages to find the destination, type and rough price of holiday you are looking for.

2. Choose. Pick an advertised holiday, call the travel agent and discuss what's available. If one suits, take down as many details as possible and find out the price and what's included. Often airport transfers, meals on the plane and credit card booking fees are separate, so ensure you find the total cost. (For example, £692 per person for a fortnight all-inclusive in the Dominican Republic.) (For the cheapest travel insurance, see page 266.)

263

3. Find competitor agents. Note the phone numbers of all the Teletext travel agents specialising in that destination. Pick one, call it and describe the holiday you've been quoted on – date of travel, airport and flight times. This way you're certain both of you are talking about exactly the same holiday.

4. Sneakily shave prices down. Take the quote you've got and – now for a bit of subterfuge – ask the agent to beat the price, but shave just a little bit off the quote you were given: it speeds the whole process up (for example, tell them £660 per person for this fortnight in the Dominican Republic). They should match it. Also try to ask the agent to write off the extras such as transfers and in-flight meals – this is worth a further £30 per person.

5. Start to play. Play companies off against each other by continuing the gradual bartering process to get the price down as low as possible (for example, £630 per person). You'll need to talk to a few agents to do this. Always talk per person price not 'total holiday' cost as it makes the amount it is discounting seem smaller.

6. Try price-beater agents. Once it looks like the price won't drop any more, go to the specialist agents on Teletext who offer to beat any price – they may be able to cut a last few pounds off (for example, final price down to £615 per person).

7. Book with the cheapest agent. Remember, it's exactly the same holiday you originally fancied, just at a reduced price.

CALORIE COUNT

The example prices above are real, done as part of my

appearance on ITV1's *Package Holiday Undercover*. The brochure start price was around £900 per person; the original Teletext discount price £692. It took an hour-and-a-half to get it to £615 per person. The holiday was for a couple, so the total saving from the already discounted price was £154.

SUGGESTED INGREDIENTS
Teletext travel agents.

ADDED SPICE
Flights only: use the web to grab the cheapest.
For booking scheduled or 'no frills' flights, the rule is simple: book as early as possible. There's more predictability in the scheduled flights market so bargain offers are better managed and quickly consumed. There are a number of very good websites for getting cheaper flights. (It's a very different business to package holidays.)

- *If you have a definite time frame.* If you know exactly when you want to go then a range of websites offer price comparisons of both flights and brokers (www.skyscanner.net, www.travelsupermarket.co.uk, www.traveljungle.co.uk).

- *To find the cheapest flights over a wide time frame.* It always seemed to me it'd be a good idea for those with flexibility to be able to say 'I can go anytime in April or May. When's it cheapest?' As this didn't exist I set up a non-commercial one at www.moneysavingexpert.com/flightchecker You can put in a date range and maximum price (for example, £5 plus taxes) and either a specific or broad destination and it'll find all the flights that fit.

- *Long haul.* If you want a long-distance flight, there are no comparison services. Thus the brokers – travelocity.co.uk, expedia.co.uk, lastminute.com and ebookers.co.uk – are the cheapest option, though never be afraid to take the price to other phone brokers and try and haggle it down.

TRAVEL INSURANCE

NUTRITIONAL INFORMATION

Typical Gain: £150 per year.
Time Taken: 30 minutes.
Difficulty Level: Easy.

THE MENU

The travel insurance Green Cross Code is 'stop after you book, don't listen!' Buy a holiday at a travel agent's and the insurance they then try to flog you can cost four times as much as is necessary.

There are two cost-cutting options:

- **Annual multi-trip.** This covers all travel during a year for a one-off fee. The number of days away is limited, usually to 30, 45 or 60. Travel is defined as the moment you leave home until you return, on any travel overseas, even a day trip, and possibly more than two consecutive nights away in the UK at prepaid accommodation. If you go away more than twice a year, it's worth considering.
- **Single trip.** This is what travel agents sell you: the cover is specific for the journey. Single-trip cover is fine if you're only going away once a year – just usually not through travel agents, as it's often available for a fraction of the cost elsewhere.

■CHOOSING YOUR DISH

While many supermarkets now sell 'off the peg' travel insurance for substantially less than most travel agents, going through specialist cheap travel insurers is even cheaper.

- ■ *Check what's covered.* The big areas are usually standard. Medical expenses are the most important and should be at least £2 million. Also ensure policies include personal liability and cancellation and curtailment insurance. Plus, if you will do winter or dangerous sports, check that such activities are included.

- ■ *Don't over-cover.* Getting £25 million rather than £5 million medical cover is pointless as the number of claims over that amount are negligible. One insurer with half a million policies once told me it hadn't received a claim over £200,000 in the last two years, yet insurers aren't shy about pushing expensive 'gold cover' with soothing but completely irrelevant maximums.

- ■ *Where possible use a couple or family policy.* These are cheaper as providers assume you're usually travelling together. Some risks depend on the trip not the people, so increasing the size of the party doesn't increase all risks. However, if you travel independently, check the cover still applies.

- ■ *Excesses.* Most policies require you to pay an excess of, for example, £35 on each claim. If you are willing to pay a higher amount you should be able to cut the costs.

- ■ *Baggage, personal possessions.* This insurance is often optional, and if you're not taking much of value with you, exclude it.

- ■ *Check credit card and bank account cover.* Some of these may offer free travel insurance with card protection, but remember it usually only applies if you buy the holiday on the card. Plus the actual cover tends to be limited, so check what's on offer before assuming you're covered.

■ *Stick with Europe-only cover.* When you buy an annual policy, you can choose between European and worldwide cover. Unless you know you're going outside Europe during the year, stick with European cover as it's much cheaper. If necessary, you can upgrade the policy or get a stand-alone policy for a specific trip.

CALORIE COUNT

Buying the right travel insurance will save you serious cash. For a family of four taking a fortnight in the USA and a week in Europe using a tour operator's single-trip insurance the total would be around £200, yet the cheapest annual family policy would be just £55. A saving of £145 – maybe enough for a quick break in Paris, which of course would be covered too.

Travel insurance for a family of four				
	Fortnight USA	Week Europe	Annual total	Annual saving
Bought with holiday*	£120	£80	£200	–
Cheapest annual policy	–	–	£55	£145
*Typical cost from high-street travel agent				

SUGGESTED INGREDIENTS

www.direct-travel.co.uk, 01903 812345; www.insureandgo.co.uk, 0870 901 3674; Travel Plan Direct, 0800 018 8737; www.atlas direct.net, 0870 811 1700; www.cheapannualpolicy.com, 0870 7700 943; www.simpletravelinsurance.co.uk, 0870 444 3778; www.travel-insurance-web.com

Updated info: www.moneysavingexpert.com/travelinsurance

■ADDED SPICE

Most policies start increasing premiums for the over-65s (sometimes even younger), but at the time of writing, travel insurer Netcoverdirect's and Rapid Insure set the age limit for their normal policies at 70.

The following suggested ingredients are for annual travel insurance for the over-70s: www.allianzdirect.co.uk; www.simpletravelinsurance.co.uk, 0870 444 3778; www.cis. co.uk, 08457 464646; www.rac.co.uk; www.helptheaged. co.uk; www.atlasdirect.net, 0870 811 1700; www.james hampden.com, 020 7398 8080; www.saga.co.uk, 0800 056 5464; www.ageconcern.co.uk

GET MORTGAGE ADVICE FOR FREE

■NUTRITIONAL INFORMATION

Typical Gain: £750.
Time Taken: 20 minutes.
Difficulty Level: Easy.
(Read the 'Healthy Eating' guide to remortgages/mortgages, (page 322) first.)

■THE MENU

When it comes to mortgages, the right brokers can quickly source a top product, offer an extra layer of protection if things go wrong and carry more clout with lenders, easing the acceptance on otherwise unobtainable mortgages. However, they can cost a fortune, but here's a sneaky way you can cut that cost.

■ *First check how much they'll charge you.* Brokers have two sources of income:

1. Commission. Lenders pay brokers a 'procuration fee', a whopping 0.3 per cent to 0.5 per cent of the mortgage's value, rising to 1 per cent for mortgages for those with poor credit. On a £150,000 mortgage, that's £375 to £1,500.

2. Fees. Most brokers also charge a fee directly, but it is possible to find those who don't charge at all and who just earn commission. No reputable broker will charge more than 1.25 per cent, even for poor credit scorers – never use anyone charging more. Fees can legally be charged upfront, but if that's the case, again run away. Most decent brokers will only charge when you complete, which is much better for you – no mortgage, no payment.

■ *Then check whose mortgages they advise on.* The main criterion you need to check in a broker is that it is 'whole of market' (this is a regulated term so it must answer the question). This means it will look at all the available UK lenders to source you a mortgage. If it isn't whole of market and just operates on a 'panel of lenders', ditch it – you'll be missing out on many of the best deals.

Actually, if I wanted to be really, really finicky, I would say the following (and obviously, as I'm going to say it, that means I do want to be really, really finicky). Even 'whole of market' isn't perfect, as they only have to look at the lenders who sell through brokers, which admittedly is more than 90 per cent of them – but there are a few such as (at the time of writing) HSBC and Egg who don't. So perfect practice is to go to a broker, then check these lenders yourself on top.

■ *Two golden rules for choosing a broker.* To summarise you want your broker to be
1. Whole of market
2. Fee-free
That way you get a wide-ranging choice and don't pay for it.

CHOOSING YOUR DISH

Smaller brokers, chosen carefully, will often provide an excellent service and have the advantage of being local, while big brokers can have more influence, research resources and market power.

Obviously it's impossible for me to review every one of the thousands of smaller brokers, so I concentrate on the four predominant UK-wide mortgage brokers: John Charcol, Savills, Chase de Vere Mortgages and London & Country. If you're choosing a local broker, just follow the two golden rules above.

All are completely 'whole of market' operators. The difference is in their charges. The first three primarily operate face-to-face and are 'independent' as they go via the fee/commission route. The fourth, London & Country, provides a telephone-only service, which is cheaper to operate, so it can afford not to charge a fee, just take the commission. This is much cheaper but sadly regulations mean it can't call itself independent (see 'Quick Fact Snack' below).

Here's the sneaky bit; best practice is to talk to a few brokers, to explore various options. This also allows a MoneySaving tactic. These large brokers only charge when you complete the mortgage. Therefore go to a few of them, but regardless of which advice you prefer, complete via London & Country for free. This way you get the best advice, and the protection of a broker.

Money Diet Quick Fact Snack: Grrrrr. 'Independent' isn't Always Good

Sometimes regulation is farcical. Recent Financial Services Authority (FSA) regulation of the mortgage market, while good news on the whole, produced a few ridiculous anomalies. The main one is about who can call themselves an Independent Mortgage Broker.

The rule's simple: they must include an option to allow someone to pay via fees only – with any commission earned rebated. Yet this is bunkum. For example, you may be given the option either to pay a typical 1 per cent fee in full and get the 0.35 per cent commission rebated or just pay a 0.65 per cent fee with the broker keeping the commission – in other words, no difference.

Worse still, it means a truly whole-of-market broker, taking only commission, can't call itself independent even though it's providing the same advice more cheaply. Bit of a farce really, hence choose a whole-of-market broker on the basis of what you'll pay.

Yet don't think this means London & Country itself isn't worth listening to; it's only that to fine-tune the very best deal you should try more than one broker. However, the quick and easy option is to go straight to L&C as you won't pay a fee and it's 'whole of market'.

■ *Exclusive Info.* All these four brokers (and others) sometimes offer exclusive deals with some of the bigger lenders, available neither direct nor via other brokers. These are often competitive and worth checking out and weighing up if it's worth paying the broker's fee to get the exclusive.

If it's John Charcol, which tends to have many exclusives, there's another trick. While it charges for face-to-face advice, it is free via its www.charcolonline.co.uk website (which unlike face-to-face is a panel of lenders – yet if it's an exclusive it's likely to be part of that panel). So you could speak to one of its advisers, and if there's a suitable exclusive, go to the website to get it and avoid the broker fee. You will have to pay around a fiver initially to access the site, but this will be refunded on completion.

■CALORIE COUNT

On a £100,000 mortgage with relatively straightforward issues, fee-based advice would cost you roughly £500. On a £200,000 complicated mortgage, it could be £2,000. Process via London & Country or Charcol Online and there's no charge.

■SUGGESTED INGREDIENTS

London & Country, www.lcplc.co.uk, 0800 953 0304; www.charcolonline.co.uk, 0800 358 5885; FPD Savills, 0870 9007762; Chase de Vere Mortgages, 0800 3585533.
Updated info: www.moneysavingexpert.com/mortgagebrokers

MORTGAGE PAYMENT PROTECTION INSURANCE

■NUTRITIONAL INFORMATION
Typical Gain: £240 per year.
Time Taken: 30 minutes.
Difficulty Level: Easy.

■THE MENU

Accident, sickness and unemployment can devastate your finances. State help is limited, especially for anyone who took out a mortgage after 1995 – it only kicks in after nine months and just pays the interest; and this only for those with limited savings and a partner who doesn't work full time.

Mortgage payment protection insurance (MPPI) ensures your mortgage repayments, and possibly other related expenditure (such as buildings insurance), will be met if any of these circumstances occur. Most MPPI policies are bought with mortgages, and though a few building societies offer low-price policies, lenders usually charge way over the odds.

Policies start to pay out 30 or 60 days after you become unable to work. They last for a limited term, usually 12 months, though after that state help should start. Those with savings that can cover this period probably don't need MPPI.

It is possible to opt out of the 'unemployment' element of MPPI cover – worthwhile if you're self-employed and the policy wouldn't pay out anyway.

CHOOSING YOUR DISH

Getting a policy from a specialist provider rather than the mortgage lender is normally much cheaper.

The price of MPPI surprisingly depends simply on the mortgage payment size rather than the usual risk factors like age, sex and health. There are a rare few age-related policies, and these are well worth having if you're under 35.

The only reason not to change is many policies operate initial exclusions so you can't claim within a set period – usually three to six months – after switching, and some policies don't pay out to anyone where there was foreseeability of unemployment or pre-existing medical conditions when the policy was taken out – so don't switch if you're likely to be in these categories.

CALORIE COUNT

To cover a £1,000 monthly mortgage repayment a standard mortgage lender's policy could cost £60 a month, £720 a year, but with a typical specialist provider it is £30, just £360 a year.

SUGGESTED INGREDIENTS

www.helpupay.co.uk, 08000 350292; www.paymentcare. co.uk, 0870 428 4088; www.moneysupermarket.co.uk; Paymentshield, 0870 7594010.
Updated info: www.moneysavingexpert.com/MPPI

LEVEL-TERM ASSURANCE: PROTECTING YOUR FAMILY IF THE WORST HAPPENS

NUTRITIONAL INFORMATION
Typical Gain: £240 per year.
Time Taken: 20 minutes.
Difficulty Level: Easy.

THE MENU

Roughly one in twenty adults dies whilst they have a dependent child. Potentially dire financial consequences can add to the devastation. Level-term life assurance is the one policy you hope is never used. It protects your family's income if the worst happens. Whether you're looking for a new policy or already have it, you can cut your costs by half.

It guarantees a fixed lump-sum payout upon death within a set time. Don't confuse it with either mortgage decreasing term-assurance (see page 279) or whole-of-life insurance – an investment-based policy used mainly for inheritance-tax planning.

> ## Money Diet Quick Fact Snack: Writing in Trust
>
> If you die, the life assurance forms part of your estate, and this could mean your family is hit with a huge whack of inheritance tax. In many cases you can avoid this by writing the policy in trust.
>
> Do that and it pays out directly to your dependents, so it never becomes part of your estate, avoiding inheritance tax. This is relatively easy to do. When you get most insurance policies they include the option (and papers) about writing in trust directly at no extra charge.

There's no investment element with level-term assurance because the payout is fixed and there's no argument over whether someone is dead, so providing the assurer is reputable it's simply a case of the cheaper the better. However, do ensure the premiums are fixed, meaning they never rise, rather than reviewable.

■ *How much cover?* The cost increases with the size of the lump-sum payout – you need enough to pay off outstanding debts and provide your family with a reasonable standard of living. Cover should also be taken out for a non-working spouse, especially when children are young, because if they die, the main earner may need to stop working. A rough rule of thumb for either parent is 10 times the highest earner's income. You can choose either to cover alone or to take out a joint policy with your partner that pays out on 'first death'. It's worth getting both separate and joint quotes.

The cost also increases with the likelihood of death within the term – age, health, being a smoker, having a risky occupation or undertaking dangerous sports can increase the price. So if you're an 88-year-old tobacco-chewing sword-swallower with a penchant for freefall aerobics, don't boast about it to the life-assurance company.

- **How long should the policy last?** If the cover is to protect children, it should last until they finish full-time education. If it's for a partner, cover until the earner reaches pensionable age. The shorter the term, the cheaper the policy. There's no need to stick to a round number of years – a 17-year term, for example, is fine.

- **Switching your existing policy.** If you already have level-term assurance, there's no problem changing. Just stop your existing policy and start a new one for the remaining time, though a quick check of the terms and conditions never goes amiss – and never cancel the old policy until you've started the new one. Existing policyholders who bought policies a long time ago or have experienced health problems mightn't find the cost decreases significantly – or perhaps no saving is possible at all, as these impact the risk pricing of a policy.

It is, however, always worth getting a quote as term assurance prices have dropped rapidly over the last few years. Anyone who's quit smoking should save a lot. (See the 'No-Butts Guide to Smoking', page 74.)

CHOOSING YOUR DISH

Life-assurance brokers trawl all the non-direct-sales insurance companies to find the cheapest policies. They will cut the cost, but don't think all brokers are equal. They make money by taking commission from policy providers. Most keep all this commission, and sell themselves as 'searching for the cheapest provider'. However, some brokers both shop around and rebate some or all of this commission to make your policy cheaper (those rebating all commission charge a fee). As the commission is massive, this cuts the cost hugely.

Yet, when getting assurance is complicated – if you've got health problems or inheritance-tax issues – then the very cheapest brokers won't help, but there are still some who provide advice and rebate commission.

CALORIE COUNT

The savings are huge. A 40-year-old male smoker getting a policy direct from a bank would pay £68 a month. Use a standard broker and this could be down to £48, but with the cheapest broker it drops to £32 a month. Over 25 years that's a saving on the policy of over £10,000.

£150,000 level-term policy over 25 years						
	Go to the bank direct		Full-commission broker		Cheapest broker		Saving
	Per month	25 years	Per month	25 years	Per month	25 years	25 years
M30 Non-smoker	£14	£4,200	£11	£3,300	£9	£2,700	£1,500
F30 Smoker	£18	£5,400	£15	£4,400	£11	£3,300	£2,100
M40 Smoker	£68	£20,400	£48	£14,400	£32	£9,600	£10,800
F40 Non-smoker	£22	£6,600	£19	£5,700	£13	£3,900	£2,700
Joint 40 Smoker	£110	£33,000	£82	£24,600	£54	£16,200	£16,800

SUGGESTED INGREDIENTS

www.cavendishonline.co.uk, 08456 4742544; www.money world-ifa.co.uk, 0808 118 1400; www.theidol.com, 01931 71 11 71; www.tqonline.co.uk, 0800 0723186 (advisory).

MORTGAGE LIFE ASSURANCE

NUTRITIONAL INFORMATION
Typical Gain: £200 per year.
Time Taken: 20 minutes.
Difficulty Level: Easy.

THE MENU

Mortgage decreasing term life assurance (MDLA), to give it its correct name, pays a lump sum to cover the mortgage debt if you die during the term. It's 'decreasing' because the mortgage debt, and therefore the potential payout, decreases over time. It ensures your dependants needn't worry about paying off the mortgage. Unfortunately, many people are automatically sold over-expensive policies when getting a mortgage, yet it's possible to cut these costs in half.

For the rest of the recipe and suggested ingredients simply follow 'Level-term Assurance' on page 275, as the rationale and providers are identical.

One final thought. If you're looking to cover your mortgage, check out using a level-term policy instead. If the cost isn't much more, it's worth plumping for as the payout is fixed rather than decreasing; if you increase your mortgage it may mean you've still got enough cover.

GIVING TO CHARITY

NUTRITIONAL INFORMATION
Typical Gain: £80 per year.
Time Taken: 15 minutes.
Difficulty Level: Easy.

THE MENU

The Money Diet isn't about being tight. Frankly, I'd love it if everyone gave a small slice of what it saves them to charity. Whenever you donate always max it out by doing it the right way. It's possible to give over 60 per cent more at no extra cost by forcing the tax system to help.

Any charity registered with the Charity Commission (it'll have 'registered charity' on its literature) can take advantage.

CHOOSING YOUR DISH

The simplest way to give is via 'gift aid'. This allows charities to claw back on both one-off and regular donations. There's no minimum contribution, so tax is reclaimable even on a pound. All the charity needs is your name and address and a declaration that you're a UK taxpayer: as this can be verbal, it can even be done over the phone.

Charities reclaim the tax you have paid at the basic 22 per cent rate, which actually means they get around 28 per cent more than you donate (because of mathematical reciprocals – if you don't understand don't worry, just think it gets more). People paying higher-rate tax are able to reclaim the extra 18 per cent tax they've paid for themselves. The tax self-assessment form includes a note of charity gifts so higher-rate taxpayers may choose to keep this extra tax money or automatically have it donated too.

CALORIE COUNT

Donate £20 a month to charity and it only costs you £15.60 if you're a basic-rate taxpayer or £12 if you're a higher-rate taxpayer. Over a year this means a higher-rate taxpayer would give £240, while it'd cost them only £144 – a massive difference.

Give more than you pay for: the cost of donating £20 a month to charity						
	Monthly			Annually		
	Basic-rate taxpayer pays	Higher-rate taxpayer pays	Government adds	Charity receives	Basic-rate taxpayer pays	Higher-rate taxpayer pays	Charity receives
Gift Aid	£15.60	£12	–	£20[1]	£187	£144	£240
(1) Assumes higher-rate taxpayer donates all tax gains to the charity						

ADDED SPICE

Easy giving. The Charities Aid Foundation (www.allabout giving.org, 0800 993311) runs a special Charity Account. Pay money in through either gift aid or payroll giving, and it automatically collects the tax and the state bonus and adds it to your account. After this, use its special card or chequebook to donate to a charity of your choice. The big advantage is you can donate tax efficiently on impulse, even putting the special cheques in collection tins so the charity gains the maximum amount.

The Hungersite. On the Hungersite's (www.hungersite.com) main page map, a different country flashes black every 3.6 seconds. The colour is symbolic. It signifies someone dying from hunger. Yet the website isn't just informative; every day it raises thousands, providing aid for over 23 countries. All you have to do is click on the site's emblazoned message 'give free food – click here' and a cup of staple foodstuff is then bought for someone somewhere who is hungry. The way it works is simple. The donations are sponsored by a variety of companies each day. The sponsor's names are prominently displayed after you've clicked the button. The more sponsors on any given day, the more is donated per click. It should be pointed out, though, that only one click per computer per day is counted. It's interesting to note that the organisation behind the site these days is not a charity; it's a profit-making company which makes its cash by selling merchandise on the back of the site itself. However, as clicking costs you nothing, and the charities themselves do confirm they get the cash and it helps the starving, it works. Try it.

LOAN INSURANCE

NUTRITIONAL INFORMATION

Typical Gain: £200 per year.
Time Taken: 30 minutes.
Difficulty Level: Mid.
(See 'Healthy Eating', page 398, for a full guide to personal loans.)

THE MENU

Whether it's a big dodgy bloke called Ron or a high-street bank, beware the 'protection business'. Financial services providers push customers borrowing money to get their (usually expensive) loan insurance. Yet it's possible to slash the cost, both for new and existing loans.

Payment protection insurance (PPI) is a welcome comfort for some people. It ensures your repayments are made, usually for a year, if you're unable to work due to accidents, involuntary unemployment or sickness; some also include full repayment if you die.

Lenders usually add PPI straight to a loan. However, it is possible to get a loan from one company and PPI from another.

These stand-alone PPI policies tend to be much cheaper than a lender's own policies.

CHOOSING YOUR DISH

First decide whether you actually need PPI. Those with small debts or anyone who could cover their repayments using savings, relatives' help or other financial protection policies may be better off without the huge expense of PPI. For the self-employed, the unemployment element is often useless, as most policies' self-employment benefits are poor.

While most policies are pretty similar, whether the PPI is with the loan or stand-alone it's always important to check policy terms for personal suitability as bizarre clauses are common. For example, some policies exclude motorbike riders or extreme sports enthusiasts from accident cover.

The only time it may be worth not using a stand-alone policy is with a flexible loan, as in this case the insurance cost is only for the outstanding amount of the loan. Stand-alone PPI policies don't have such flexibility.

■ *Switching PPI on existing loans.* Some, though not all, lenders will permit PPI cancellation while keeping the loan, though watch for redemption costs. If this is the case it's possible to switch PPI to a stand-alone provider without changing the loan. Lenders mightn't make it easy, though, and getting illustrations to see the benefits is never simple. Yet it is possible, and worth a go.

The only time not to try it is if your circumstances have changed – a 'foreseeability of redundancy' or 'pre-existing conditions' when you take a new policy out usually invalidate claiming. Switching if this applies to you could mean you lose cover.

CALORIE COUNT

For a £5,000 high-street loan, the insurance alone would add an extra £29 a month, so together with the interest, the total cost over five years is £3,800. Even with the cheapest insured loan on the market, the total cost would be just £1,700. Yet use the cheapest uninsured loan, coupled with a stand-alone PPI policy, and the cost is just £1,240, beating all else.

£5,000 loan over 5 years	Monthly loan cost	Insurance cost	Monthly total	Total 5-year interest & insurance cost	Saving
High-street loan	£119	£29	£148	£3,820	None
Cheapest loan with insurance	£102	£10	£112	£1,720	£2,100
Cheapest uninsured loan and stand-alone PPI	£98	£6	£104	£1,240	£2,580

SUGGESTED INGREDIENTS

www.goodinsurance.co.uk, 0870 2420015; www.payment care.co.uk, 0870 428 4088; www.payprotect.co.uk, 0845 061 8822; www.moneysuper market.co.uk; www.burgesses.co.uk, 0870 242 0015.

CAR INSURANCE

NUTRITIONAL INFORMATION

Typical Gain: £300 per year.
Time Taken: 1 hour.
Difficulty Level: Easy/Mid.

THE MENU

Car insurance is inescapable, compulsory and expensive, and

finding the cheapest can be hell. There is never simply one cheapest provider, as there are too many variables – location, driving history, who drives the car, whether it's used for commuting and, of course, its make and model. However, I've got a strategy ...

CHOOSING YOUR DISH

To find the cheapest insurer takes work. The only way to guarantee the cheapest is to get a quote from every one of the many hundreds of insurers and brokers. Yet my drop, shop, double and haggle system should cut both time and costs (and if you're reading at speed, the powerhouse in Step 2).

- **Step 1: Drop – *lower the price regardless of policy.*** Ensure you're the lowest risk possible. If you can, fit an alarm or an immobiliser; don't overestimate the annual mileage you tell them; keep your car off the street and in a drive, or better a garage overnight. Choose whether you really need to pay extra for a policy with a courtesy car. Decide how much you're willing to pay towards any claims – the higher this 'excess', the less you'll pay. The final choice is comprehensive or third-party insurance: here, weigh up the cost of repair versus the increased cost of comprehensive insurance; those driving old bangers are often best sticking to third party.

- **Step 2: Shop – *have your shopping around done automatically.*** The aim is to cover as many underwriters as possible. These are the companies who assess the risk of covering any individual, yet they all do it differently. These assessments are then supplied to the insurers themselves – yet even with providers using the same underwriter the price can differ due to how competitive they wish to be in various market sectors.

1. If you're on the internet. To do this quickly and easily involves using two internet sites. These aren't brokers – they work off a limited panel of insurers and have their own pricing and supply arrangements with insurers – they are effectively car insurance search engines. You fill in your details and they submit them to a large number of providers and brokers and feed you back the results. In return, they are given a small commission if you get a policy via their search.

Think of it like this. A broker is like a shop; let's say it sells 15 loaves of bread that it prices accordingly. Yet these two sites simply wander round checking the price of loaves in a range of shops, a much more efficient system. The two sites are www.confused.com, which provides a detailed and accurate search, and www.insuresupermarket.com, which provides a quicker search of more providers, but is less accurate, especially for drivers who've had an accident or motoring conviction in the last few years, in which case the quoted price can be way off.

2. If you're not on the internet. If you're not on the net, you are severely disadvantaged. The sheer speed and power of the internet means it is worth asking a friend who does have it to help, as once you've got the policy, you can simply operate it by phone. However, if that is not possible, the insurers I would suggest you get phone quotes from first are in 'Suggested ingredients' below.

■ *Step 3: Double – double-check and get the discounts.* Once you have the search results, note which providers come top of both. It's not just the prices that are important here; it's also the order, as that shows you their attitude to your risk. Pick the top three from each site and go separately to their websites. This way you may be eligible for further direct sales discounts on top of the quotes.

■ *Step 4: Haggle.* The car insurance market is very competitive and haggling is possible as companies aim to retain business. Once you've found the cheapest quote, take it to your existing insurer or a broker to see if they will beat it.

CALORIE COUNT

For a young couple, going direct to an insurer, the quote was £800. Using a broker the price quoted was £703. However, following Drop, Shop and Double, the best price found was £450 and that's before Haggle. Incidentally the highest quote found was £910.

SUGGESTED INGREDIENTS

Search sites: www.insuresupermarket.com; www.confused.com.
Insurers themselves: Direct Line, www.directline.co.uk, 0845 246 8701; Direct Choice, www.directchoice.co.uk, 08451 285 285; Esure, www.esure.co.uk, 0845 603 7874; Tesco, www.tescofinance.com, 0845 300 4400; Sainsbury, www.sainsburysbank.co.uk, 0845 608 6034; Budget, www.budgetinsurance.com, 0800 072 0644; Co-op Insurance, www.cis.co.uk, 08457 46 46 46; Diamond, www.diamond. co.uk, 0800 362436; Endsleigh, www.endsleigh.co.uk, 0800 028 3571; Elephant www.elephant.co.uk, 0870 013 1072.

ADDED SPICE

Further tricks and tactics include these:

- *New may be better than renewal.* Applying to your existing insurer as a new customer often produces a cheaper price than its renewal quote.

- *Add a second person.* Adding a second driver with a good record, even if they won't often use the car, will, surprisingly – sometimes, but not always – reduce the premium as it smooths out the average risk. It's worth a try.

- *Don't pay insurance interest.* Most policies allow you to pay either per month or per year. Pay by the month and they effectively loan you the lump sum, so you pay instalments with interest at up to 20 per cent on top. If you can, pay it as a lump sum. If not and there's cheaper borrowing available elsewhere – even a 0 per cent credit card – use that to pay the lump sum instead.

- *Younger drivers – check out free insurance with a new car.* Some cars include free insurance, worth only a few hundred a year to an experienced driver, but to a young car owner it could be worth thousands.

- *Gender specific isn't always best.* Don't fall for the 'we know women drivers are a lower risk, so we specialise in them' hype. Yes, women are a lower risk, so all insurers factor this in to their pricing structures. Gender-specific policies aren't automatically cheaper than unisex ones.

- *No-claims discounts don't necessarily reduce the premium.* For every year you don't claim you get a no-claim discount, which often makes a substantial difference to the overall cost. If you do claim, two years is usually taken off this discount; deliberately to discourage claims. It's also possible to get a 'protected no-claims discount', so that claims don't impact this discount. Remember, though, even if your discount is protected, the actual price of the policy may still rise if you have an accident as you will be assessed as being at higher risk of future claims.

CHEAPEST ROADSIDE RECOVERY

■ NUTRITIONAL INFORMATION

Typical Gain: £120.
Time Taken: 30 minutes.
Difficulty Level: Easy/Mid.

■ THE MENU

It may be *the fourth emergency service* (though don't tell the Coast Guard) staffed by *very, very nice men,* yet breakdown insurance is a commercial business like any other. Neither the AA nor the RAC are the mutual members organisations they once were, having between them changed hands many times between big corporations and venture capitalists.

Thus this is a pure, clinical decision about getting a decent service and peace of mind at a rock-bottom price.

■ CHOOSING YOUR DISH

■ *Don't fall for the traditional approach.* The two big beasts in the motor assistance world have, over the years, persuaded us there's only one way to operate. When you've a problem, call them, they send their patrols and sort it out. Yet these *'automatic service'* policies are just one option.

The alternative is 'pay and claim' policies. You call them when there's a problem and rather than sending their own patrols, they utilise a local recovery firm (either selected by you or allocated by them) to sort out the problem for you.

You have to pay for the repairs there and then, and afterwards send in receipts to claim the money back. However, this doesn't mean constantly carrying cash. If you're without notes, inform the insurer and they'll ensure the recovery firm offers credit or debit card payment service or can invoice later.

This may lack convenience, but the price is often a fraction of that of the big insurers and the call-out times are very similar. So if you don't break down you've a much cheaper policy, and if you do, the maximum hassle is putting a stamp on an envelope.

However, there's a warning: one of the reasons the cashback method is so cheap is that some people forget to claim, and this helps substantially offset the providers' costs. If that's likely to be you, forget it; stick to the autoservice type instead.

- **Do you need European cover?** If you know you're going to take your motor into Europe, then it's worth considering a special policy which includes that cover. However, if you're not sure, don't pay the extra; stick with a UK policy and then get a special extension (or even separate stand-alone cover) if you do travel.

- **Who or what are you covering?** There are some policies (often pay and claim) that cover the person rather than the car. This is especially advantageous for older cars as it means mileage and reliability are irrelevant.

CALORIE COUNT

The price differences are staggering. A couple wanting the full spiel – recovery and tow, relay cover and home-start from the AA or RAC – would pay around £150. Yet the same cover is available from pay-and-claim companies for around £30 a year.

Annual Breakdown Recovery Policy Cost for a Couple					
System	Recovery & Tow	Relay Cover	Home Start	Cost	Saving
Standard Policy	YES	YES	YES	£150	–
Cheapest pay & claim	YES	YES	YES	£30	£120

SUGGESTED INGREDIENTS

Pay and claim: AutoAid, 01277 235500 (no website, a small subsidiary of a large insurer); GEM Insurance, www.motoringassist.com, 01342 825 676.

Cheaper autoservice: www.quotelinedirect.co.uk, 0870 444 0870; www.autonational.co.uk, 0845 9100 345.

Breakdown recovery comparison site: www.insuresupermarket.com (only offers a limited selection and misses some of the best deals, but if you're looking for a quick one-off travel policy, it's very useful).

Updated info: www.moneysavingexpert.com/breakdown

HOME INSURANCE

NUTRITIONAL INFORMATION

Typical Gain: £250–350.
Time Taken: 1 hour.
Difficulty Level: Easy.

THE MENU

Buildings and contents insurance quotes involve enough variables to shave a slide rule's edges off. Much like with car
insurance (see page 284) I've a four-step plan to quickly find
the cheapest policy, possibly halving your costs.

Start by deciding whether it's buildings, contents or
combined insurance you need. The difference? If you turned
your house upside down, everything that falls out is covered
by contents, whatever stays firm by buildings.

Logic suggests combining building and contents will make
it cheaper. While this assumption's often correct, it's not guaranteed. If you've time, get quotes for stand-alone policies as
well. It's especially important when you're in a high-risk category for one type of cover, such as burglary for contents or
flooding for buildings. However, those living in rented or lease-
hold accommodation should find the landlord/freeholder is
responsible for buildings insurance.

If the price variance isn't great, combined policies have the
advantage that if a claim falls between the two stools, there's
no 'jurisdiction' argument and less admin.

CHOOSING YOUR DISH

This is all about Drop, Shop, Double and Haggle.

■ *Step 1: Drop – lower the price regardless of policy.* All
insurance policy prices are based on risk assessments, so to
cut the cost, cut the risk. It's especially important for
contents insurance – fitting approved locks, neighbourhood
watch, fitting alarms and getting a dog all make policies
cheaper, although the cost of increased security can
outweigh the reduction in insurance cost (see 'Added
Spice' for more details). Increasing the policy 'excess', the

Money Diet Quick Fact Snack: How Do I Value My Things?

You normally define a specific 'sum insured' – the maximum the insurer will pay out. If this is too little the full claim mightn't be met; too much and it's overly expensive. Under-insuring can be devastating. For example, insure contents worth £15,000 for only £10,000 and, even for claims on one individual item, they may pay out only a proportional amount.

Contents insurance: To work out the correct amount to insure, walk from room to room, not forgetting lofts and garages, noting down what everything would cost on a new-for-old basis, including fittings. It soon adds up. For those on the internet, the trade body, the Association of British Insurers (ABI), has a useful spreadsheet on its website www.abi.org.uk and broker Hiscox has a calculator, www.hiscox.com/calculator, though it tends to overestimate.

There are a few alternative options.

■ *Bedroom rated* – here the 'sum insured' is automatically defined depending on your location and the number of bedrooms. It's convenient, but those with valuable contents may be under-insured.

■ *Unlimited sum* – more rare, these cover all possessions regardless of value (though ultra-high value contents homes are often refused cover). For those with higher than average value contents, worth around £50,000, these can be great value as their price is based roughly on the average £35,000 sum insured contents value, so you are subsidised by those with lower value contents.

Finally, very expensive individual goods like antiques and paintings should be professionally valued and listed separately. As their value increases over time, either reassess or get a policy where the 'sum insured' rises annually.

Buildings insurance: It's important to remember you are insuring the house's 'rebuild value', not the price you bought it or could sell it for. This amount is usually lower, and detailed in any survey of the property. Alternatively the ABI has a calculator at http://abi.bcis.co.uk.

amount you must pay towards any claim, also cuts the cost: £50 to £100 is usual.

■ *Step 2: Shop – get the shopping around done automatically.* Shopping around as many providers as possible is the only real way to find the best price, as there are too many variables to make 'best buy' tables relevant. Many people use brokers, yet these usually work off a limited panel of insurers and add their own fees, hence different brokers quote different prices for the same insurer. More importantly, many competitive companies only sell direct to consumers and thus aren't covered by brokers.

The internet solution. Web users have an easy solution using two special 'screen scraping' websites. Screen scrapers mean you put your details in, and then it zips to a larger number of insurers and brokers and automatically fills in their forms for you, and 'scrapes' the details back to you – effectively allowing you to get quotes from most of the market in minutes.

Quick and wide-ranging: Insure Supermarket scrapes a large number of sites, and the whole process takes just a few minutes. This is because it makes some basic assumptions, so for people outside the normal range of answers it can be less accurate.

Detailed and thorough: confused.com is a newer scraper and searches less providers. Yet it is more thorough (and takes longer) so the answers are more accurate.

Both screen scrapers make their money if you get a policy: providers pay them a small 'lead fee'.

If you're not on the net. The sheer power and speed of this process means you should ask a friend who is online to help. Then once you have a policy it can be phone operated. However, if that's not possible, then simply call at least five providers (good ones include Tesco, Direct Line, Elephant, the AA and Co-op insurance) and get quotes.

■ *Step 3: Double – double check and get the discounts.* Once you have the screen scraper results, who comes out top is as important as the price as it shows their attitudes to your particular risk. Pick the top three and go separately to their websites, check the policies are suitable and requote – the more detailed information entered means the price may vary, plus you may be eligible for further direct or especially internet discounts on top of the quotes you've got.

■ *Step 4: Haggle.* There's no such thing as a fixed price when it comes to insurance. The final step is get on the phone and try to haggle. There is often massive price flexibility, but be fully armed with the cheapest standard quote first.

Always try taking it to your existing insurer and a broker to see if they will beat it, and perhaps try shaving a few extra pounds off when you mention your best quote.

Also, beware: opt to pay monthly rather than in a lump sum and it costs more. In effect the insurer lends you the money for the lump sum and you pay back in instalments plus interest (it can be 20 per cent). For those with good credit scores, if you need to borrow it's much cheaper just to pay on a 0 per cent credit card.

■ **CALORIE COUNT**

Using this four-step solution works. For buildings and contents insurance for a four bedroom semi-detached house in Manchester with £35,000 worth of contents: going direct to an insurer the quote was £600; using a broker the price dropped to £500; yet the screen scrape found similar cover for £300. A saving of £300 before haggling.

SUGGESTED INGREDIENTS

Screen scrapers: www.confused.com; www.insuresupermarket.com
Updated info: www.monysavingexpert.com/homeinsurance

ADDED SPICE

Extra tricks can shave up to 20 per cent off the cost of your premium.

- *Approved locks on all doors and windows.* Then ensure they stay locked. Otherwise it may invalidate your claim, even if that isn't the cause of the problem.
- *Approved alarm.* Fitting NACASS standard burglar alarms reduces premiums. However, these are expensive alarms which require an annual checkup.
- *Increased excess.* You will usually have to pay the first £50 of any claim, but the more you're willing to pay, the lower your premium.
- *Neighbourhood Watch.* Some insurers offer discounts if you live in a Neighbourhood Watch area; however, this is becoming less common as premiums already factor in the lower risk of theft in such areas.
- *No claims.* Insurers factor in your claims history, so a record of no previous claims will reduce your premium substantially. When you've a claim, consider whether it's actually worth doing, as it may be cheaper to pay it yourself and avoid an increase in the policy cost.
- *Age.* The older you are, the less likely you are to make a claim, which makes premiums lower. However, a 'special

price' for older customers doesn't mean it won't be beaten by a non-special quote from somewhere else. All insurers use risk-based price assessments so this is factored in anyway.

■ *Special precautions.* Notify insurers about any special safety precautions for your valuables, such as a home safe.

■ *Lifestyle.* Having a dog/being teetotal/not smoking are all used by some insurers to reduce premiums. If this applies to you it's worth asking insurers whether it impacts their pricing.

■ *New may be better than renewal.* Applying to your existing insurer as a new customer occasionally produces a cheaper price than its renewal quote.

PART 3

HEALTHY EATING

DEBT ISN'T BAD ...

What? Shock! Horror! Think you misread it? Well, let me say it again. Debt is not bad. There is nothing wrong with rationally deciding to pay more to get something now you would otherwise have to wait for. Governments borrow, companies borrow and individuals borrow; it's a financial necessity.

In our funny world, recently the cause célèbre has been 'over-indebtedness'; prior to that it was disenfranchisement from credit. There's verbal dexterity here – debt is bad; credit is good – yet they're almost identical.

Get debt right and you profit, or at least have easy access to cheap lending. 'Healthy Eating' is about how to do just that.

... But There Are Bad Debts

Before you smile lovingly at credit cards, loans, mortgages and HP agreements – while debt isn't bad, this doesn't mean all debt is good. Overly expensive debts, ill-thought-out debts and, worst of all, debts you can't afford to repay are hideous.

Get debts wrong and it's a nightmare. In a worst-case scenario, you will become financially crippled. Home, cars, families and lives have been lost due to debts.

While 'Healthy Eating' is about prevention more than cure

– how to do it right in the first place – I have also included a special section on what to do if you're in debt crisis.

Why 'Healthy Eating'?

For many people, borrowing, like eating, is necessary. Even some who consider themselves debt-free actually have a mort-gage, often the biggest loan of all. Do it right and you'll be healthy and fit, get it wrong and you'll be obese and ill. The reason I wanted to dedicate an entire section to debt is that you're paying for money itself, rather than any intrinsic goods, so reducing its price is MoneySaving purity.

one
WHEN TO EAT WHAT

I want to cover two main areas in this chapter:

How Debt Works

Ten years ago mortgages, credit cards and personal loans were different beasts – now they merge into one. Before looking at the different types, it's necessary to choose what's right for you.

How They Decide Whether to Lend You Money

Beneath all debt is the murky world of credit scoring, a secret scheme lenders use to decide if they want to lend you cash. Knowing how they decide, and what you can do about it, is laying the table for healthy eating.

So without further ado ...

THE CRUCIAL COMPONENTS OF ANY DEBT

Debt is simply any type of borrowing. The reason it causes problems is that, unlike a newspaper subscription or gym membership, when times are tough you can't just cancel it and stop repaying. Once you know you need to borrow and why, whatever type of debt you incur, it's time to start thinking or you'll overpay a fortune.

There are three things that impact the cost of borrowing:

1. Borrowing more
2. A higher interest rate
3. Borrowing over a longer time

It's the last point that people forget. The longer you borrow, the more you will repay. Debt costs rely on length of time as well as rate. While a mortgage at 5 per cent looks cheaper than a personal loan at 10 per cent, don't forget the time factor.

Repay £1,000 at 10 per cent over five years and it costs £260 in interest. Repay the same at just 5 per cent over a 25-year mortgage term and it costs £740.

Admittedly, the impact of inflation diminishes the difference slightly. Even so, always remember the longer you borrow, the more it costs.

Quick Wealth Warning: Secured v. Unsecured

'Don't worry, your loan is "secured",' they tell you. Doesn't that sound good – far better than a risky old 'unsecured loan'. Nooooooooo! Don't fall for it. It's not you it provides security to – it's the lender. A secured debt is one where the loan is secured on your home (or some other potential valuable asset). This means if you can't pay off the debt, ultimately they can throw you out of your house. Admittedly, fail to pay off an unsecured loan and after a substantial legal process your home could ultimately still be at risk, but it is much less clear-cut – if other things are equal, stick with 'unsecured'.

One tricky thing to watch: are there any fees or other charges? Watch for annual fees, insurance costs, penalties tying you in and administration costs. Financial services is a creative industry, especially when lenders are thinking up new ways to charge us.

One personal choice: how much flexibility do you need? Pay something off more quickly and you pay less interest on it. Ensuring you have access to borrow more when necessary means you can avoid penalties or fines for going over the limit, or ruining your credit score. Flexibility pays.

AN INTERESTING TALE

Interest is the cost of borrowing money. Unfortunately, there are more ways to express it than positions in the *Kama Sutra*. To help, we have the wonderful term 'APR – Annual Percentage Rate' to guide us. The APR is a great idea. It nets together all the costs of borrowing money over the full term of a loan. Unfortunately, the reason I say it 'nets' is because APRs are full of holes, and therefore often misleading, irrelevant, confused or all three. So let's ignore APRs and go ...

Back to Basics

An interest rate of 5 per cent over a year means borrow £100 and by the end of the year you will need to repay £105 on it. If only it was always this simple:

Interest compounds: Borrow over a longer time and you need to pay interest on the interest that's already been charged. An example. Borrow £100 over three years at 10 per cent a year and:

■ After year one, the total interest is £10

- After year two, the total interest is £21 (£10 from year one, £10 from year two, plus £1 – the interest on the interest from year one)
- After year three, the total interest is £33.10 (£21 from years one and two, another £10 for year three, plus the interest on the £21 – £2.10)

This little piece of maths means debts don't just get bigger if they're not repaid; they get bigger more and more quickly.

Fees: To make interest look cheaper, lenders sometimes lower the rate but charge fees on top instead. Don't be fooled.

Can you spot what's wrong? Can you spot what's wrong with this sales patter, common in the car trade? 'It's a really cheap loan. Look, you borrow £5,000 off us over three years, with 36 monthly payments of around £160. That means you'll be paying us £5,750 in total. Which is a total of 15 per cent over three years or about 5 per cent a year.'

This all sounds perfectly reasonable and cheap. Yet it's dodgy, dodgy, dodgy. Did you spot the problem? It's not the figures – they're roughly right. It's the entire concept.

Borrow £5,000 over three years and repay a lump sum at the end of £5,750, then indeed it is roughly equivalent to an annual interest rate of 5 per cent. Yet you aren't borrowing

Martin's Money Memories: £2500 for 3 missing letters!

While filming *Make Me Rich*, one of the families was trying to buy a new people carrier. The finance quote said 6 per cent, which sounded cheap. They were happy. Yet I noticed there was no 'APR', which meant it was the flat rate and £2500 more expensive than it appeared.

> **Money Diet Wealth Warning: Be a Round Peg in a Square Hole**
>
> The debt industry is damn clever. It's aware people don't understand it, and to 'help' has developed different products for different circumstances: a mortgage for your home, a secured loan to consolidate debts, a credit card for spending, a personal loan for a lump sum, overdrafts to extend the monthly pay packet. This is its way of boxing you in and charging you more. Don't fall for it.
>
> There's no reason not to use a credit card rather than a loan to buy your new kitchen, if it's cheaper. There's no need to get a 'secured' consolidation loan for your debts, when a mortgage is the same thing at a much lower rate. A 'car loan' for a car isn't the only choice. Know what you're doing and choose the product that means you pay less!

£5,000 over the whole three years, as you're paying it off as you go. Halfway through the loan period, nearly half the loan is cleared so you should only pay interest on around £2,500. In fact, the annual interest rate on this loan is roughly 10 per cent, not 5 per cent. Watch out.

A Simple Solution?

After all these complications, the solution is actually quite simple. One question beats all these tricks. When you get a loan just ask, 'What is the total cost of borrowing this money over the time period, including all fees and charges?' And compare the answer.

FLIPPING THE TWO-SIDED MONEY COIN

I've said it before, and I'll say it again: debt and savings are two sides of the same coin. Both are paying a set amount out of your salary each month, except that debt pays for something you've already had, while saving is for something you will have. The big difference is: with savings they pay you a little interest; with debt *you* pay *them* a *lot* of interest. Therefore to flip the coin in your favour, pay off the debts with the savings.

In even the best savings account on the market, £1,000, after tax, will probably earn you only around £40 a year in interest.

On a typical high-street credit card, £1,000 debt will cost you around £170 a year in interest.

So pay off the credit card with your savings and you'll be roughly £130 a year better off. It staggers me that many people have both debts and savings.

Of course it's always important to have some cash available for emergencies. Yet to be sophisticated, remember a paid-off credit card can provide an emergency facility too. So pay off your credit-card debts with your savings and you're better off. If in the future you need emergency cash and have to use the card for it, you are no worse off than you were in the first place, yet in the meantime you have had a good few months paying less interest, leaving you overall in ruder financial health.

Freak Interest – Occasionally Debt is Better than Savings

'Damn you Lewis, I'd just understood that. Now you're changing your mind!' Okay. I'm aware of the contradiction, but in some very specific circumstances the aim is to borrow as much as you can and save it. Those circumstances are the rare occasions when the after-tax interest earned on savings is higher than the cost of borrowing.

This may sound like madness, but it happens. Interest-free credit is a common enticement to borrow, so why not earn interest on money they're lending you for nothing by saving it in a high-interest instant savings account? This 'freak interest' situation predominantly happens in five areas, four of which are covered elsewhere – student bank accounts (see page 242), graduate bank accounts (see page 244), and introductory credit card and overdraft offers (see 'Free Cash', page 387). The only one left is student loans, so let me quickly tick that box before going on.

The student loan interest rate is set at the rate of inflation. Usually this is lower than the best savings account rates, though once tax is taken into account it can be close. While it may not always be worth playing the game, it does mean there's very little point in paying student loans off early as, effectively, the real cost stays the same. It's much cheaper debt than pretty much anything else, so there's not too much harm leaving it over a long period. Plus, it may mean you don't have to take other expensive commercial loans out to replace it.

Cheap Debt is Better than Expensive Debt

I know this is obvious. Yet you'd be amazed how many people get this wrong (not you, of course, but why not read this bit, just to tell your friends). The classic mistake is with over-drafts, as people often don't see this as debt. Yet it is, and it's often expensive. Of course, the first step should be to move to a better bank account (see 'Crash Diet', page 238), but we'll ignore that for a second.

Let me give you a scenario:

Ms Irma Big-Spender
Take-home salary: £1,500 per month after tax

Credit Card: Moreballs Misercard
Rate: 0 per cent for six months, then 13.9 per cent
Current balance: £1,500
Credit limit: £3,000

Overdraft: Barstools Bank Account
Rate: 17.9 per cent authorised
Current overdraft: £1,300
Overdraft limit: £2,000

Irma has debts on both her credit card and her overdraft. However, the overdraft debt is substantially more expensive, even after the credit card interest-free period is over. Irma would pay around £200 a year in interest in this scenario. There are some sophisticated ways to move debts from a current account to a credit card (see 'Super Balance Transfers', page 374), but for the moment let's take the easy route.

If Irma spends on her credit card rather than from her bank account (and just makes the minimum repayments), her wages will start to pay off the overdraft. Even without actually paying any debt off, after a couple of months she'd be in the following situation:

Credit Card: Moreballs Misercard
Rate: 0 per cent for four months (all that remains of the 0 per
     cent period), then 13.9 per cent
Current balance: £2,800
Credit limit: £3,000

Overdraft: Barstools Bank Account
Rate: 17.9 per cent authorised
Current overdraft: £0
Overdraft limit: £2,000

She's now borrowing the same, £2,800, but not paying any interest on it. Even when the credit card reverts to its standard rate, it is 4 per cent cheaper than the overdraft borrowing, so Irma should keep her debts there, rather than going overdrawn to feed it. Of course, it still needs repaying, but that will be quicker as there's less interest accruing. However, never let the fact that it is a card not your bank account let you think you can spend more.

WHERE IT ALL BEGINS – CREDIT SCORING
How They Decide Whether to Lend You Money

Let me start with a pet peeve. There are two commonly used terms that simply don't exist. Newspapers use them, and people use them in conversation. To make my point properly I'm going to use very big letters.

YOU DON'T HAVE A CREDIT RATING
There is no central list anywhere which says whether you should be lent money.

THERE'S NO SUCH THING AS A CREDIT BLACKLIST
Equally, there's no list of 'no-go people'.

Try to borrow money or get a credit agreement and the credit company tries to work out how you measure up against its 'wish list'. To make this decision they use a secretive technique known as credit scoring. Every lender uses its own bespoke system. This affects not just whether you get a loan, but sometimes the actual rate you get.

Now do note, I didn't say they weigh you up to decide whether you're a good or bad 'risk'. Actually they weigh you up to decide whether they can make a profit out of you. This is so important, let me shout again:

IF THEY THINK YOU'LL MAKE 'EM PROFITS, THEY'LL LEND YOU CASH

This is the basis of the decision. Remember, lenders have absolutely no obligation to give us their money. All this doesn't mean risk isn't a big factor. Giving money to someone who isn't a good bet to pay it back is not a potentially profitable transaction, which is where the idea of a blacklist comes from. Those with a poor credit history will score badly on most credit-scoring systems, and will usually be turned down.

However, believing the blacklist concept is dangerous. Assuming that if one company turns you down they all will is wrong. Of course, if your credit history makes Nick Leeson look solvent, then most mainstream lenders will turn you down. But for those who are middling, it's worth considering that some lenders' scoring policies are more forgiving than others.

Who Will Lend to those with a Poor History?

I just used the phrase 'mainstream lenders', and this is important. There are also 'sub-prime' or 'adverse credit' lenders, who target people who have had problems. For these companies, a poor risk makes them salivate with the thought of huge profit, so they're happy. Their business models are built on the fact that they can lend money to people who can't get it elsewhere, and at vastly inflated rates. What is profitable for one isn't profitable for another – that's why there's no such thing as a credit rating, just a different score with each and every lender.

Money Diet Quick Fact Snack: Info for Tarts

The risk that tarting will impact your credit score isn't always because a lender can see 'they've got loads of 0 per cent debt – they're trying to scam us'. Often they don't know what rate you're paying or who with. Actually it tends to be a symptom of some other factors.

■ *Over-indebtedness:* If you are holding £50,000 on 0 per cent cards, all a lender sees is you have £50,000 debt. This in itself may be a reason for rejection. Tarts with lower balances are less likely to be rejected.

■ *Lots of credit searches:* If you apply for many cards in a short space of time it'll be a problem – try and keep card applications as far apart as possible.

■ *The sheer number of cards:* If you have many outstanding cards with lots of available credit you will again be likely to score lower.

Most credit-scoring systems are not currently sophisticated enough to score out 'tarts' specifically. However, this is changing and their aim is to do so, so be careful.

Does Credit Scoring Impact Tarts?

For super tarts like me, who serially rotate 0 per cent cards (see page 372), the 'profitability clause' also causes problems. There's no fixed rule on how many times you can rotate debts before lenders get wise. Yet, anecdotally, few people have problems until they've had 10 cards in a row (especially if they cancel the unused old ones). Still this means be careful about applying for cards willy-nilly. A free camera may sound a good freebie, yet if it's the straw that breaks the credit-scoring camel's back, and you then can't apply for any more cards, you may have wasted access to £6,000 of interest-free credit for a quick snap.

This may all seem tremendously unfair, reminiscent of the 'I am not a number' cry of The Prisoner. However, it works well for the credit industry. Of course, they make mistakes, but why should they care? Applications are aggregated into millions, so the mistakes cancel each other out. And, overall, credit scoring is easier, cheaper and, crucially, more profitable than either lending everyone money indiscriminately or doing a manual personalised assessment.

THE PRACTICAL PROCESS

Credit scoring is a number-crunching attempt to predict your potential behaviour from the vast range of data they have. The actual scoring systems are never published and differ from lender to lender and product to product.

What They Know About You

Their info is gleaned from three primary sources:

1. The application form. Fill it out precisely as it's the primary source: salary, family size, reason for the loan and whether you're a home-owner. Many people don't get credit because of filling in forms incorrectly. Adding (or missing) an extra '0' to your salary would probably leave you rejected for security reasons. Be careful.

2. Past relationships with the lender. Any previous dealings you've had with a lender will help inform them. For those with a poor credit history but better recent behaviour, this can mean existing providers are a better bet than complete unknowns.

3. Credit reference agency files. Three companies, Equifax, Experian and Callcredit, compile data from three sources:

a. Electoral roll information: contains people's address details and the details of who lives with whom.

b. County Court Judgements (CCJs) and bankruptcies: used to indicate if you have a history of debt problems.

c. Financial data from banks, building societies and others, compiled from all payments and transactions. Around 200 million records a month are tracked.

Credit Reference File Errors

Before worrying about a poor score, there's a possible chink in the armour. It could just be they've scored you incorrectly due to a data error. Lenders should recommend you check your credit reference file upon rejection. It's very important at this point not to apply for other credit until you know. If there is a hideous error, and you keep applying, it's likely most lenders will turn you down. This means you'll have pointless applications on your file, which won't help your score even once the errors are fixed.

You have a legal right (to be technical, but only in brackets so it's not too bad, this right is currently contained in the Data Protection Act 1998) to see your credit reference files. The three agencies, Equifax, Experian and Callcredit, all allow this. The quickest method is online or by phone but you can also write – it should cost around £2, which can be paid using a debit or credit card. You will need to tell them details of your six previous addresses and postcodes. Even if you're not applying for new products it's worth checking your file for errors every 18 months or so.

Things to check include your present and past address and your family details. (I once lived in Cardiff – not a good thing for your credit score when your name is Lewis. One of the agencies decided that I was the son of some Lewis who'd lived there four years before, and linked our files. This Lewis had a County Court Judgement (CCJ): I was rejected for credit. Thankfully, the rules allowing this linking have now changed.)

If you disagree with anything on your file, contact the agency and ask that it be changed. The entry will be marked 'disputed' and the agency will contact the organisation that provided the information. If it's agreed it's wrong, the file will be amended, though always check this is actually done. Sometimes it'll be necessary to talk directly to the organisation that supplied the incorrect information to the agency in the first place. Normally, however, this will be done for you. Unfortunately, at times the information provider may disagree with you and be unwilling to allow the credit reference agency to amend your file. If this happens, unless you take them to court or try to kick up a stink, your only option is to add your own comments to the file to explain your side. Do this carefully, keeping your entry concise and factual.

CREDIT REFERENCE AGENCY DETAILS

Experian: www.experian.co.uk, PO Box 8000, Nottingham N61 5GX; Equifax: www.equifax.co.uk, PO Box 3001, Glasgow G81 2DT; Callcredit: www.callcredit.co.uk, Callcredit plc, One Park Lane, Leeds LS3 1EP.

A Secret – Credit Ratings Actually Do Exist

Don't worry, I'm not being duplicitous. It's extremely important for people to understand there's no universal rating on everyone, yet now you've read on a bit, I can get just a wee bit more technical. There's a growing trend in the debt industry to use a 'credit rating' from one of the credit reference agencies as a part of their credit score.

Should I Buy Credit Rating Data?

This trend means the credit reference agencies have developed a profitable new business for themselves, selling 'find out your credit rating' for much more than the old-fashioned £2 to get your credit file info. Yet this rating still only tells you one score, not that of all the agencies. The info can often be reasonably useful, but remember many lenders don't use the rating, and even for those that do, it's only part of your score. Doing this may save you time, but the old-fashioned file method is cheaper and still contains the info.

What this means is rather than just getting a data sheet from Equifax or Experian, they get a score, which is then used alongside their own application form data, past dealings and other info provided by the credit reference agencies, to build their own final credit score.

Now this trend has become much more common recently, but by no means is everyone doing it. And it still means every lender scores you differently. The credit rating, if used, is just one stat and never the be-all and end-all. This is especially true of those you have an existing relationship with (previous dealing data) as that is always the most important factor.

How to Improve Your Credit Score

If you've just scanned down the page to this bit – the exciting bit – then, sorry, but before you read it, please go back and read the above on how credit scoring works – or you just won't get it.

At this point I need to say something which will disappoint – there's no magical way to improve your credit score, unless there is a factual mistake in the credit reference agencies' files. However, even though there's no exact science, there are things that will help.

Electoral roll. Always ensure you are on the electoral roll – it is the bedrock of all credit scores. If you're not, you will struggle. For those not eligible, send the credit reference agencies proof of residency – they will then add a note saying they've seen and verified this. This will slow down the process as the application will be dealt with manually, but it should still improve your chances.

Keep up payments and never be late. Always try to follow at least the minimum repayment plan for your financial products. Even if you're struggling, don't default or miss payments. Doing this once or twice will cause problems that can cost you for years. Think of it like this – every late payment is effectively costing you £100 on top of the debt; every missed payment £250. In truth I've plucked these numbers out of thin air, as there's no way to quantify a poor credit score, but it's the right way to think.

If you are in difficulties, the clichéd 'contact your lender' is still the best advice. Hopefully they will try and help a little, as changing your repayment schedule is preferable to you defaulting – and though it will hit your credit score, it's better than a County Court Judgement (CCJ) against you.

Don't apply too many times. Lenders don't just look at your current situation. They try and predict your future behaviour. Potential over-indebtedness can cause rejection – scoring looks not only at your repayment history but at the likelihood you will repay in future. Multiple credit applications can count as evidence of possible over-indebtedness.

It is important to note that there is a distinction between a 'credit enquiry' and a 'full credit check'. The latter goes on your file, the first doesn't, so if you just want a quote, get one, but ensure you ask what type of checks they will make. Providing it's not a 'full credit check' it is fine.

Avoid too much potential credit. Access to too much credit, even if it isn't used, can be a problem. If you have a range of unused credit cards, cancel most of them; this lowers your available credit and should help. As an added bonus, once you cancel unused cards, in approximately (though there's no guarantee) 18 months you should count as a 'new customer' again and be able to reapply for 'special introductory offers'.

Moving house hurts. If you're moving house, this usually scores you lower. If a move's on the cards, apply beforehand.

Marriage doesn't hurt – joint finances do. Marrying or living with someone who has a bad credit score shouldn't impact your finances, as recent changes mean third-party data (i.e. someone else's info) doesn't appear on your file. However, if you are 'financially linked' then it can have an effect on your score. Therefore, even having a joint bank account for bills can mean you are co-scored. If your partner has a poor score, keep your finances rigidly separate and then at least one of you should have access to good credit.

Apply while in work, not after. Many people leaving work to study, have a baby or travel round the world try and sort out adequate credit after leaving. Yet you score much more highly when you have an income, so apply before leaving.

Don't change your mobile, home telephone, utilities or car insurance before applying for credit. All of these may mean a credit search is performed which goes on your record. When a lender sees your credit reference file, it doesn't distinguish between whether this is a search from a mobile company or a loan company. As having many searches in a short space of time hurts your credit score, doing all these together can negatively impact on your ability to obtain new credit.

Evidence of stability is good. Those who own their home rather than rent, or who are employed rather than self-employed, tend to score more highly. Putting a fixed (land) line rather than a mobile number on application forms can help with security checks and improve your chances.

Money Diet Quick Fact Snack: Credit Repair Companies

Steer clear of any company advertising it'll fix your credit score. They do it in one of two ways. The legal method is to negotiate with a company after a CCJ has been served. If you offer them a settlement (not necessarily the full amount), a condition can be that the CCJ is wiped. Many companies do this for you, though they make you pay. However, there's nothing they can do you can't do for yourself, and if you need help, Citizens Advice Bureaux, Independent Advice Centres and the Consumer Credit Counselling Services should assist for free anyway.

The other method is illegal. Some credit repair agencies advise you to perjure yourself and swear you didn't receive a CCJ even when you did. Once it's illegally wiped they try to quickly negotiate a settlement with the lender, before it is re-served. Don't just steer clear – turn the car right round and drive away at speed!

Credit Score Myths: The Following Do NOT Impact Your Credit Score

■ **Others' info:**
Information about other people who live with you who aren't financially linked.

■ **If you've been declined by someone else:**
Only the fact a credit search has been done is recorded.

■ **Your sex, race, religion or politics**

■ **Who your current providers are:**
Your new lender won't know who you are with.

■ **Checking your credit reference files:**
Lenders are not informed as to whether you check the files – it doesn't hurt.

No history can be a problem. A limited credit history is a problem as it means lenders cannot predict your behaviour. This is a 'chicken and egg' situation – you can't get credit without a history; you can't get a history without credit.

IF YOU CAN'T GET ACCESS TO CREDIT

A few lenders, like Capital One, Monument and even Barclaycard, have special 'rate for the risk' credit cards. These have extremely high rates of interest, and should be avoided except for the specific purpose of building or rebuilding your credit history.

To do this use the card for a little spending each month, but always pay it off in full so there is no interest charged. Do this and after a year or two you should have a sufficient credit history to enable you to move towards more normal products.

And a final thought – although it may be tempting, lying on your application form won't help. First, it's an offence, but also, if lenders can't corroborate your information, it's normally not used for credit scoring anyway.

two

THE BIG MEAL

THE COMPLETE, NO-HOLDS-BARRED, COMPREHENSIVE GUIDE TO SAVING MONEY ON MORTGAGES AND REMORTGAGES

Mortgage debts stay with us longer than badly cooked kippers. The wrong mortgage can add tens of thousands to your costs over the years. This chapter takes you through getting the very best-value mortgage possible, and how to improve your current home loan.

WHY BOTHER?

If someone walked up to you and offered you a legal 20 grand in cash with no strings attached, it's likely you'd grab it – in your teeth if you had to. Shave one percentage point off a £100,000 mortgage with 20 years left and you'd lower your repayments by £80 a month. Save this, and by the time the mortgage is paid off, you could have well over 20 grand.

It's just a stat, but shows the scale of gain available. Paying off your home loan is the biggest financial burden you're likely to have, and by tackling it, you're likely to make the biggest single saving going.

The last few years have been an amazing time to get a mortgage or remortgage. Interest rates briefly touched their lowest for over 50 years and house prices rocketed. All this means those remortgaging are often borrowing a smaller proportion of their house's value – which should enable them to get, relatively, an even better rate than when they first took the house on.

Getting a Mortgage

Funnily enough, deciding whether to get a mortgage or not is easy. If you want to buy a house – unless you're very lucky – someone will need to loan you the money, and that means a mortgage, as a mortgage is a home loan.

The bigger the deposit you can put down, the easier it is to get a mortgage. Lenders will usually lend people on their own up to three-and-a-half times their income. These days some lenders will give more – in fact on rare occasions it is possible to borrow up to six times your earnings. For two people getting a mortgage together, it's normally possible to borrow either three times the income of the highest earner plus one times the income of the other, or two-and-a-half times their joint income. There are also a few lenders who don't use 'earnings multiples', but instead simply ask the question, 'What can you afford to repay?'

Money Diet Quick Fact Snack: Special Recipes to Create a Deposit

Raising a deposit to get on the housing ladder can be tough. Not having a deposit leaves a 100 per cent mortgage as the only option and these are usually very expensive – meaning the interest rates are higher. While standard options involve help from your family – either they act as guarantors, so that if you can't pay they have to, or you get a loan from them – many people simply don't have this option. There are, however, a couple of more creative solutions that are possible.

Use a cheap credit card or personal loan. This should only be used by those who can keep a tight hold on their budget management. The idea is simple. Rather than an expensive 100 per cent loan, borrow some or all of the deposit on a credit card (depending on your credit limit and the amount you need), preferably at 0 per cent. A 95 per cent mortgage is substantially cheaper than a 100 per cent one, so overall you will be much better off. Even if the credit card rate is more than the mortgage rate, because the mortgage borrowing is so much larger, as long as you are borrowing the deposit just for the short term, and can prioritise paying it back, it's generally worthwhile.

Use a cashback mortgage. Some mortgages offer cashback to help with a new home's expenses when you get a mortgage. This can be up to 6 per cent of the mortgage value. Providing the mortgage is HLC-free (free of a Higher Lending Charge, see page 331), and extended-redemption penalty-free (see page 338), this can be used creatively to act as an effective deposit. If the cashback mortgage, as they sometimes are, is much cheaper than a 100 per cent mortgage, then when contracts are exchanged (towards the end of the home-buying process) if the seller agrees, it is not necessary to hand over the full deposit then, but at completion. In this case the cashback may be used as the deposit and the overall mortgage will be at a cheaper rate.

Remortgaging

You don't have to move home to remortgage; all you're doing is swapping your current loan for a new one. Ask the question 'Is there a new mortgage available that's better and/or cheaper than my current one, where the benefits of switching outweigh the costs?' If the answer is yes, then buckle up and prepare for the ride, as it's time to switch.

However, there are more reasons to think about changing your current home loan than just the savings available. So let me try and anticipate a few of these reasons and see if any fit you.

THE SLAP-ON-THE-WRIST

'I've had my mortgage for years, why should I change it?'
Inaction is expensive. If you haven't touched your mortgage in years, it is likely you are paying your lender's Standard Variable Rate (SVR). These rates tend to move with the UK base rate (see page 333), which is set by the Bank of England. However, they don't necessarily move in exact proportion, as lenders can choose to move the rate willy-nilly, making themselves either more competitive or more profitable. Each lender's rate varies, but as a very rough rule of thumb it's 1.5 percentage points above the UK's bank base rate. Frankly, if you are paying the SVR and have been for years, then with only a few exceptions you're flushing cash down the toilet.

Money Diet Quick Fact Snack: Remortgaging – a Definition

Remortgaging simply means changing your mortgage deal, whether with your existing lender or a new one. The main reasons it is done are to get a cheaper rate, because you are moving house, or to be able to borrow more on top of your existing mortgage.

> ### You're Not as Rich as You Think You Are!
>
> So your house is worth a quarter of a million! Sounds a lot and indeed it is, yet only on paper. It's not cash in the bank. Years of house-price rises in the early noughties made people feel rich, which meant they spent more.
>
> Yet incomes didn't go up so this spending was on plastic. Soon that plastic debt was plonked on to the mortgage, meaning it's likely to take 20 years to repay and you now own less of your house.
>
> And all this without discussing the potential for house prices to fall ...

THE SOFTLEE-SOFTLEE-CATCHEE-MONKEE

'I want to increase my borrowing and consolidate my loans.'
Rocket-paced house-price rises mean your home may be worth substantially more than the size of your mortgage. Remortgaging allows you to increase the size of your mortgage and borrow more at the low mortgage rate. Yet, remember, you are choosing a very long-term form of borrowing which will leave you actually paying quite a substantial amount in interest. It's also worth remembering that interest rates can rise sharply, so always ask yourself if you could afford to make the repayments if interest rates rose by three percentage points, or perhaps even more.

THE OUCH

'My endowment probably won't pay off my mortgage.'
Not fun, this one. If you are one of the millions of UK homeowners who have received letters from your endowment company warning your investment may not repay the mortgage in full when it matures, then remortgaging can provide a couple of useful solutions – see 'Interest-only mortgages', page 328.

THE WHAT-CHOICE-DO-I-HAVE?

'I'm moving house.'

It isn't always necessary to remortgage when you move; many modern mortgages are 'portable', which means they can move with you. However, increasing the loan to do it will need agreement from your current lender. A house move is a good time to look at remortgaging as you may save substantial cash when you check out what is available.

It's worth noting that your existing lender cannot force you to stick with it, though it could force you to pay any contracted redemption penalties (more on that in a moment). On occasion they may not give you their best bureaucratic efforts to help you move, but if things don't go smoothly the Financial Services Authority lays down a complaints procedure for such an eventuality.

Money Diet Quick Fact Snack: Loan-To-Value ('LTV')

The actual interest rate paid on a mortgage depends on your LTV. As it sounds, this is the size of the loan compared to the value of the house. There are different LTV bands, and the lower the band you are in the cheaper the mortgage – bands are such things as a sub-75 per cent LTV, or between 80 and 90 per cent LTV, or over 95 per cent LTV.

For first-time mortgage holders, working out the LTV is easy. Simply take the value of your deposit away from 100 per cent. For example, a 10 per cent deposit is a 90 per cent LTV. It is slightly trickier for those who are remortgaging. To find the LTV, divide the amount you have left to pay on your mortgage by the current value of your home. This means if your house's value has risen, your LTV will have decreased, which should mean you are able to get a better deal.

CHOOSING A MORTGAGE

Each individual lender's competitiveness varies depending on its current business priorities, but there's always one lender desperate for new business and willing to undercut its competitors. This means there's no such thing as the top mortgage provider.

A lender topping the mortgage table six months ago is likely to have done so to increase its share of the market, and once it has hit its target, the probability is it will push its rates up, leaving it no longer the best.

Mortgage Type: Repayment or Interest Only

Mortgages come in two flavours – which to choose is the most important decision to make. When you remortgage, there is the opportunity to change the type, though.

REPAYMENT MORTGAGES

Here you repay the lender each month, and this pays both the original money borrowed (the capital) and the interest the lender is charging on the loan. At the end of the mortgage term you will automatically have paid off the mortgage in full.

INTEREST-ONLY MORTGAGES

Here, you pay the lender only the interest cost of the loan, while you agree to pay off the capital at a later date. Some people don't look at paying off the capital, and hope that moves in property prices or other investments will cover it, but the usual method is to set up an investment vehicle. The traditional one has been an endowment policy, which is a life assurance investment plan; however, ISAs, pensions and previously PEPS have been used to do the same thing.

People *incorrectly* name such mortgages 'endowment mortgages', 'pension mortgages' or 'ISA mortgages'. This isn't just me being picky, but an important concept. The two products are not linked. You have an interest-only mortgage and, separately, an investment to pay it off. You needn't use that investment to pay off the mortgage; you could choose to use cash from another source. Sometimes endowments are 'assigned' to pay off a mortgage, but this should be changeable.

The big sales plank for interest-only mortgages is that if the investment performs well, the lump sum may be more than the amount needed, giving you a windfall at the end of the term. This is why many endowments were sold – yet the suggested repayment level of the combined interest and investment was usually set lower than a repayment mortgage.

Unfortunately, this often meant not enough money was invested, which is why, especially if the investment performed poorly, for many people the endowment isn't coming close to repaying the mortgage.

If you have an endowment shortfall. There are a number of options, which can be either used separately or combined.

■ Remortgage, and use the benefit of a cheaper interest rate to make up the shortfall.

■ Switch either completely or partially to a repayment mortgage. This may be more expensive, but it means that at the end of the term your mortgage is guaranteed to be paid off.

■ Pay more into the endowment. Well, I have to mention it as a possibility, though for almost everyone it's likely to be a terrible idea. However, to be ultra-thorough, get an Independent Financial Adviser to assess how well the endowment is likely to do.

■ Set up a savings plan to make up the shortfall. Here you simply start paying money into another account to make sure you'll be covered. One way is to use a mini cash ISA (see 'Crash Diet', page 223) to get tax-free savings. This is quite a simple plan. And if the shortfall isn't as bad as expected, you'll have extra funds.

One final quick point. Many people, when annoyed at a poorly performing endowment, decide to surrender it. This is often a bad idea. Most of the benefit from an endowment is due to the bonus paid at the end of the term – surrender and you lose that. Endowments are one of the few subjects Independent Financial Advisers shine at. (See 'Financial Fitness', page 110.) However, as a rule of thumb, if you are looking to surrender, you may be better off 'selling' the endowment. There is a market for second-hand endowment policies; buyers commonly advertise, and if you sell, you can get up to 30 per cent more than surrendering. So always, always, always check this option out if you are considering getting rid of the endowment.

DOES THIS MEAN NEVER GET A NEW INTEREST-ONLY MORTGAGE?

No. It's been a very bad decision in the past, but that doesn't mean automatically exclude it. The keyword is 'risk'. Take an interest-only loan and you must be aware of the 'risk' it may not be paid off in full. However, once you're aware of the risk, have considered it, understand it and planned for the worst, then an interest-only mortgage is still acceptable. Endowments have lost their sheen, and most new interest-only mortgages will be ISA-backed, taking advantage of ISAs' mostly tax-free ability to fund the mortgage. Yet this option

Money Diet Quick Fact Snack: Higher Lending Charges (HLCs)

HLCs are outrageous fees some lenders charge with mortgages where the loan-to-value (LTV) ratio is more than 90 per cent. It is an insurance policy, yet – although you pay for it – it's not you it protects but the lender, in case you default.

They used to be called 'Mortgage Indemnity Guarantees (MIGs)' or 'mortgage indemnity premium' or MIP, but it all amounts to the same thing. Avoid them.

Not all lenders charge HLCs and that makes a huge difference. Someone with a 95 per cent LTV would pay an HLC of around 1.5 per cent of their house's value, or £1,500 on a £100,000 home. If you're mathematically minded then you can work out the HLC using the following equation. If not, just know that HLCs are complicated, expensive and should be avoided.

The Maths. You usually only pay an HLC if you're borrowing more than 90 per cent of a house's value. The amount you pay is commonly defined as 7 per cent of the amount borrowed above 75 per cent of the house's value. To find out the cost of a HLC, key the following into your calculator:

$$(0.XX - 0.75) \times 0.07 \times \text{house value}$$

where XX is the percentage of your house's value that you're borrowing. (i.e. Borrow 98 per cent and you do 0.98 – 0.75, then multiply the result by 0.07 and then by the house's value.)

suits very few – most people should stick with a repayment mortgage.

Types of Mortgage Special Offers

Mortgage 'special offers' is an unfamiliar term for a familiar mortgage phenomenon. Companies try to tempt us in, hoping later they'll be able to bung the rate up and leave us clinging on, paying more for the rest of the term.

Money Diet Wealth Warning: From Small Changes Do Big Savings Grow

While differences in mortgage percentage rates sound small – they have ENORMOUS impact. Cut the rate by one percentage point on a £100,000 mortgage and you save £80 a month.

These special offers are the classic terms you'll have heard of: the 'fixed', 'discount' and 'trackers' or a combination of these. They usually last for two to five years, though they can be as short as six months or as long as 25 years.

FIXED RATES

As the name suggests, the rate doesn't change, and UK interest rate moves are irrelevant. The best time to get a fixed rate is when UK interest rates are about to rise, as your rate remains static while others move higher.

Sweetener: the certainty of knowing exactly what you'll pay during the entire special-offer period. This means you can plan. If you choose a fixed rate, simply be satisfied you can make the repayments, and even if rates drop don't worry. If the decision is made based on certainty, you still have it, so there's no point regretting what may have been. No one has an interest-rate crystal ball – so any choice you make is a gamble.

Rotten eggs: if rates drop, you're paying more than you need to. Fixed rates almost invariably stop you changing deals within the special-offer period, so get a fixed rate and you're stuck with it.

Final thought: many people wrongly assume the price fixed rates are initially offered at moves up and down with base rates. While there is some relationship, actually fixed-rate prices depend on the City's predictions of long-term rates. This means fixed-rate offer prices can be rising while UK base rates are falling. So be careful.

Money Diet Quick Fact Snack: Know the Difference

The Bank of England base rate. The basic cost of UK money is set by the Bank of England's 'Monetary Policy Committee'. Their job is to try and keep the country's inflation rate on a steady course. Their only weapon is the ability to change the rate at which the Bank of England lends money – the base rate.

When inflation (the rate at which prices rise) is too high, to slow the economy and stop people spending, they increase the cost of borrowing by raising the base rate. When inflation is too low, they need the economy to grow, so they decrease the cost of borrowing, reducing the incentive for people to save and encouraging them to borrow to spend.

When the Bank of England rate moves, other interest rates tend to move, too. This is because the base rate is roughly 'the standard price' for lending money. A good way to measure how competitive loans or savings rates are is to compare them to it.

Lenders' standard variable rates (SVRs). Each bank or building society sets its own SVR; often it's referred to as the bank's standard mortgage rate. These move both when the Bank of England changes interest rates and if the lender wants to change its competitive stance. So if you're with a lender that's sold a lot of mortgages recently, it may increase its rate. Yet willy-nilly moves are uncommon; lenders are sneakier than this. They tend to move at the margins, taking advantage of changes in the Bank of England rate. If the Bank of England drops by 0.25 per cent, a lender may subtly only drop its rate by 0.2 per cent. Much more difficult to spot, but effectively rate rises. Watch out for these moves.

DISCOUNT RATES

The important question is 'What is it discounted off?' The answer is usually it's a temporary discount off the standard variable rate (SVR). This is confusing as it depends on what level lenders set their SVR. For example, a one percentage point discount from a lender with an SVR of 7 per cent is more expensive than an undiscounted mortgage from a lender with an SVR of 5.5 per cent. Therefore with discounts it's not just size, but the usage that counts.

Sweetener: when the UK's interest rates are falling, your mortgage rate drops too, so if it looks like rates are due to drop, a discount is the one to go for. As it moves with base rates you won't feel you are paying much more than the market rate.

Rotten eggs: if interest rates rise, so does the cost of your mortgage. This means there's no security with a discount mortgage.

Final note: some discount mortgages have a 'collar', a set minimum rate, and if the SVR drops below that, you won't benefit. If you're getting a discount mortgage because rates are going to drop, avoid collars like the plague.

DISCOUNT TRACKER RATES/TRACKER RATES

Here rather than the discount being off a bank's SVR, these discounts are off the Bank of England base rate itself. So a 0.5 percentage point tracker discount when the base rate is 5.5 per cent means you pay 5 per cent (though paradoxically even a tracker at +0.5 percentage point, in this case a rate of 6 per cent, could still count as a discount mortgage if it's lower than most SVRs). There are also now long-term tracker rates where, after the special offer, rather than reverting to the SVR it reverts to a tracker rate, for example, base rate plus one percentage point.

Sweetener: the lender can't interfere with the rate to suck in some extra profits. All the gain or pain of base rate moves is passed on directly.

Rotten eggs: like normal discount mortgages – no surety and if rates rise you will pay more.

CAPPED RATES

The rate is variable – either based on the SVR, a tracker, or a discounted version of either of those – yet the maximum rate you can pay is fixed. In reality capped rates usually work like fixed rates, as the only time you don't pay the top rate is if the rate the loan's based on drops below the cap, and they're designed so this rarely happens.

Sweetener: you effectively have a fixed rate if rates are rising, but a discount if there's a substantial drop. Great in theory.

Rotten eggs: capped rates are usually higher than fixed rates, so you are consistently paying more. And if the rate never drops, you'd be better off with a fixed rate. However, if (as it'll rarely be) it's a straight choice between fixed and capped with exactly the same rate, go for capped.

LOW SVR MORTGAGES

Not, strictly speaking, a special offer, it's a relatively new beast in the mortgage market. Rather than a cheap rate for a couple of years, the low rate lasts the entire mortgage term. The internet banks Egg and Intelligent Finance, coupled with HSBC, lead the way on these.

Sweetener: there's no need to switch lenders every few years. So for those who really don't want hassle, this is the way to go.

Rotten eggs: the SVR may be low, but it isn't anywhere near as low as the best special offers. Those willing to ride the waves of the best mortgage rates are much better off sticking

To Fix or to Discount, that is the (Big) Question.

To answer this, let me first ask you another question.

'WHICH IS MORE IMPORTANT TO YOU – SURETY OR CHEAPNESS?'

This is because discount rates are usually (though not always) cheaper, but fixed rates are safer, as, well …. they're fixed aren't they! You know exactly what you're getting, exactly what your mortgage repayments will be over the whole of the special offer period.

This therefore boils down to the 'how close to the edge are you?' question.

If you're close to the edge, fix it! Those who can only just afford mortgage repayments shouldn't gamble on interest rates. This means a fixed rate is likely to be a better option as it means you'll never be pushed over the brink if interest rates increase.

If you do go for a fixed rate for surety, then forget looking at other mortgage rates during the fix. It's pointless and you'll only regret it. Even if taking a discount might have been cheaper, it doesn't mean a fixed rate was wrong. You chose for peace of mind.

An analogy! (Primarily because I've just thought of it, and it'd be a waste not to use it!) You're in Martin's Casino, an unsophisticated place as I offer you a bet based on the toss of a coin. 'I'll give you £10 if you win, but you only need pay me £1 if you lose.'

This is a fantastic bet for you, not because the chances of winning have increased – they haven't – but because the reward for winning is much better than the cost of losing. This means, even if we tossed the coin and you lost, it was still a worthwhile bet.

The same is true with opting for a fixed rate. If it's because 'surety is important', the fact that with hindsight a discount would've been better doesn't make it the wrong decision.

Discounts are often cheaper, but it's a gamble. Yes, that's what I said, 'a discount is a gamble'. This doesn't mean I'm equating it to the roulette table, but with a discount there's a risk interest rates will change.

Those who can afford substantial increases in interest rates are more able to take the gamble of a discount rate, in the hope it'll prove to be better value. Often this does work out to be the case, but not always.

Now let me get a bit more technical. I'm about to get a bit nerdy. If that worries you, skip this bit, it isn't necessary.

It's worth considering the differential between fixed and discount rates available at any one time. Let's assume *ceteris paribus* (that's my A-level economics course coming back to me; it means 'all other things being equal') that the mortgage choice is simply between

- Two-year discount currently at 5.3 per cent
- Two-year fixed rate at 6.0 per cent

Therefore the difference between the two rates is 0.7 per cent.

Now let's factor in what happens to interest rates in the UK. Generally when they move they do so in increments of 0.25 per cent. So, for the discount to be more expensive than the fixed rate, UK base rates must rise three times.

Yet, we must also factor in the time frame. If it took the whole first year for base rates to rise three times, then the discount rate would still have been an average 0.375 per cent cheaper than the fixed rate.

And if base rates were then stable for the next year, the discount rate would only be 0.05 per cent more expensive. Over the two years in this case, the discount would still have been cheaper overall.

This means it's not just a question of 'will base rates rise three times?' but '*when* will base rates rise three times?' to make up the difference.

The surety differential. Overall this indicates the importance of what I call the 'surety differential', how much are you willing to pay for surety? The more comfortable your finances are, the less you should be willing to pay for surety.

to the short-term special offers. Plus, these tend to be SVRs, not trackers, so at some stage the bank may choose to make it

---

Money Diet Quick Fact Snack: Redemption Penalties

Many mortgage lenders tie you to their mortgage by contractually obliging you to pay a fine if you remortgage or repay the mortgage before the end of a set period. Redemption penalties are also known as 'tie-ins'. These penalties may be substantial, up to 5 per cent of your mortgage's value (in certain circumstances even more), and can seriously impede any remortgaging benefits.

There are two types:

Not so bad: Standard Redemption Penalty. Here the penalty only lasts during the initial special offer period. This used to be the norm; now some new mortgages don't have any penalties at all. However, pick a good mortgage and you won't be looking to move until after the special offer period anyway. Though if you intend to overpay (in order to pay it off more quickly) in some circumstances redemption penalties may prevent that. The main time that standard redemption penalties are a real problem is with a five-year or longer fixed-rate offer, as there's a greater likelihood your situation will change over that time.

Always avoid: Overhanging or Extended Redemption Penalties. Here you pay a penalty for switching even after the special offer has ended. This often means that even though you're paying a high SVR you are still tied in with penalties. This can completely stymie remortgaging, even for those paying massively over the odds.

Other penalty triggers. Unfortunately, it is not just remortgaging that may trigger redemption penalties. It is possible that overpaying, relocating or splitting with your partner (or anyone else on the mortgage with you) will do too; check these when you take a mortgage out.

---

less competitive. Even if you pick this nice easy mortgage life, you'll still need to keep an occasional eye on the market to make sure you are not overpaying.

Always Make Sure the End is in Sight

Whether you've a discount, fixed or tracker special offer, the most important thing is to keep a note of when it ends. It's very likely your mortgage repayments will then shoot up, as you will be moved to the standard variable rate. When this date is a minimum of three months away (after all, mortgage moves are easy to delay but difficult to speed up) look at the mortgage market and consider remortgaging (again).

Flexible Mortgages

Mortgage flexibility is chic, and rightly so – this innovation will save many people money. However, it's not necessarily for everyone. Flexible mortgages are usually at a higher rate than inflexible ones, and as each flexible feature tends to add to the cost, pick only those you'll actually use.

Money Diet Quick Fact Snack: Using a Flexible Mortgage to Get a High Rate on Your Savings

It's possible to morph your flexible mortgage to earn more on your savings. This involves combining the use of overpayment and borrow-back facilities. To do it, pay all your excess savings into your mortgage, providing they can be withdrawn whenever you choose.

As the savings temporarily pay off some of the mortgage, you pay less interest. The overall impact is the same as *earning* interest on the savings, at the mortgage rate, plus there's no tax to pay on this. Therefore, your savings should easily outperform even the highest-paying savings account on the market.

Flexible mortgages have four essential characteristics:

Overpayments. You can pay more than is needed, so the mortgage is repaid more quickly, and less interest accrues.

£100,000 repayment mortgage over 25 years at 6.5 per cent interest
- NO OVERPAYMENT – repay a total of £202,000
- OVERPAY £1 a day (£30 a month) – repay a total of £191,000 (pays off the mortgage two years earlier)
- OVERPAY £100 a month – repay a total of £172,000 (pays off the mortgage six years earlier)

Underpayments, or taking a payment holiday. Decrease your payments, or even stop them completely if you have other more pressing financial commitments or a lifestyle change, such as a new baby. Remember, though, the more slowly a mortgage is repaid, the more interest you pay in the long run.

Borrow-back. Allows you to reborrow money already repaid at the mortgage rate. This effectively allows you a personal loan – admittedly secured on your property but without application and credit score and at a much lower rate than would be available elsewhere.

Daily calculated interest. The interest on a flexible mortgage should be calculated daily, or at least monthly. This way, as soon as you contribute, the amount owed decreases and so does the interest. Calculating interest daily as opposed to annually can be the equivalent of a 0.15 per cent decrease in interest rate.

Current Account Mortgages – 'Hmmmmm'

Current account mortgages, originally popularised by the then Virgin One, are 'super-flexible'. A current account, mortgage and debts are wrapped together.

As your salary is paid directly, it automatically decreases the mortgage debt, so the interest decreases too.

You may note my 'hmmmmm' in the title: this is because while the concept is clever, the marketing of these accounts makes the benefits look a lot bigger than they really are. The most common trick is to sell them based on benefits available with all flexible mortgages, not just the additional current account features.

For example, £100,000 repayment mortgage over 25 years for someone with a £30,000 salary.

Standard mortgage: at 5.5 per cent you'd pay £614 a month.
The hype: with a current account mortgage at the same rate, pay your salary into your account and spend all of it, apart from £100 each month, and you'd save £26,000, paying the mortgage off three years and five months earlier. This is equivalent to a standard mortgage at just 4.05 per cent.
The reality: most of this gain is due to the fact the £100 left in the account each month is an overpayment – in other words, it's equivalent to upping your monthly contributions. This feature is available with any flexible (and some not so flexible) mortgage. Strip this out and you are left with the pure benefit from putting your salary in, which is just £8.70 a month, £2,600 over the term.

This means the 'current account' bit is only equivalent to a gain of 0.1 per cent in the interest rate, so if a current account mortgage is much more than 0.1 per cent more expensive than a standard flexible mortgage, which they almost always are, the gain is wiped out. Only those earning big lump sums will find the 'current account' bit more substantial.

What about Offset Mortgages?

These work in a very similar way, except rather than bundling everything up together, there are separate pots for debts and savings so you can see the difference. However, your savings are still 'off-set' against your debts.

Money Diet Money Magic: How to Flex the Inflexible

Like a chiropractor's manipulation, it is possible to encourage brittle old mortgages to bend in ways they weren't designed to. It isn't always easy, foolproof or perfect. Yet it is worth thinking about.

Overpayments. Nearly half of all flexible mortgage holders are only really concerned about the ability to overpay. By happy coincidence, this is by far the easiest to replicate, without any tricks at all, as most modern 'inflexible' mortgages permit overpayments, though lenders don't shout about it. The rules usually stipulate overpayments must be lump sums of a minimum of £250.

Always ensure it is put towards paying off the capital, as only this decreases the interest charge. The only sticking point is if the mortgage is within its redemption penalty period. Technically, overpayments may count as redeeming before the agreed time. However, it's becoming increasingly common for mortgage companies to make exceptions.

If redemption penalties hamper overpayments: There's one other trick to play. Request a decrease in the term length of your mortgage. This means the necessary monthly payments will increase, effectively working like an overpayment. It's worth noting permission to alter the term is at the lender's discretion: they'll consider whether the new repayments are affordable or if you're overstretching your finances. Usually, though, it isn't a problem. There is also sometimes a one-off admin fee of roughly £50. However, term changes tend to be permanent – they may let you switch back, but there's no guarantee – so all this needs careful consideration.

Underpayments. It's the opposite of overpaying: just lengthen the mortgage's term. It's worth remembering a longer term means permanent underpayments, and therefore the total interest charged on the mortgage will increase, but if it stops you defaulting, it may be worthwhile.

£100,000 Repayment Mortgage at 6% interest

Term (years)	Monthly repayment	Total repayment	Total interest	Compare to 25-year term
30	£605	£218,000	£118,000	£22,500 MORE
25	£652	£195,500	£95,500	N/A
20	£726	£174,000	£74,000	SAVE £21,500
15	£858	£154,500	£54,500	SAVE £41,000
10	£1,132	£136,000	£36,000	SAVE £59,500

Payment holidays. Thank heavens we're over half-way through the diet before I admit failure. I've squirmed, shaken and wriggled, but I'm scuppered. There really isn't a way to replicate a payment holiday. It is possible to use interest-free credit card special offers to pay the mortgage in the short term, but this leaves you with a debt repayment glut in the future. If you're in dire need, speak to your lender. They may allow some repayments to be missed, but it is likely this will harm any future applications for credit.

Borrow-back. To borrow back with a bog-standard mortgage, simply apply to the lender to increase the loan's size. Most allow this up to 75 per cent of your house's current value, and with the rise in house prices, for most people this isn't a big problem. For more than that, the lender may well question the loan's purpose – however, if it's for home improvements they should be more generous.

If the amount required is less than £25,000, it can put lenders off slightly as they then need to comply with the bureaucracy of the Consumer Credit Act, though again household improvement loans are exempt from this.

Barring overpayments, these solutions don't come with the ease and fluidity of a pre-packaged flexible mortgage, and those who are genuinely likely to make regular use of the features should stick with those.

While this aids financial management as everything's easier to see, the problems are identical to normal current account mortgages.

HOW MUCH WILL IT COST ME?
The Costs and Fees

1. STAMP DUTY

When you buy a property, the government usually gets a cut in the form of stamp duty. This is calculated on the value of the house, not the size of the mortgage. And it's the purchaser who pays the stamp duty.

2. PENALTIES ON YOUR CURRENT MORTGAGE (REMORTGAGES ONLY)

It's important to check there are no redemption penalties to pay your current lender. If there are, ask exactly what they will be and factor this against the gain made due to the cheaper rate. If you are close to the end of the penalty period it may be worth waiting a couple of months.

Unfortunately, if the penalties are too large it won't be worth remortgaging. But don't give up hope – a few lenders allow their 'trapped' customers to switch to a limited selection of their other mortgages – not perfect, but definitely an improvement.

If not, 'holler' (see page 129): threaten you'll pay the fine and move regardless, in the hope they'll make you a special offer. Opposite is a short letter I've drafted for you. No promises it'll work, but it definitely shouldn't hurt. Though if it doesn't work, don't feel duty bound to follow through on your threat if it'll cost you more. This is all about posturing.

Have-a-Go Hero!

Sample Letter for Those Trapped by Redemption Penalties

Mortgage Lender	My name
Profit Making House	My address
Extortionate Interest Lane	My street
Poundchester	My town
DOU 12P	My postcode

Today's date

Dear Sir/Madam,

I am writing to request further information on my mortgage policy. I currently have a **[NAME AND DETAILS OF MORTGAGE HERE, WITH REFERENCE NUMBER]**. I took this policy out on **[DATE MORTGAGE STARTED]**.

I am considering switching to another lender, as the rate it will charge me is much less than what I pay you. Please will you tell me:

a. What the redemption penalty cost will be if I switch my mortgage to another lender.

b. If there are any other costs you will add if I move mortgage.

c. If I do choose to stay with you, what better mortgages will you able to offer me than my current uncompetitive package? Please send me full details on each of these, together with examples of the new monthly costs, and details of redemption penalties or switching costs involved.

I would be very grateful for your help. I would appreciate a reply within the next 30 days.

Many thanks,

Me

Money Diet Quick Fact Snack: Get-Out-of-Jail-Free Card – 'Super-Portability'

There is a possible loophole for people trapped by redemption penalties. Some loans are 'super-portable', which means move house and you are eligible to continue with the current deal or switch to any of that lender's other offers without penalty. If you have a mortgage with penalties, simply use super-portability to move to a non-penalty mortgage, and then remortgage with another lender. One person I mentioned this to saved £4,000 on redemption penalties and cut their rate. It's a small, but valuable, loophole.

---

3. OTHER REMORTGAGING FEES

It ain't just redemption penalties. There is a range of further costs to remortgaging:

Money Diet Quick Fact Snack: Rough Guide to Remortgaging Fees

	Approximate Cost
Administration fee: this is your old lender's last snack on your cash. It charges you for the bureaucracy and paperwork involved in letting you go. (It's often also called a sealing or deeds transfer fee.)	£0–£150
Arrangement fee: paid to your new lender for setting up the mortgage. It's increased a lot in recent years.	£300–£600
Legal fee: you will need legal conveyancing when you remortgage.	£250–£400
Valuation fee: to assess whether your property is adequate security for the mortgage, the new lender will want a valuation. The bigger the house value, the bigger the fee.	£150–£500
Others: there may also be small fees for telegraphic transfer and checking insurance policies.	
TOTAL	£700–£1,650

FEES-FREE DEALS

Fees have a significant impact on working out the best deal. Many lenders offer special deals where their own fees are waived and cash is provided to pay the other fees. Fees-free mortgages tend to be, though aren't always, at a slightly higher interest rate.

Rule of thumb: the bigger the mortgage and the longer the special offer, the better off you are focusing on interest rates rather than fees-free option. As a very rough rule of thumb, with mortgages under £100,000 fees-free is better.

The Proof of the Fees-free Pudding

FEES-FREE WINNER: THE BORROWERS

Omar and Irma Borrower have a £50,000 repayment mortgage lasting for 20 more years.

Current mortgage: Barstools Bank at standard 5.95 per cent rate; no redemption penalties for moving.

Monthly repayments: £362.

Remortgage Option 1: Hardleyfixed Bank Fees-Free – 4.25 per cent fixed for two years.

Fees: no arrangement fee; legal and valuation fees are paid for you; leaving just a deed transfer fee of £50.

Fee cost: £50.

Monthly repayments: £313.

Saving over two years: £49 x 24 months = £1,180 minus £50 fee.

TOTAL SAVING = £1,130

Remortgage Option 2: Notionwide Building Society – 3.89 per cent fixed for two years.

Fees: arrangement fee £300 + combined £600 legal, valuation and deed transfer fee.

Fee cost: Estimate £900.

Monthly repayments: £302 a month.

Saving over two years: £60 x 24 months= £1,440 minus £900 fees.

TOTAL SAVING = £540

And the winner is ... the Borrowers would be £590 better off over two years taking the fees-free mortgage, compared to the cheapest-rate mortgage.

PAY-THE-FEES WINNER: THE SWITCHERS

Wanda and Walter Switcher have a £200,000 repayment mortgage lasting for 20 more years.

Current mortgage: Barstools Bank at standard 5.95 per cent rate, no redemption penalties for moving.

Monthly repayments: £1,447.

Remortgage Option 1: Hardleyfixed Bank Fees-Free at 4.25 per cent fixed for two years.

Fees: no arrangement fee; legal and valuation fee are paid for you; leaving just a deed transfer fee of £50.

Fee cost: £50.

Monthly repayments: £1,254.

Saving over two years: £193 x 24 months = £4,630 minus £50 fee.

TOTAL SAVING = £4,580

Remortgage Option 2: Notionwide Building Society at 3.85 per cent fixed for two years.

Fees: arrangement fee £300 + combined £650 legal, valuation and deed transfer fee.

Fee cost: estimate £1,000.

Monthly repayments: £1,207 a month.

Saving over two years: £240 x 24 months = £5,760 minus £950 fees = £4,810.

TOTAL SAVING = £4,810

And the winner is ... the Switchers would be £180 better off going for the cheapest rate Notionwide mortgage compared to the fees-free mortgage.

HOW MUCH WILL I SAVE?
First-time Mortgage

Ask the lender for the cost of monthly payments including any Higher Lending Charge (see page 331), and compare. Ensure you are comparing like with like, though. For example, if you are planning to pay a higher deposit with one than the other, it's unfair to compare the monthly payments.

Remortgage Savings: Calorie Counter

There are some simple steps to follow to find out a rough answer. To aid in the calculation there's a Money Diet Mortgage Calorie Counter. Though before committing get accurate figures done.

Step 1. Use the Ready Reckoner in the following pages to find the size of your mortgage and the decrease in interest rates the new mortgage offers over the old one.

E.g. £65,000 repayment mortgage decreased by two percentage points is a saving of £76 a month.

Step 2. Multiply the monthly saving by the length of the special offer.

E.g. The special offer lasts two-and-a-half years (30 months), so the saving is £2,280.

Step 3. Take off the cost of any redemption penalties.

E.g. There are redemption penalties of 1 per cent of the mortgage size, which equals £650. Therefore the saving is reduced to £1,630.

Step 4. Take off the cost of any remortgaging and broker fees for the specific mortgage.

E.g. This mortgage is mostly fees-free, so the total fees add up to only £200. Therefore the saving is reduced to £1,430 over the two-and-a-half years. This is equivalent to an actual saving of £48 a month or £570 a year. Well worth it.

Money Diet Mortgage Calorie Counter

These tables are based on an original mortgage rate of 6 per cent. They are not completely accurate for other interest rates, but should give you an idea.

Repayment, monthly interest

	£20,000		£30,000		£50,000		£65,000	
	Monthly Saving	Annual Saving	Monthly Saving	Annual Saving	Monthly Saving	Annual Saving	Monthly Saving	Annual Saving
0.25%	£4	£46	£5	£55	£8	£91	£10	£119
0.50%	£8	£91	£9	£109	£15	£181	£20	£236
1.00%	£15	£179	£18	£215	£30	£358	£39	£466
1.50%	£22	£265	£27	£318	£44	£531	£58	£690
2.00%	£29	£349	£35	£419	£58	£699	£76	£908
3.00%	£43	£510	£51	£612	£85	£1,021	£111	£1,327
4.00%	£55	£661	£66	£794	£110	£1,323	£143	£1,719

	£100,000		£150,000		£200,000		£500,000	
	Monthly Saving	Annual Saving	Monthly Saving	Annual Saving	Monthly Saving	Annual Saving	Monthly Saving	Annual Saving
0.25%	£15	£182	£23	£274	£30	£365	£76	£912
0.50%	£30	£363	£45	£544	£60	£725	£151	£1,813
1.00%	£60	£717	£90	£1,075	£119	£1,433	£299	£3,583
1.50%	£88	£1,062	£133	£1,592	£177	£2,123	£442	£5,308
2.00%	£116	£1,398	£175	£2,096	£233	£2,795	£582	£6,988
3.00%	£170	£2,041	£255	£3,062	£340	£4,082	£850	£10,205
4.00%	£220	£2,645	£331	£3,968	£441	£5,291	£1,102	£13,227

Interest only

	£20,000		£30,000		£50,000		£65,000	
	Monthly Saving	Annual Saving	Monthly Saving	Annual Saving	Monthly Saving	Annual Saving	Monthly Saving	Annual Saving
0.25%	£5	£63	£6	£75	£10	£125	£14	£163
0.50%	£10	£125	£13	£150	£21	£250	£27	£325
1.00%	£21	£250	£25	£300	£42	£500	£54	£650
1.50%	£31	£375	£38	£450	£63	£750	£81	£975
2.00%	£42	£500	£50	£600	£83	£1,000	£108	£1,300
3.00%	£63	£750	£75	£900	£125	£1,500	£163	£1,950
4.00%	£83	£1,000	£100	£1,200	£167	£2,000	£217	£2,600

	£100,000		£150,000		£200,000		£500,000	
	Monthly Saving	Annual Saving	Monthly Saving	Annual Saving	Monthly Saving	Annual Saving	Monthly Saving	Annual Saving
0.25%	£21	£250	£31	£375	£42	£500	£104	£1,250
0.50%	£42	£500	£63	£750	£83	£1,000	£208	£2,500
1.00%	£83	£1,000	£125	£1,500	£167	£2,000	£417	£5,000
1.50%	£125	£1,500	£188	£2,250	£250	£3,000	£625	£7,500
2.00%	£167	£2,000	£250	£3,000	£333	£4,000	£833	£10,000
3.00%	£250	£3,000	£375	£4,500	£500	£6,000	£1,250	£15,000
4.00%	£333	£4,000	£500	£6,000	£667	£8,000	£1,667	£1,667

WHERE TO GET FURTHER ADVICE – INDEPENDENT MORTGAGE BROKERS

Mortgage brokers are specialist advisers; it's well worth getting their help. For more details, see 'Get Mortgage Advice for Free' (page 269).

ADVERSE CREDIT MORTGAGES: HOW TO GET A MORTGAGE IF YOU HAVE A POOR CREDIT HISTORY

Normally mortgage companies lust after your business, but if you've a poor credit history they often won't play. It's not personal, just the result of computer predictions of your behaviour (see page 310 for more details).

What is Adverse Credit?

Adverse credit means anything that doesn't follow the usual pattern. The absolute worst case is a history of repossession, though a CCJ (County Court Judgement) or debt arrears can count too. Annoyingly, just being self-employed could mean you need to get a specialist mortgage.

Adverse credit doesn't always mean you are forced to pay hugely over the odds. These days even some high-street lenders will still give you a mortgage, though their criteria are strict. In all cases a big deposit will help.

WHAT TO DO?

Using a mortgage broker (see page 269) is a big advantage, though you need to be careful. In general, avoid those that 'specialise' in adverse credit; often they're just there to take advantage. Some dodgy mortgage brokers are fronts for expensive sub-prime lenders. These offer mortgages to higher-risk borrowers rejected by the high-street lot, and stay profitable because they charge higher interest rates (which, they argue, reflect that risk).

Of course, the worse your credit history, the more they charge. If you do have an adverse credit history it is often worth waiting a year before trying for a mortgage and making treble-sure you meet all your repayments and use some of my credit score improvement tricks (page 316) in the meantime. This can make a big difference to the mortgage cost.

ADVERSE-CREDIT MORTGAGES AREN'T GOALS IN THEMSELVES

I tend not to think of sub-prime mortgages as a goal in themselves, but a sometimes-necessary way of rehabilitating credit. If it is necessary to get one of these higher-rate mortgages, ensure all the payments are met. Then, after a few years, you should be able to remortgage to a normal lender.

However, it's time for a BIG warning: there are some real sharks in this game, aiming to screw people in vulnerable situations and squeeze hideous amounts of cash out, so be incredibly careful.

THINGS TO WATCH FOR IF YOU'RE GETTING A 'SUB-PRIME' MORTGAGE

Interest rate. At its extreme this should never be more than four percentage points above UK bank base rates (see page 333) and even that's pushing it. If possible try for a lender whose standard mortgage rate is set in relationship to either UK base rates, or the interbank lending rate (known as LIBOR), rather than an SVR.

Redemption penalties (see page 338). They're almost unavoidable in the sub-prime market, but ensure they don't last for more than three years. Longer penalties would prevent you from remortgaging after rehabilitating your credit.

Avoiding missed repayment penalties. Another big warning: don't ever get a mortgage with increased-interest penalty clauses for missed repayments. These can spiral you into disaster, heaping on bigger debts at the worst time. Some nasty operators structure their loans to maximise the chance of repossessing your property.

Do You Really Need a Mortgage?

I don't like being a party pooper, but if the mortgage is expensive it's very important to question whether it's worth buying a home at all. Stop and clinically consider if you can truly afford the repayments and, more importantly, whether you could afford them if interest rates rose by, say, 3 per cent. If not, you're trapping yourself into further debilitating debt and running the risk of losing any home you buy.

three

SNACKS

THE PRECISION PLASTIC GUIDE TO THE PERFECT CREDIT CARDS

They say don't show favouritism to any of your children, but, alas, I can't help it. This chapter is my baby. There are three types of credit-card user. I'll show you how to work out which type you are and then how to play the system in each case.

WHAT'S THE BEST CREDIT CARD?

On the bus, at a party, on a television programme, eating at a Chinese restaurant, talking to a taxi driver or buying something at my local shop – there is one question I'm asked without fail. 'What is the best credit card?' I've learned to stifle the exasperated scream trying to erupt from my stomach.

Don't think I mind being asked questions; I love what I do and am happy to help. People recognising me on the street and saying hello is a compliment (much better than surreptitious glances which leave me wondering whether it's because they've seen me on the telly or because my flies are undone). No, the reason I hate this particular question is I don't know the answer!

Before you cry, 'Fraud! I've heard him introduced as the Dumbledore of Debt and he knows nothing,' the reason I can't answer is ...

There is no one-size-fits-all credit card.

Credit cards involve not just multiple interest rates, but a range of benefits, gimmicks and fringe uses too. All these factors can be used to sell us a card, but most cards are worthwhile for only one or two purposes. To beat the system you need a number of different ones – personally I keep six or seven active cards, but three is fine.

Yet don't just jump straight in and turn to the 'what to do' bits. The most important thing is to know what type of credit card person you are. Read the 'potential player', 'credit survivor', 'debt crisis' test on page 364.

BACK TO BASICS: WHAT IS A CREDIT CARD?

The plastic in your pocket is one of two very different animals: debit or credit cards. A debit card is a bit like an electronic cheque, so when you pay, the money is taken straight from your bank account. With a credit card (or store card, which is a limited-use credit card) you run up a bill for the month's spending. Then you either pay it off in full, so there's no interest charged, or you pay off a proportion of the bill, and interest is charged on the entire month's borrowing.

Use the right card correctly and credit cards have many advantages over debit cards: extra consumer protection, the ability to delay payment, earn rewards and more (all are covered

---

Money Diet Quick Fact Snack: Hurdle Over a Cash Hump with a Credit Card

Almost all credit cards are interest-free for short-term borrowing – regardless of the published interest rate. Use it to buy something and the cash stays in your bank account until you pay it off. This is a useful way to delay or spread payments over a short time at no cost. It is possible to have nearly 60 days from the time you spend until the time the money must leave your account (about two weeks after you receive your statement). However, ensure you can pay off the entire bill in full, as leave even just £1 unpaid and you will be charged interest on the whole outstanding amount – negating any benefit.

---

here). However, use the wrong card badly and all these are massively outweighed by one big disadvantage: expensive debt.

As a footnote, there is a third type of plastic – charge cards, the most famous of which is the green American Express card (though Amex also has credit cards, don't get confused). These are a hybrid between debit and credit cards. You spend, build up a bill, and every month must pay it off in full. However, in truth, except for business people, this type of card has limited merit.

Visa and MasterCard (and Amex)

'What credit card do you have?' If you just answered 'Visa' or 'MasterCard', we've work to do – almost undoubtedly you've the wrong plastic. You should've answered who the provider is. Is it a Barclaycard? HSBC? First Direct? Associates? They set the interest rates and terms, so this is where the difference lies. If you don't know, then undoubtedly you chose it for the wrong reason.

Visa and MasterCard are card-transaction companies; they do the processing when you buy or pay for things, and send

> **Money Diet Quick Fact Snack: When is it Right to Answer 'Visa' or 'MasterCard'?**
>
> While the rate you get depends on the card brand, its acceptability relies on the type of card. Therefore when you're paying for something and someone asks, 'What's the card type?', then it's correct to answer 'MasterCard', 'Visa', 'Amex' or 'Diners Club'.

back the details to the card-provider. The actual differences between them are virtually nil; just a few technical issues. There may be slightly more significant issues of acceptability when you travel abroad, but I wouldn't let it impact the choice of card.

American Express (Amex) is slightly different. It generally offers its own and affiliated cards, so you can't get a Barclaycard Amex, for example. Also, American Express is accepted less often in the UK than Visa or MasterCard, so sometimes paying for a meal on it is tough. Most of this revolves around the way the three companies charge retailers, but I shall restrain myself from information overload on that right now.

HOW CARD PROVIDERS MAKE THEIR MONEY

The big bucks come from interest earned on money lent. And when I say big, I mean BIG! Some cards have more interest than Melinda Messenger would generate at a stag night.

> **Martin's Money Memories: Oops, Oops, Grin! Sorry Melinda**
>
> I've just had one of those 'oh no' moments, updating the book. After the first edition was published I worked with the lovely Melinda a couple of times and she asked to read the book. I'd entirely forgotten the above sentence. Let's hope she skipped it.

Fines, Grand Designs and Transaction Fees

Interest isn't the only credit-card-provider income stream:

Fines. Late-payment fines, cash-withdrawal fees and other penalties all add to their coffers. The easiest way to avoid a late-payment fine is to use a direct debit. For those who automatically pay off the bill in full, this is easy. If you can't afford to do that, at the very least set up a direct debit to make the minimum repayments. You can (and should where possible) always add to the payment by sending a cheque each month, but at least this way you'll never be fined.

If you are fined, most lenders will usually wipe the fee (the first time at least) if you call them and say you honestly forgot; just ask – surely £25 is worth the phone call.

One final thing to check: some providers want 'cleared funds' in their account by the deadline day. This means your cheque needs to reach them at least three days before the deadline date, to prevent a fine.

Grand designs. To squeeze every last pound from us, plastic-providers try to flog us two additional extras.

■ *Repayment protection insurance, in the event of accident, sickness or unemployment.* Often this is automatically included, so you actively need to tell them if you don't want it. This is expensive protection; it's usually proportionally much cheaper to use a general 'income-replacement policy' which pays a proportion of your salary if such problems arise.

■ *Card protection* is the other oft-sold plan. Here if you lose your card(s) and make one call, all will be cancelled. You can always call all of your card providers yourself, but some

---

Money Diet Quick Fact Snack: WOW! How Much They Charge in Interest

This really is worth a moment's consideration. The average high-street bank charges around 17 per cent on credit-card debts, yet pays just 0.1 per cent on interest on the money kept in its current account. Now think about this: when you keep money in a current or savings account, you are effectively lending the bank money. It can take this cash and lend it out to someone else, or, worse still, back to you, as credit-card debt. Admittedly banks have expenses, but in simple terms, over a year:

Lend it £1,000 in your current account and it pays you £1 (80p after tax).

It lends you £1,000 as credit-card debt and you pay it £170.

Almost makes you want to become a banker, doesn't it?

---

like the peace of mind. Remember, as they usually deal with all your cards, don't sign up for a policy with more than one card provider. Plus 'advanced' and 'premier' packages are often pants, offering little more for a lot more cost. Be careful – sometimes you'll find your cover is automatically 'upgraded'; do always check whether there's a cheaper option available and ask to downgrade.

Transaction fees. Almost every time a transaction is made, retailers pay up to 2.5 per cent of the spending to the card company, generating revenue even from those people who never pay interest. Ultimately we pay for this in the form of higher retail prices. However, the transaction fee is often used to offset the cost of credit-card reward schemes. Use one of these correctly and you'll gain. (See page 377.)

There's a final, less tangible, benefit for providers – credit cards allow banks to 'cross-sell'. This means they use the data gleaned from your credit-card custom to build a profile on you and try and flog you other goods.

Martin's Quick Fact Snack: Minimum Payments – Danger, Warning, Red Flag, Careful, Stop, Watch Out. Noooooooooo!

You may've just gathered by the title that I've a tiny wee issue with only making minimum payments on a credit card. You see they're a deviously clever scheme designed by mathematicians to make you think you're paying off your debts, while secretly allowing the debt to linger ... and linger ... and linger (and linger).

A definition. The minimum payment is the amount you must pay off a credit-card debt each month or you'll be fined. Rather than a fixed payment it is usually a set percentage of the outstanding debt, commonly 2 or 3 per cent with a £5 minimum. On direct debit forms it's always included in the options as it's by far the most profitable for credit-card providers.

Why is it dangerous? You're only repaying a percentage of your outstanding debt, so as your debt decreases, so does the amount you repay. This has some startling consequences when you look at the numbers.

The Example: Mr Roger De Bydebt
Credit Card Interest Rate: 17.9 per cent (pretty standard).
Outstanding Balance: £3,000.
Minimum Payment: The higher of 2 per cent or £5.
Roger's strapped for cash and has therefore decided he can only afford the initial £60 minimum repayment. Unfortunately, he hasn't read *The Money Diet* so he doesn't know cheaper debt's available elsewhere.

Roger's debt repayments decrease with his debts. At first this doesn't look too severe, as the table opposite shows.

Roger De Bydebt's Repayments
£3,000 debt at 17.9% minimum payments 2 per cent.

After	Minimum Payment
1 Month	£60
2 Months	£59.60
12 Months	£56
60 Months (5 years)	£41
120 Months (10 years)	£28
240 Months (20 years)	£14
360 Months (30 years)	£6

Yet the amount repaid quickly drops too. As the payments get smaller the interest continues to compound. This means even if Roger never spent on the card again, and just made the minimum repayments, it would take him 40 years and 5 months to pay off the debt and cost £6,300 in interest. Minimum repayments are credit-card companies' perfect method to keep us perpetually in debt, and them reaping the interest.

The only time it is worth sticking with them is if you are following the 'free cash from credit cards' technique (see page 387).

An easy solution. Okay, Roger's got no cash – so telling him to pay it all off now won't work. Yet there's a simple trick that makes a huge difference. We know he can afford to repay the £60 a month, as that was the first month's minimum repayment. If he sticks with paying a fixed £60/month, rather than the minimum payments, it would have a massive impact, saving him over £4,000.

Time for another table:

What a Difference 'the Pay' Makes
£3,000 debt at 17.9%

Repaying	Time Taken to Repay in Full	Interest Cost
Minimum (2% or £5)	40 years	£6,300
£60/month	7 years	£2,100
£80/month	4 years 6 months	£1,250
£120/month	2 years 7 months	£700
£240/month	1 year 3 months	£315

By simply repaying the initial £60 a month every month, his debts are repaid in seven years, not 40, and the interest cost is reduced by two-thirds.

ARE YOU A POTENTIAL PLAYER, A CREDIT SURVIVOR OR IN DEBT CRISIS?

To decide the way to play the system, first work out exactly what type of credit-card user you are. This, unfortunately, isn't your choice; it's determined by your financial situation.

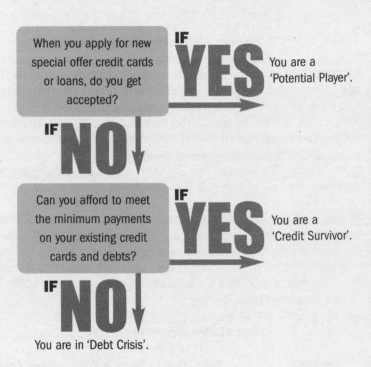

When you apply for new special offer credit cards or loans, do you get accepted?

IF YES You are a 'Potential Player'.

IF NO

Can you afford to meet the minimum payments on your existing credit cards and debts?

IF YES You are a 'Credit Survivor'.

IF NO

You are in 'Debt Crisis'.

To Explain:

POTENTIAL PLAYERS

Who? Anyone who can apply for new credit cards, and scores well enough to get introductory offers.

Why? You're a 'player' because do it right and you can beat the system.

What to avoid? Choosing the wrong cards – worse than allowing your children to turn your cash into papier-mâché (at least that way they get some enjoyment out of it).

What to read? 'The Potential Player's Precision Plastic Guide' (page 366). 'Free Cash' (page 387). However, even potential players can gain by reading 'The Credit Card Shuffle' (page 391) too, as it offers good hints for general credit-card housekeeping and saves you over-applying for credit.

CREDIT SURVIVORS

Who? Anyone meeting their current debt repayments, but who is rejected from all new special-offer cards.

Why? You're surviving – but could thrive, by rejigging existing debts and minimising your interest.

What to read? 'The Credit Survival Technique' (page 391).

DEBT CRISIS

Who? Those who can't meet current debt repayments and can't get any new mainstream credit (ignoring specialist consolidation or 'rate for risk' loans).

Why? Missing repayments causes debt problems to spiral. The amount owed could increase due to fines, and unless you act, the debts could get critical. Deal with it immediately; it's a priority.

Is it unsolvable? No. There are no quick fixes, but people do successfully improve their situation, rehabilitate their credit and get back on track. Realising you are in debt crisis is a massive first step.

What to read? 'Food Poisoning' (page 411).

THE POTENTIAL PLAYER'S PRECISION PLASTIC GUIDE
Be at the Cutting Edge

There's no such thing as a bad credit card, just a bad credit-card user. Use the right card for the right purpose and you'll win. Get it wrong and they'll skin you for every penny. Shifting when it suits you, not them, makes you a 'credit-card tart'. If you're a potential player (see page 364), then pick a card, any card.

DIY Credit Card Rough Calorie Counter – How Much Will You Save?			
Decrease in interest	£1,000 debt over 1 year	£5,000 debt over 3 years	£10,000 debt over 5 years
1%	SAVE £10	SAVE £151	SAVE £510
3%	SAVE £30	SAVE £463	SAVE £1,592
5%	SAVE £50	SAVE £788	SAVE £2,763
10%	SAVE £100	SAVE £1,655	SAVE £6,105
18%	SAVE £180	SAVE £3,215	SAVE £12,877
32%	SAVE £320	SAVE £6,500	SAVE £30,075

How to Be a Tart: Picking Your Premier Plastic
(card types detailed in following pages)

Do you already have debts on your current cards?

IF YES

Balance Transfer Card
Shift your debt to a new card with a special rate. Use a separate card for spending on – follow the 'NO' path to decide which one.

IF NO

Do you regularly spend on a credit card?

IF NO

Reward Card
Even if you've never used a credit card before, providing you have a little discipline, you should start. Credit cards paid off in full each month are a more rewarding weapon than cash or debit cards and you gain additional consumer protection.

IF YES

Do you pay off the bill in full each month?

IF YES

Reward Card (see above).

IF NO

Are you happy to change cards every six months or so?

IF YES

Purchases Card: Best Intro Rate
Be a tart. Use the card which offers the best introductory rate for purchases – hopefully at 0%.

IF NO

Purchases Card: Lowest Standard Rate
If you prefer a 'stable relationship', stick to the credit card with the lowest possible standard rate.

Who's My Baby? Picking Cards for Specific Uses
(card types detailed in following pages)

Your main card isn't right for every use. I'm not suggesting you have every type of card, but think through which of these events are common in your life, and pick secondary cards accordingly.

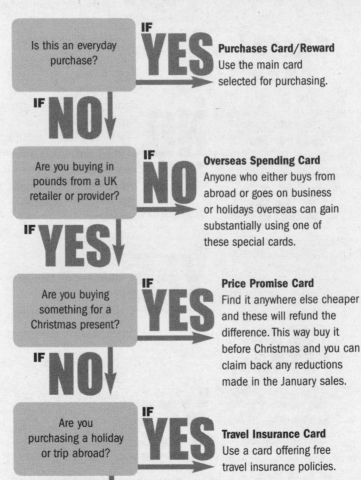

Is this an everyday purchase?

IF YES → **Purchases Card/Reward**
Use the main card selected for purchasing.

IF NO ↓

Are you buying in pounds from a UK retailer or provider?

IF NO → **Overseas Spending Card**
Anyone who either buys from abroad or goes on business or holidays overseas can gain substantially using one of these special cards.

IF YES ↓

Are you buying something for a Christmas present?

IF YES → **Price Promise Card**
Find it anywhere else cheaper and these will refund the difference. This way buy it before Christmas and you can claim back any reductions made in the January sales.

IF NO ↓

Are you purchasing a holiday or trip abroad?

IF YES → **Travel Insurance Card**
Use a card offering free travel insurance policies.

IF NO ↓ **Main Card**
Stick with your main card for all other transactions.

The Card Types: Detailed Recipes

The very best card of each type changes with pulse-raising speed. As in the Crash Diet, each category has 'suggested ingredients', yet things change, so always follow the logic when you pick and I include direct links to articles on my website which are updated weekly with the top picks. I compile the best buys there manually, not by computer selection. This is important. Cards are too complicated to categorise by numbers.

PURCHASES CARDS

Credit cards are perfect for borrowing as they're extremely flexible, allowing you to borrow what you need and pay back when you can. They charge interest on the entire amount borrowed if you don't clear the debt in full. Therefore borrow £1,000 and repay £950 and you will pay interest on the entire £1,000 for that month. If you had been able to find the extra £50 you wouldn't have paid anything at all. For anyone who borrows without always clearing the debt in full, even for just two or three months a year, then by far the most important consideration is the interest cost.

If you've got a good credit-card score and are willing to put the effort in to play the system, then follow the tarts system below. If not, go for the stable relationship option.

Money Diet Quick Fact Snack: Cards that Charge Even When Paid Off in Full

A very small number of cards charge interest even if you pay the bill in full. These should be avoided. The way to tell is if they don't have the usual 40–60 day interest-free repayment period that is standard on most cards (separate to interest-free introductory offers). Lloyds TSB, Halifax and MBNA have some of this type of card on offer.

Purchases: be a tart. This is the cutting-edge method, and it's way cheaper than any other. If you want to be a tart (and who wouldn't?), the rules are simple. Be wantonly disloyal and brazenly switch to the best new offers. There are usually more than 40 mainstream cards offering 0 per cent introductory interest rates.

Top tarts can keep the interest they're charged at 0 per cent as at the end of the special offer, they simply apply for a new offer and shift the existing debt. This doesn't mean they don't pay the card back – there is always a necessary minimum monthly repayment (usually 3 per cent of the outstanding balance or £5, whichever is greater). It's also necessary to be careful of the impact on your credit score (see page 312). Choosing the right tart card is easy – just ask 'Who gives new cardholders 0 per cent interest for the longest amount of time?' A standard offer is six months, but nine months and a year are becoming more common.

Tarting takes effort and organisation, but it pays. Always remember to take precautions, though: note down when the

Calorie Counter: Purchase Card		
Spend £500/month over a year, repaying only the minimum each month [1]	Interest rate	Interest cost
High-street card	18.9%	£540
Stable relationship card	7% [2]	£200
0% intro rate for 6 months followed by 15%	0%, 15%	£300
Tart: Two 0% intro rates for 6 months	0% [3]	£0

(1) making 3% or £5 monthly minimum repayments (2) lowest possible rate (3) debts shifted to a new 0% intro offer started after first intro rate ends

> **Money Diet Wealth Warning: Store Cards – The Devil's Debts**
>
> With store cards like Burtons, BHS or Kwik-Fit you can spend only in a specific store or group. Interest rates can be upwards of 30 per cent. There is never an excuse for borrowing on a store card; even the very few that don't charge horrendous rates are no better than average high-street credit cards. For stores these cards are gold dust. They sell you the goods, get their cut of the interest, and can build up valuable information on your spending. Avoid them or, better still, get your own back (see 'Financial Fitness', page 147).

0 per cent rate ends in your diary; put it on a Post-it stuck on the wall or write it on a loved one's forehead; and make sure the debt is paid off or moved. Fail to do this and all your tarting gains will be washed away as the interest rate shoots up and you have to pay. (See 'Know Thyself', page 63, for the impact of bad tarting.)

Suggested ingredients. NatWest; Egg; Mint; Sainsbury's; Halifax; Morgan Stanley; MBNA; Tesco; Nationwide; Lloyds TSB; Accucard; RBS

Updated info: www.moneysavingexpert.com/purchases

Purchases: stable relationships. Tarting isn't easy in any walk of life; it takes time and effort and can impact your reputation, in this case to gain credit. The alternative is a stable relationship; simply find as low a 'non-promotional' rate as possible – under 10 per cent is a must but under 7 per cent is sometimes possible. Do remember most standard rates are variable, so technically they could change over time, though competitive standard-rate providers tend to stay competitive – but still always monitor what you're paying.

Tart Alert .

If you're on the internet go to www.moneysavingexpert.com/tart for a free e-mail/text reminder six weeks before your card ends.

Suggested ingredients. Capital One; Co-Op; Northern Rock; Cahoot; Intelligent Finance; Smile.

Updated info: www.moneysavingexpert.com/purchases

BALANCE TRANSFER CARDS

Anyone paying interest for existing debts on a credit card or, worse still, on a store card should immediately consider a balance transfer – a shrinking potion for interest bills. Transferring a balance means the new provider pays off the debts on your current cards for you, so you now owe it the money instead, at a hopefully lower interest rate. When you apply for a new card with a balance-transfer special offer, tell the new provider what cards and debts you have and it should pay them off for you up to its credit limit.

Tarts' transfers. There's a horde of cards offering 0 per cent transfers for six to nine months for new cardholders; after that the interest reverts to the card's standard rate. Work out if you can pay the debt off within the 0 per cent time period. If the answer is yes, then whether you want to tart or not this is the right method, as since you're not being charged interest it's easier to pay off more quickly.

If you can't repay within the 0 per cent period, these cards can still be useful. Shift your debt to another 0 per cent balance-transfer card every time the special offer ends. Those with good credit scores can continue to use this method for a substantial number of years.

Money Diet Quick Fact Snack: Practical Balance Transfers

As balance transferring is so important, let me re-emphasise the ease of the process.

Current debt: £3,000 on Richbank card at 17 per cent.

New card: Coolbank with a 0 per cent nine-month balance-transferring offer. What happens? You ask Coolbank to do a balance transfer to your Richbank card. Coolbank then pays £3,000 into your Richbank account. Now Richbank is paid off and you owe Coolbank the money.

You should always transfer in the month before the special offer ends, to avoid all interest charges. Therefore apply for a new card around four to six weeks before the introductory offer ends. One common mistake is to think that as the interest is 0 per cent you needn't repay anything; you still need to meet the card's minimum repayments.

Choosing a card. It used to be a simple question of the longer the 0 per cent offer the better, yet many cards now have balance-transfer fees.

This means while you're not charged interest you pay 2 per cent (usually capped at £50) of the amount of the money transferred as a fee. This fee is added to your 0 per cent debts.

It's the BEST 0 per cent no-fee that counts. Go for the longest 0 per cent period possible with no fee. Even a short 0 per cent that's fees-free still beats a long 0 per cent with fee, as you can always transfer again to another interest-free card when the special offer ends.

Two quick tips. Before your special offer period ends, try calling the card company and asking for an extension. It doesn't always work, but you may just find you get 0 per cent for longer with no extra effort (see 'The Credit Card Shuffle', page 391 for more details on existing-customer balance transfers).

Be mindful when transferring balances to different cards which are managed by the same company; for example Virgin, Alliance & Leicester and Abbey cards are run by MBNA (look in the terms and conditions to find out). This can impact on the offer you are given, as the company will look at its total exposure to your risk.

Suggested ingredients. Capital One; Halifax; Morgan Stanley; Tesco Visa; Nationwide; Lloyds TSB; NatWest; RBS

Updated info: www.moneysavingexpert.com/balancetransfers

Lazy transfers. For anyone with longer-lasting debts for whom tarting by rotating 0 per cent offers isn't going to happen, use 'life-of-balance' transfer cards, where the special-offer rate lasts

---

Money Diet Quick Fact Snack: 'Super Balance Transfers'

A number of cards offer what I call 'super balance transfers'. This means that rather than just allowing balance transfers to pay off another card's debts, they also provide a facility officially demarcated to pay off an overdraft, which actually allows you to pay the money into your current account. This is a very effective mechanism for getting cheap and flexible debt, as once the money is in your current account you can use it to pay off whatever you want. Or you could just earn interest on money lent to you for 0 per cent (see 'Free Cash', page 387).

Suggested ingredients. Egg; Abbey; Virgin; Mint. (However, do check this counts as a balance transfer. Some of these providers have hinted they may stop allowing free SBTs soon.)

Calorie Counter: Balance Transfer Cards			
£5,000 debt over 6 months (just making the minimum 3% repayments)			
Card	Interest rate	Interest cost	Saving
High-street card	17.4%	£390	–
Transfer to a 0% rate for 6 months	0%	£0	£390
£7,500 debt paying £225/month until balance is cleared			
Card	Time taken to repay	Interest cost	Saving
High-street card (18.9%)	46 months	£2,840	–
Life-of-balance transfer at 4.9%	37 months	£560	£2,280
Continual tarting at 0% (if possible)	34 months	£0	£2,840

until the entire balance transferred has been paid off. The rates
can be as low as 2.9 per cent during special promotions, but the
usual best offer is around 4.9 per cent. These represent an easy
and very effective way to cut the cost of debts. Again, you must
make the minimum payments, but it is a way to be assured of
low interest if you are prepared to transfer.

Interestingly, the best life-of-balance transfer rates are lower
than the lowest standard rate for purchases. This means if
you're not a tart but need to make a big credit-card purchase,
spend on your normal card, then move it to a life-of-balance
transfer card immediately for a perpetually lower rate.

Suggested ingredients. Blue American Express; Lloyds TSB
Advance; British Airways American Express; Capital One
(certain cards); HSBC; Barclaycard; Mint.

Updated info: www.moneysavingexpert.com/balancetransfers

Money Diet Wealth Warning: Misbalanced Transfers

There are two major potential problems with balance transfers. Both occur when the special offer is only for balance transfers, not normal spending – something especially common with 'Lazy Transfers'.

Problem 1: The Obvious. Balance transfers and purchases count as separate transaction types. Therefore things bought on the card are NOT at the cheap balance transfer rate (e.g. 4.9 per cent), but at the higher spending rate (e.g. 18 per cent).

Problem 2: The Devious. When you repay the card, the card company can choose what happens to your repayments. Usually it chooses to pay off the cheap (4.9 per cent) debt first. This means you're not repaying the expensive (18 per cent) spending debts at all. They sit there with the interest growing and growing, and there's nothing you can do apart from pay all the balance transfer debts first.

This has such an impact that in most circumstances even using your balance transfer card only for balance transfers, and another card at a higher interest rate (e.g. 20 per cent) for spending is actually cheaper – as you can choose to prioritise paying off the more expensive debts first.

So, how do I put this subtly ...?

Never, ever, ever, ever, ever, ever, ever spend on a card with a special offer only for balance transfers. Just transfer the balance, then lock the card away, cut it up or eat it. *(Safety note for any precocious children reading – 'eat it' is just for emphasis, not genuine advice!)*

Similarly, though it's less common, if a card just has a special rate for purchases, never do a balance transfer on it. If the special-offer rate is for both, you're fine, providing it lasts the same length of time. (See 'The great Barclaycard 0 per cent for life loophole', page 152.)

REWARD SCHEME CARDS – SOMETHING FOR NOTHING

This is where it gets fun. Anyone who doesn't need to borrow on a credit card can make money in a simple way, so if you don't have plastic, it's time to get it. (For a less easy, but more profitable way, see 'Free Cash', page 387). Credit-card reward schemes provide flights, days out, vouchers or cash to reward you for spending on the card. The more spent, the more you collect.

Pay in full or be a fool. There's a golden rule – only ever pick a card based on loyalty schemes if you pay the balance off in full every month without fail. Then you avoid any interest charges. Crucial, as the gains from even the best reward schemes are massively outweighed by any interest.

To avoid accidental interest charges, set up a direct debit to automatically pay off the card in full. This isn't always easy – providers' forms may just have boxes for 'minimum monthly repayments' and 'pay a fixed amount'. However, cross these out and write 'pay off in full each month' and most card companies will honour it – but do always phone to check it has been set up.

The other possible hurdle, an annual fee, is mainly a thing of the past. If there is an annual fee, it will suck back any reward gain, so keep away.

You're paid to spend. For those who do pay in full, reward schemes are something for nothing as you gain each time you spend on the credit card. Therefore forget cash, forget debit cards; always use your reward credit card! And be paid every time you spend. (It is very rare for rewards to be paid on balance transfers or cash withdrawals.)

Money Diet Quick Fact Snack: It's Always Good to Have Protection

Another advantage of credit cards over cash or debit cards is an additional legal protection due to Section 75 of the Consumer Credit Act, cunningly known as 'Section 75 protection'. While the name isn't sexy, the result is. Buy anything costing over £100, and pay even just some of it on a credit card, and the card company is jointly liable with the retailer for the sale. Thus, if the retailer goes bust or the goods aren't delivered, the credit-card company may have to step in to compensate you.

When points don't make the prize choice. There are two types of credit-card reward scheme – cashback and points. Cashback is simple: a proportion of your spending is returned to you in cash. Usually it's totalled up and paid annually, either on the anniversary of the account opening or a fixed date. With points schemes, points or miles are awarded for spending and may be used to redeem gifts, flights, trips, days out or holidays. The reason most reward cards pay points is because this completely mystifies the actual value of the reward itself. There's a feel-good factor for getting points, but it's often false.

On the other hand, cashback has two huge advantages: you know exactly how much it is worth, and it's flexible. Even the widest-ranging scheme, AirMiles, is massively restrictive compared to the spending range of cold hard cash.

Actually comparing rewards schemes is excruciatingly difficult. Trust me, I've now spent more than one depressing Christmas fortnight analysing the real value of the 50-plus different schemes on the market. (It felt like even if I picked my nose, points would drop out.) The results further bolstered the standing of cashback, its average value being substantially higher than rewards. The reason is simple: it's easy to see if you're getting a bad cashback deal, so they don't try it on as much.

Suggested ingredients: **the best-paying reward schemes.** Reward-card schemes tend not to change too often, but when they do the changes can be substantial. Traditionally the best-paying reward schemes come from companies where the rewards are their own products, as therefore they are actually only forking out the cost price, not the retail value, plus they get ancillary marketing gains.

Updated info: www.moneysavingexpert.com/rewardcards

For a number of years the GM Visa card has been top of the tree, paying £3 per £100 spent – twice as much as the next best; however, this cash only counts as a discount off a new

Calorie Counter: Reward Credit Cards			
The return on £15,000 a year on various standard credit cards as at 1/6/05			
Card	Scheme	Return per £100	Return per £15,000
GM Card	Discount off Vauxhall cars	£3	£450
Tesco	Clubcard points (only if redeemed off Clubcard Deals scheme)	£1.70	£255
NatWest	AirMiles (flights, days out, shopping)	£0.47	£70
Sainsbury	Nectar (flights, days out, shopping)	£0.27	£40.50
HSBC	No rewards	None	None

Money Diet Quick Fact Snack: Should I Cut Up Old Credit Cards?

No. You should cancel them. Cutting it up simply stops you using it. Instead call up the card company and tell them you want to cancel. If possible, request confirmation of cancellation in writing, as sometimes they don't action it.

Cancelling has three major benefits over cutting.

- *It improves your credit score.* By cancelling cards you have less available credit. This means potential over-indebtedness is less of a problem.
- *You can be a 'new customer' again.* The best deals on the market are always the preserve of new customers. Cancelling existing cards means after a time (roughly 18 months but there are no hard-and-fast rules), you'll be re-eligible for new customer deals.
- *New cheap credit may spontaneously appear.* The mere act of attempting to cancel may mean the credit-card company will try and tempt you to stay with some form of special offer deal allowing you to shift other debts to it cheaply. This has another benefit to your credit score; it means you won't need to apply for a new card, thus there'll be no more searches on your file.

Be careful – cancelling doesn't automatically close an account. Card companies leave accounts dormant in case any payments you've made still need to come through. It's worth making a call a few months later to double-check it's all done and dusted. So, just to make things difficult, cutting up doesn't mean cancelling, and cancelling doesn't always mean closure.

Some cards are always worth keeping. Quite a number of cards have special qualities, which means they're worth keeping regardless.

There are two types of cards to consider keeping:
- *Cards consistently offering existing customers balance transfers.*

Some cards, such as Egg and Barclaycard, will consistently allow existing customers to move debts to them cheaply. This is great for protecting your credit score. See Credit Card Shuffle (page 391) for more details.

■ *A super-balance transfer card.* For those willing and able to play the debt system with a greater sophistication, a super-balance transfer card is a very powerful weapon as it is a conduit for allowing other cards to give you cheap debts (see page 374).

If you're debt-free and going to stay that way. In this case, you've the ability to play the system and use either cashback cards or the right cards for making free cash from the system (see page 387).

For those still in debt. Some cards are better to keep than others, but it's important you understand this isn't an encouragement to keep borrowing; it's how to keep your current borrowing cheap so you can pay it off more quickly.

Vauxhall car bought from a dealership. Well worth it for Vauxhall buyers – pointless (forgive the pun) for anyone else.

The big card that is very worth considering for rewards is the Tesco credit card. This pays Clubcard voucher points, which in themselves are only worth 50p per hundred pounds of spending when used for in-store Tesco spending. However, redeem them on Tesco 'Clubcard Deals', which are days out and entertainment vouchers, and the return increases to £1.70 per £100 spending.

If none of these tickle your fancy, then it has to be cashback, the very best of which pay a 2 per cent return on your spending, or £2 per £100 spent in cash, but only for those making substantial spending each year. AirMiles lovers may gnash teeth at this, but AirMiles cards actually tend to reward less than 50p worth per £100 spent – not a bargain. The only

---

Money Diet Quick Fact Snack: Cut Up Your Charity Affinity Credit Card

No, I'm not Scrooge; by all means give to charity – but for the same effort you can give much more by scrapping these cards.

Sign up for a charity card and the charity usually receives between £2.50 and £18. After that, most charity cards donate around 0.25 per cent of the purchase value – that's 25p per £100 spent. This is a very small amount, and as technically it's a royalty from the bank, not a donation from an individual, the charity can't reclaim tax through the gift-aid scheme (for full details see 'Crash Diet', page 279).

Instead, use a cashback reward card, paying, for example, one per cent, and donate this cash to charity. As well as getting more, it gets the tax break too. While this takes more discipline, the difference is huge. For £16,000 spending a year (not unreasonable if it replaces debit-card and cash transactions) on a charity card it would receive around £40 including the sign-up fee.

Use a one-per-cent cashback card and you'll receive £160 cashback; donate this and the charity can reclaim £45 on top, or £105 more if a higher-rate taxpayer donated all their gains. In total, that's £265 rather than £40. Of course, the 'pay in full or be a fool' reward-card rule still applies, so only do this if you pay off your card in full.

---

thing to watch for with cashback is if you are a very high spender – some cards have maximum cashback limits; it may mean you need two cashback cards to cover a year's spending. *Suggested ingredients, cashback reward cards:* American Express; Nationwide Cashback; Conran Card; Abbey; Bank of Ireland Card; Morgan Stanley Cashback Card; Accucard; More>Than; Easy Money.

Updated info: www.moneysavingexpert.com/cashbackcards

OVERSEAS SPENDING CARDS

Going abroad doesn't mean taking a holiday from being ripped off. There are tons of hidden charges on credit cards used abroad, in addition to the normal interest charges. Yet, with the right card, plastic is the cheapest method of overseas spending. There are, however, some hidden and unbidden charges.

A hefty 'load' on the exchange rate: card exchange rates are based on the highly competitive Visa or MasterCard wholesale rates. Yet almost all debit and credit cards secretly add a 'load', which makes the exchange rate around 2.75 per cent worse. This 'load' isn't billed as a separate item on your statement; it's invisibly smuggled into the exchange rate and just adds to what you pay.

They snack when you withdraw cash: withdraw cash when abroad and as well as the 'loading' there is a fee on top. This is usually either 2 per cent or £2, whichever is the higher. On credit cards this fee applies in the UK too, yet most of us never experience this as we use debit cards at home, so we avoid it. However, some debit cards don't work overseas, and those that do almost always add the cash-withdrawal fee too. This fee is separate from

---

Money Diet Quick Fact Snack: Spend on the Card, not with Cash

The fact that there's an additional cash-withdrawal charge and, potentially, interest means using the card to pay for things abroad is always cheaper than withdrawing cash and spending it. Spend as much as you can on the card, using it to pay for even very small purchases. Though a few banks, notably NatWest and Halifax, have now outrageously added a fee of roughly £1 each time you make a purchase too, meaning with them there's no escape.

---

anything the overseas bank may charge you on top for using their machines, something especially common in the USA.

An 'interesting' addition: there's another danger to credit-card cash withdrawals – those who are usually protected from any interest charges, because they pay off their balance in full each month, may lose this protection when withdrawing cash.

Money Diet Quick Fact Snack: The Cheapest Way to Get Overseas Cash Before You Go

While the right credit card is the best way to spend abroad, it's often useful to have at least enough foreign currency to get you from the airport to your final destination when you travel. This means buying it here. For either traveller's cheques or foreign currency, beware the over-hyped 'commission-free'. This is pretty much irrelevant; it's the exchange rate that really impacts on the cost. Let me show you by example:

Sneakyboy Travel: Commission-free
Exchange rate: £1 buys 17 Money Diet dollars
Pay £100 and get MD$1,700

Honest Martin's Bureau de Change: Commission charge £1.50
Exchange rate: £1 buys 18 Money Diet dollars
Pay £100 and get £98.50 worth of currency, which at this exchange rate buys MD$1,770

So Honest Martin's pays more even though it charges commission. As exchange rates change daily, there is no hard-and-fast rule of who's cheapest. Ignore all sales pitches and simply ask what you will get for your cash, including all commissions or fees – 'How many US dollars for £100, after all charges?'
Suggested ingredients. Travelex; Post Office; Marks & Spencer; Thomas Cook.

Most cards charge interest on cash withdrawals even if you pay off the balance in full – it's another sneaky terms-and-conditions note.

WARNING: DEBIT CARDS

Let me just make doubly sure this isn't missed: loading and overseas cash-withdrawal fees apply to debit cards (such as your bank account card) as well as credit cards. Here they're not the good guys.

Therefore, there are three things to ask credit- and debit-card providers before going overseas:

■ What is the foreign-exchange loading? Is it different in Europe compared to the rest of the world?

■ What is the cash-withdrawal fee?

■ If I withdraw cash on my credit card, and pay off the balance at the end of the month, will you still charge me interest?

The only problem is many card companies' customer service staff mightn't know the answers to these questions, especially to the last one – I've been misanswered a number of times. So get them to check rather than just answer off the top of their heads, and if necessary ask for proof in writing.

Abroad saving: **the right card for the job.** Some cards reduce their overseas charges and sell themselves based on this. Often there is no loading at all on these cards, making the exchange rate ultra-competitive, and the cash withdrawals are cheaper too. This is very sassy marketing – the aim's to put the card in your pocket when you go abroad, and hope you'll use it all year round in the UK. Money Dieters will realise that isn't the right thing to do – instead just get these cards for use only when you are abroad.

Calorie Counter: Overseas Spending Card

Spend £1,000 and withdraw £750 worth of overseas currency

Card	Load	Cash withdrawal fee (higher of)	Load on £1,000 worth of Euro spending	Cash withdrawal of £750 worth of Euros (A)			Total cost
				Load	Cash withdrawal fee (A)(B)	A month's interest (if paid off in full)	
Standard card	2.75%	£2.50 or 1.75%	£27.50	£20.60	£19.50	£13 (C)	**£80**
Specialist overseas card	0%	£1.50 or 1.5%	£0	£0	£13.50	£0	**£13**

(A) 2 x £200, 2 x £100, 3 x £50 worth of Euros; (B) ignores any overseas bank charge; (C) 17% interest

Not only do these cards beat other credit cards (you'll be roughly 5 per cent better off), they also usually beat every other holiday cash method. On a day when the exchange rate was $1.42 to the pound, an American Express Bureau de Change charged £735, including commission, for $1,000 in traveller's cheques, while spending the same amount on an overseas specialist credit card cost just £705.

Suggested ingredients. Four cards consistently trumpet their overseas charges: Nationwide; Liverpool Victoria; Saga, and Lombard Direct. Also current account holders with Nationwide may find its debit card best of all.

Updated best buys: www.moneysavingexpert.com/over seascard snacks

POTENTIAL PLAYERS:
FREE CASH – BE THE ULTIMATE TART

I started explaining this technique in the year 2000, when the first 0 per cent balance transfers started. Since then, coupled with other ad-hoc credit-card cash tricks, I estimate I've made over £1,600 in pure profit from my plastic. Others have gained too. My favourite e-mail came a year after I wrote about this technique in my *Sunday Express* column. It went something like this: 'When we first read about Free Cash, we didn't think it would really work, but gave it a go anyway. We've spent our lives being skint, but we've made about £400 each since and are taking our five- and seven-year-olds on holiday for the first time in their lives. Thank you.'

Though it's not difficult, Free Cash isn't for the forgetful – it requires care and attention. If you've any doubts, don't do it, as play it badly and you'll pay. Also if you've any other credit-card debts, forget it; concentrate on minimising their interest costs. As this isn't for beginners I'm assuming you've read the rest of the credit-card section before reading this. For those ready to take credit-card companies for every penny, this is how.

The Basic Premise

Credit-card 0 per cent offers mean they lend you money for free. Save that money at the highest interest rate possible to earn on it, plus get cashback if possible.

STEP 1: GAME

To start you need to max out your new special-offer 0 per cent card and get that money in your current account. There are two routes.

■ *Balance-transfer bonanza.* A number of credit cards, such as Mint and Abbey, allow 'super balance transfers' (see page 374), allowing you to move money directly into your bank account. Providing this is at 0 per cent, and there's no balance transfer fee (sadly this is becoming more rare), game on. Get it to pay the maximum amount into your current account.

■ *Alternative: The purchasing prizes method.* Use a 0 per cent-for-purchases card for all spending instead of debit cards, other credit cards and cash transactions, but make only the minimum monthly repayments. This leaves your wages unspent, allowing the equivalent amount to build up in your current account. (Warning: this requires self-discipline. Seeing the money build up is very tempting, but it isn't the same as real money; it's just that the debt is elsewhere – don't spend it.)

Cashback bonus. A few cards offer cashback on spending and 0 per cent interest. If you're using the 'purchasing prizes' method, it means you can earn cashback on top.

Money Diet Refined Food: Use a 'Mule' Card

If you want to get clever there's a way to really step this up. As the number of super-balance-transfer cards is limited, this restricts the amount of 0 per cent debt that can be created using this method.

Yet, you can use any super-balance-transfer card, new or old, as a 'mule', simply to transport 0 per cent debt from a non-super-balance-transfer card to your bank account. As I write, the best card for this is Egg, as it allows existing customers to do it with no fee.

An example will help:

Old card: Super-balance-transfer 'mule' card. APR 15 per cent; credit limit £5,000; current debt £0
New card: Non-super-balance-transfer card. 0 per cent for 9 months; credit limit £5,000; current debt £0

Before doing this, ensure you've got the new card set up. Then balance-transfer £5,000 from your mule card to your bank account. This means you now owe your mule card the £5,000 at 15 per cent. Then immediately balance-transfer £5,000 from your new card to the mule card. So now you owe the new card the £5,000 but don't owe the mule card anything.

You may incur a few quids' interest on the mule card while the debt was there, but providing you do it quick, the cost should be negligible.

STEP 2: SET
The extra cash in your current account should now match the 0 per cent debts on the card. Move the cash into the highest-interest, safe, easy-access savings account you can find – either a mini cash ISA (see page 223) or a savings account (see page 215). Then you'll earn interest on it while the credit card charges you nothing. However, remember you still need to meet

---

Money Diet Quick Fact Snack: Make Even More With an Offset Mortgage

Those with mortgages or loans allowing the use of savings to offset their costs should instead put the money in there (providing you can access these savings instantly) for even more gain – as the 0 per cent money will be temporarily paying off your mortgage (see page 339).

---

the minimum repayments on the credit card, so the debt will lessen gradually (use a direct debit to ensure it's always paid).

■ *Purchases prizes method note:* As the money will be dripping gradually into your current account, rather than wait for the whole lot to build, move lumps into your savings account as often as possible.

STEP 3: MATCH

You can bag the free cash after your card's 0 per cent period ends. However, to keep earning, shift the debt to a new card using an interest-free balance transfer offer and leave the cash in the highest-interest savings account. It's also possible to build more 0 per cent debt at the same time by starting again, using more cards. Some high-credit scorers claim to have had up to £70,000 worth of 0 per cent debts at any one time – but always ensure ready access to the same amount of cash to pay it off.

Suggested ingredients. Egg; Morgan Stanley; Tesco; Mint; Nationwide; Abbey; Sainsbury's; Halifax.

Updated info: www.moneysavingexpert.com/stooze

Martin's Money Memories: All Your Baskets in One Egg

At one time, internet bank Egg paid the highest credit-card cashback and at 0 per cent interest, whilst also offering the highest-paying savings account. This meant it lent me money for free, and then paid me 6 per cent on it. Poetry.

Ready Reckoner: Roughly How Much Free Cash You Can Make Per Year				
	The amount of interest-free debt			
Savings rate (after tax)	£1,000	£5,000	£12,000	£30,000
3%	£30	£150	£360	£900
5%	£50	£250	£600	£1,500
7%	£70	£350	£840	£2,100

THE CREDIT SURVIVAL TECHNIQUE: WHAT TO DO IF YOU CAN'T GET ANY NEW CARDS

All the 'precision plastic' tricks and potential profits are stymied for those with a low income, or less than perfect credit history. Funny how lenders like to give money to those who already have it ...

Yet, as long as you can cover the minimum repayments, I've got a system that will cut your interest charges and repay your debts more quickly.

It's worth pausing for a second before that, though. Good financial health is precious: take a moment to consider why you're only surviving, and what would happen if you didn't? Do the Financial Blitz (page 9), work through the Money Diet Monthly Calorie Counter (page 36) and read 'Food Poisoning' (page 411) too, as there's advice there that's relevant. And even once we've reduced the amount of interest you pay, don't let it become an excuse for borrowing more.

THE CREDIT CARD SHUFFLE: SLIP, SLIDE, SHUFFLE AND GROOVE

This is my four-step interest-reduction dance. Don't confuse 'shuffling' with 'switching' – the key to the shuffle is moving money around between existing, not new, debts. The shuffle is a Money Diet workout – cue flared trousers and gyrating hips.

First, a Simple Question

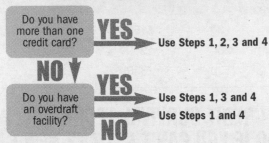

Do you have more than one credit card? **YES** ➤ Use Steps 1, 2, 3 and 4

NO ⬇

Do you have an overdraft facility? **YES** ➤ Use Steps 1, 3 and 4 / Use Steps 1 and 4

NO

Note: Don't give up at any point – Step 4 can work even if 1, 2 and 3 aren't possible.

Step 1: the Slip

Slime up to your provider and ask it to cut the rate

Call your current credit- and store-card providers and ask if they will slip your interest rate down. Some providers have automatic 'interest-rate-matching policies', so if you've other cards at cheaper rates, they will match. Even without any of that, it's truly silly but simply asking can work, and intimating you're thinking of shifting to another card works even better. Be confident, be polite, be charming and try to think of a reason your rate should be cheaper. It's amazing what deals customer-service reps have the power to authorise.

Money Diet Safety Disclaimer: The Credit Card Shuffle

The Shuffle is designed to save you money, not make you look cool at a nightclub. The author and publishers take no responsibility whatsoever for embarrassment or injuries caused by trying to actually shimmy to the Shuffle.

Step 2: the Slide

Can the debt be moved?

It used to be that all special balance-transfer offers (see page 372) were for new cardholders, whereas existing cardholders were just offered the card's standard rate. Yet momentum is changing, and existing-customer deals are springing up, as providers are scared of continually losing customers. Barclaycard started this – unsurprising, it's the biggest card so it has most customers to lose – and others are catching on. Existing-customer deals aren't as good as new-customer offers, but are much better than most cards' standard interest rates. *Updated info:* www.moneysavingexpert.com/creditcardshuffle

Official Balance Transfers For Existing Customers	
Card	**Existing customer balance transfer rate**
Abbey	Offer rate decided on individual circumstances
Alliance & Leicester	Offer rate decided on individual circumstances
American Express Blue	2.9 per cent for six months
Barclaycard	6.9 per cent life of balance
Cahoot	Standard 10–15 per cent
Egg	In the anniversary month of card being opened you receive 0 per cent for five months on balance transfers made in that month
HSBC	3.9 per cent for six months
Lloyds TSB	Offer rate decided on individual circumstances
MBNA	Offer rate decided on individual circumstances
Mint	11.4 per cent life of balance
NatWest	No fixed policy but targeted offers available
RBS	No fixed policy but targeted offers available

As at June 2005. These will change, but the table gives a rough indication of the type of offers available.

So call your provider and ask it the following questions to see if you can slide any debts over.

- If I transfer a balance from another card, what rate will you charge me?
- What is the maximum debt I can have on this card? (In other words, the credit limit.)
- Will you increase my credit limit? (Provides more flexibility for the shuffle.)

The table on the previous page indicates the types of offer available; they will change, but shouldn't move too substantially.

Step 3: the Shuffle

Move the debts

Now you've minimised all current interest rates and discovered at what rates transfers are available, shuffle the debts, using balance transfers. The aim is to fill up the credit limits on the cards charging the least interest. Even if no special rates were offered, you should still be able to shift the money to the cheapest standard-rate card.

Those with just one credit card, and an overdraft facility, should compare their rates. If the overdraft rate is more expensive, spend on the credit card instead of from your bank account, releasing the pressure on the overdraft and allowing your earnings to pay it back. Effectively this moves the debt to the cheaper rate on the credit card. If the overdraft is cheaper, then simply pay as much as you can off the credit card.

Step 4: Get Into the Groove

Focus your repayments

At this point you have the lowest interest rates possible. The final step is to focus repayments to pay off the most expensive

Credit Card Shuffle: A Possible Complication and a Possible Solution

A problem arises if a card offers a cheaper rate for balance transfers to it than the existing debts on it. This adds an expense due to the way the card companies allocate repayments (see page 376 for an explanation). It's still better to do it than not – but there is a way round it. It may sound silly, but first shift the debt to another card, and then move it back, effectively converting the 'purchase debts' to 'balance-transfer debts'. If the credit limits don't allow it, shift as much of the debt as is possible. An example should help:

Daley Grind has two credit cards:

Card 1: Obey Notional Misercard
Standard rate: 17.9 per cent; balance: £700; credit limit: £3,000.
Balance-transfer rate: 9.9 per cent until all the debt transferred is paid off.
Card 2: Critical Two Weasel card
Standard rate: 16.9 per cent; balance: £1,200; credit limit: £2,000.
Balance-transfer rate: the standard 16.9 per cent.

The Obvious Method Simply transfer the Critical Two balance to the Misercard. Total debt: £700 at 17.9 per cent and £1,200 at 9.9 per cent.

The bank will automatically allocate the repayments to the cheap debt, meaning the 17.9 per cent debt isn't paid off until the £1,200 is cleared. It's a saving, but more is possible.

Money Diet Method First transfer the Misercard debt to the Critical Two Card. Situation: £1,900 debt now at 16.9 per cent.

Then, once the debt is definitely on that account (call and check), transfer all the debt back to the Misercard.

Situation: £1,900 debt, all at the 9.9 per cent rate.

One note of caution: usually there shouldn't be any problem doing this but, very, very occasionally, providers may spot what you're doing and kibosh the transfer back.

debts first. To do this, pay the minimum repayments on all debts, except the most expensive. Throw all the cash you can at paying that off. As soon as it is paid off, shift focus to the next highest-rate debts and continue until all debts are repaid. This will reduce the interest cost, even if the other steps above aren't available. If you have an overdraft, check its rate, too – if it's the highest rate, make sure it is paid off first.

One final trick: even with minimum payments you will gradually pay some debts off the cheapest cards. Every six months or so, do balance transfers again to move debts from the most expensive card to fill up the credit limit on the cheapest.

Calorie Counter: Doing the Shuffle – a Real-life Example

A friend with some debt worries came to talk to me last August. She had a range of cards and had been turned down for new credit. After having done a budget with her (and, trust me, that makes her seriously brave – I'm tough) we managed to squeeze £300 a month out to pay off the debts. As she was worried about dancing alone, I decided to partner up and Shuffle with her. At the start her debts looked like this:

Initial Situation				
	Debt	Rate	Credit limit	The potential interest cost if cards repaid in full with £300/month payments
Barclaycard	£2,500	17.9%	£3,500	£545
Tesco Card	£1,750	14.9%	£4,500	£220
Debenhams Store Card	£1,750	29.9%	£2,000	£485
TOTAL	£6,000	18.7%	N/A	£1,250

The average interest rate was 18.7 per cent, and with the
£300/month payments it'd cost her £1,250 in interest by the
time she'd pay them all off.

What we did. Barclaycard was willing to slip down her interest
rate to match Tesco's, but this turned out to be irrelevant, as it
also offered a 6.9 per cent balance transfer for existing
customers with the rate lasting until the entire debt was paid off.

The first thing we did was move all the debt off Barclaycard
to the other cards, so it was empty. This enabled us to move
all the debts back to the card at the transfer rate, rather than
the spending rate. After Barclaycard was filled up, the rest
went to Tesco, at its standard rate. This left the hideously
expensive store card paid off. To finish, my friend started
focusing on repaying the costlier Tesco debt, with only the
minimum going to the cheaper Barclaycard.

Post Shuffle Situation				
	Debt	Rate	Interest (prioritising expensive debts)	Saving
Barclaycard	£3,500	6.9%	£325	£220
Tesco Card	£2,500	14.9%	£200	£20
Debenhams Store Card	£0	29.9%	£0	£485
TOTAL	£6,000	9.0%	£525	£725

The result. Overall, the interest to be paid until the time the
cards are paid off was reduced from £1,250 to £525, more than
a 60 per cent saving. And remember, there were no new cards
here; just using the ones she had, but more efficiently.

four

MORE SNACKS

PUKKA PERSONAL LOANS

For a simple product, when it comes to loans there are more fences to leap than the Grand National. However, get it right and loans are an effective way to borrow. This chapter also includes a sneaky way to beat even the cheapest loan on the market, by 'perverting your plastic'. Newspapers may shriek 'UK in debt crisis', but for most households it isn't debt itself but its punitively high interest that's the crisis. Yet, get a loan the right way and it's possible to cut the cost by over 70 per cent.

BACK TO BASICS

Traditionally personal loans are the way to borrow between £1,000 and £25,000. They give you cash, you spend it on whatever you want, and repay a fixed amount each month for a set term. The rate of interest agreed at the loan's start is fixed, which is useful when certainty or self-discipline is needed. So for a lump sum for a car, kitchen or even holiday, loans are a reasonably convenient way to do it.

Like credit cards, most personal loans are 'unsecured', which is good. Unfortunately, while loans should be simple, there is a range of hurdles to leap over. However, don't be too worried – read on and you can out-jump Colin Jackson. Before getting into the nitty-gritty, I want to ask you three questions:

1. *Do you really need to borrow money?* Loans are a long-term commitment – you should consider whether you can afford it, and if you are sure you'll always be able to repay.

2. *Do you have access to other borrowing that may be cheaper?* If you have credit cards, overdraft facilities and a mortgage, then it's likely you already have access to substantial amounts of borrowing. Don't plump for a loan simply because you need a lump sum. Follow the explanations in the rest of this section to see what's cheaper, plus see my half-price plastic personal loan technique (page 406).

3. *Will they loan you the money?* As with credit cards, your credit history impacts on your ability to borrow. It's necessary to work out whether you're a potential player, credit survivor or in debt crisis (see page 364). Potential players should just read on. Credit survivors shouldn't really be borrowing more, but a loan at a decent rate may be slightly easier to get than a credit card, so it can be a good way to reduce your existing debt's interest rate. Focusing on mainstream rather than cutting-edge lenders makes this more likely. Also, if you can't get loans the standard way, check out if you have a local Credit Union, a small community-run organisation that may be able to help. Those in debt crisis shouldn't be considering further debts, and should turn straight to page 411.

PERSONAL LOAN E NUMBERS: WHAT TO AVOID

Lenders have an arsenal of weapons to shoot up the price of personal loans and, rather obviously, the best way to get a cheap one is to avoid them. To push the diet theme probably slightly further than I should, they're a bit like E numbers. They may look good, may even help the taste, but can seriously damage your wealth over the long run.

E101: Insurance Costs

This is the big one – it can cost thousands. Loans are advertised based on the APR – the standard measure of interest. The lower the APR, the cheaper the loan. But (and this is a but so big even Jennifer Lopez would be impressed) this is only for loans WITHOUT payment protection insurance (PPI).

PPI covers repayments if you have an accident, get sick or are made redundant, and can cost thousands. Yet it is never included in the APR. This shouldn't happen. The law says insurance costs should only be included in the APR if the loan cost is compulsory. Lenders therefore almost never make PPI compulsory; they just push it heavily. In fact, many lenders treat it as a default setting; in other words, unless you specify you don't want it, you'll get it. All this is so they can advertise cheaper loans, and make most of their profits on expensive insurance policies. PPI is also damn difficult to cancel.

This doesn't mean PPI is bad – just be careful, and read my sneaky way to slash its cost in 'The Crash Diet', page 282.

Martin's Money Memories: I Almost Paid £550 a Minute to Hear a Sexy Voice

Sorry to disappoint; I'm not about to confess to a skeleton in my closet. This is still about PPI. I once called Northern Rock Bank's call centre to test how it sells insurance. A lovely woman answered. She was polite and charming with a voice so husky it'd make Benson & Hedges proud.

Martin: 'I'd like a loan, please. I want to borrow £10,000 over five years.'
Sexy Northern Rock Woman: 'Certainly, Mr Lewis. No problem. It's £248 a month.'

Forearmed with Northern Rock's prices, I knew this was the 'with insurance cost', though neither I nor the nice woman had mentioned PPI. As a good honest chappy I thought it best to clarify.

Martin: 'Does that include insurance?'
SNRW: 'Yes, you're fully covered with this loan.'
Martin: 'Do I need the insurance?'
SNRW: 'We wouldn't advocate you not to get it; it's advisable you do. But obviously the choice is yours.'

In the midst of this five minutes of huskiness is a teeny-weeny financial fact. She had automatically quoted a with-insurance loan. I was prepared, but how many people can work out in their head in under five seconds the cost per month of 8 per cent interest applied to a decreasing £10,000 loan balance over five years? Frankly, even with a spreadsheet it isn't easy.

Plus, she never asked whether I was self-employed, or other issues which potentially devalue the insurance. It was just automatically added. It would've been easy to sign for the loan, which had the cheapest advertised APR, thinking it a good deal, without realising about the extra for insurance. And don't think that this is small change; at £2,700 over the Term, the insurance cost substantially more than the interest.

E102: Penalties for Paying Off the Loan Early

Loans have redemption penalties. Did you know? Pay a loan off early and most lenders usually add a couple of months worth of interest, but you tend only to find out when you try it. If there's any chance you may want to repay before the term ends, always check, and go for the few that don't penalise you.

E103: the Rule of 78

Thankfully this is now banned on new loans, but if you took a loan out before May 2005, watch out as, until 2007, it's likely this applies to you. The rule of 78 is another form of redemption penalty.

Money Diet Quick Fact Snack: Doing the Maths on the Rule of 78

WARNING: This isn't 'need to know'. For nerds only.

Calculate the interest. Work out the total amount of interest payable over the life of the loan by taking the amount borrowed away from the total cost (for non-insured loans).

Assign each month its reverse number. Take the number of months and assign this in reverse order to each month you're due to pay off (for example, over two years, the first month is month 24, the second month 23, the third month 22, etc.).

Calculate interest in proportion. The amount of interest assigned per month is worked out by dividing that number (e.g. for the fourth month over two years it's 21) by the total of all these numbers (i.e. 24+23+22+21 ...+3+2+1 = 300). So, in this example 21/300th of the total amount of interest. Told you it was complicated.

P.S. It's called the Rule of 78 because the total of all the months (1+2+3 ... up to 12) in one year adds up to 78.

It's a hideously complicated hidden formula, which means early repayments are artificially allocated towards repaying the interest, not the capital. Basically, pay the loan off early and any prior repayments won't have made much of a dent, leaving more to repay than you'd think. This can make paying a loan off in the first year or two much more expensive.

E104: Bizarre Tiers

As a general rule with personal loans, the more you borrow, the lower the interest rate. Most banks set their tiers at standard rates. For example:

- £1,000 to £4,999 – 11.9 per cent
- £5,000 to £9,999 – 8.9 per cent
- Above £10,000 – 7.9 per cent

However, a couple of lenders deliberately set theirs in bizarre places. For example:

- £1,000 to £5,050 – 12.9 per cent
- £5,051 to £10,050 – 8.9 per cent
- Above £10,051 – 7.9 per cent

Most people borrow rounded amounts for loans. Yet in the above example it would be substantially cheaper in total to borrow £5,060 than to borrow £5,000. Keep an eye out.

E105: It's Not Just the Size, but How Long it is

Remember, the loan term plays a part in the cost. The longer you borrow for, the higher the total cost you pay, as the interest stacks up for longer.

E106: It's Bloody Typical

So the loan is advertising a cracking 5.7 per cent rate! It looks cheap. Yet this is a 'typical rate', which means after you apply, it's perfectly possible the actual rate will be more, 6 per cent, 8 per cent, 12 per cent even.

The rules are that the typical rate must be the rate two-thirds of accepted customers are paying. The other third? Who cares! (Not the regulations anyway.) The worst thing is you only find out the rate AFTER you've applied. This means there's an additional search on your credit file, hurting your credit score. Outrageous, it should be stopped ...

In practice, those with good credit scores and reasonable salaries should still go for the cheapest rate, even if it's 'typical', yet others should try and find one of the few 'guaranteed' rates around that are cheap. Nationwide is a good place to start. Unfortunately, this means you're going to have to do a bit of small print-checking before you start.

Suggested ingredients: no-insurance loans. Northern Rock; Liverpool Victoria; Sainsbury; Tesco; Lombard Direct; Cahoot; Nationwide; Halifax; Moneyback.

Questions When Buying A Loan

Now you know the tricks, and have decided whether to get PPI or not, ask prospective lenders:

■ How much will I have to repay in total over the life of the loan?
■ Does it have redemption penalties?
■ Is the rate 'typical' or 'guaranteed'?
Simple as that!

Money Diet Quick Fact Snack: Flexible Personal Loans

Based on the flexible mortgage system, the idea is you have a borrowing facility where you define the amount repaid. There are three tenets.

Overpay: pay the loan more quickly without any penalties at all.

Underpay: pay less than the recommended amount, within set limits.

Borrow-back: borrow back some of the money repaid, within set amounts, if you need more.

Interest and PPI are only paid on the outstanding amount. Flexible loans can be a great deal for people with uncertain finances. The rates tend to be good, but a little higher than the cheapest standard loans. The only real negative is that the interest rate usually isn't fixed, so the lender reserves the right to increase it during the life of the loan, something you're protected from with a normal loan.

Flexibility can also be achieved using 'offset' loans. Here you have a loan linked to a savings account, so they balance each other out, and you only pay interest on the total amount you're in debt.

Suggested ingredients. Full flexibility: Cahoot. Partial flexibility: Intelligent Finance; Egg; Goldfish.

Suggested ingredients: with-insurance loans. Intelligent Finance; Nationwide; Cahoot (and try the cheapest 'no-insurance loans' as well); Leeds & Holbeck.

Suggested ingredients: loans you may redeem early. Egg; Intelligent Finance; Cahoot.

Updated info: www.moneysavingexpert.com/personalloans

Calorie Counter

Borrow £7,500 without insurance over five years with a typical high-street branch loan at 15.2 per cent and the total repayment is £10,530 – that's interest of £3,030. Use instead a provider with a cheap rate, usually around 6 per cent, and the total is £8,735, of which £1,235 is interest – substantially less than a third of the cost.

Yet it all changes with PPI loans. Here the 'cheap APR' provider charges £10,790 in total, but loans that offer cheap insurance can undercut this even if they have a higher APR. In the example below it's another £730 cheaper due to its much less expensive insurance. (Also see 'Loan Insurance', page 282.)

£7,500 over five years	Rate	No Insurance		With Insurance		
		Monthly payment	Total cost	Monthly payment	Total cost	Unnecessary cost
Branch loan	15.2%	£175.45	£10,530	£218.80	£13,130	£3,070
Cheap insurance loan	8.3%	£152.37	£9,140	**£167.60**	**£10,060**	None
Cheap APR advertiser	6.3%	**£145.58**	**£8,735**	£179.79	£10,790	£730

HALF-PRICE PLASTIC
PERSONAL LOAN OR OVERDRAFT

This is where loans get sexy – well, for me, anyway. It is possible to massively undercut even the cheapest loans on the market by perverting your credit cards. This isn't a technique for beginners. It needs an understanding of the way credit cards work. Read the credit card chapter (page 356) first, focusing especially on balance transfers, to provide the building blocks.

The Premise

The cheapest credit-card balance-transfer offers undercut the cheapest loans. Therefore use them to replicate a loan.

There are two types of balance-transfer offer to choose from:

The ultimate: Moving debt around from 0 per cent card to 0 per cent card via repeated balance transfers is always cheapest. This is the best route if you're just looking for short-term loan replication. Yet for longer-term borrowing – two years plus – there's a risk you'll forget or credit-scoring issues will deny continued access to such terms.

Cheap and safe: Life-of-balance transfers are actually very similar to loans, as the rate is fixed at the outset. The cheapest are usually 4.9 per cent (or 2.9 per cent if you're lucky) – much better than loan rates. For all but ultra-toned Money Dieters, I'd plump for this method for longer loans. And my explanation below assumes you have (see suggested ingredients on page 375).

How to Pervert Your Plastic

To create your own bespoke personal loan, apply for as high a credit limit as possible on the new 'life-of-balance' card then, if it's approved, you're ready to start. I'm assuming you already have an existing credit card; if not, then you'll need to apply for a standard card as well.

To consolidate existing credit card debts. Simply transfer the balances directly to the new card.

To make a big one-off purchase. Pay for it with your existing card and immediately transfer the debt to the new card.

To make a range of cash purchases or to cut the cost of existing personal loans or overdrafts. The cheapest option is via an existing 'super-balance-transfer' card (see page 374) so you can pay the cash straight into your current account, though sadly many of the current providers that offer this are looking to stop it. If that isn't possible, some credit cards offer cheques, usually at a charge of 1.5 per cent (even with this it should still work). Write one of these to pay into your bank account. Then simply transfer this card's debt to the life-of-balance card. (Those paying off existing loans should read the next section, page 409.)

As soon as this debt appears (speed is important, as some cards charge interest on balance transfers for every day they're in your account; don't wait for the statement), transfer it straight across to the life-of-balance transfer card. The only exception is where the debt is on an intro 0 per cent offer. However, most life-of-balance cards put a time limit on when you can make the transfer – such as not beyond six months after getting the card – so ensure you don't miss out.

Watch Out

Even at 4.9 per cent life of balance, be careful. Never use it for spending – do that and the lender biases your repayments towards paying off the cheap debts first (see page 376). So, simply transfer the balance, then stick this card in a drawer.

To Truly Replicate a Loan

Repay a fixed amount each month; this pays the debt off much more quickly than sticking to the minimum. Credit cards are more flexible than loans, so you can also pay off more if you choose. Yet always keep repaying the loan; if you just choose to make the minimum repayments you'll end up paying a stack more interest due to the extra time it takes.

Calorie Counter

£5,000 loan repaying £150/month	Interest rate	Months to repay	Total interest	Saving
Standard branch loan*	15.9%	44	£1,630	N/A
Cheapest standard loan*	6.8%	37	£560	£1,070
Life-of-balance transfer loan system	4.9%	36	£380	£1,250
0% rotating transfer loan system	0% then 0%	34	£0	£1,630

*No PPI

WHAT IF I ALREADY HAVE AN EXPENSIVE LOAN?

Prior to the Money Diet you may have signed up for an expensive personal or car loan. Now we need to cut the cost. Unfortunately, it isn't as simple as just moving to a cheaper loan. Two things may make it more expensive than you think.

Redemption penalties: pay loans off early and you can be fined (see page 402). This is worse if you have payment protection insurance (PPI) as you may need to repay the whole policy.

The Rule of 78: again, repay early and this calculation method adds to your cost (see page 402).

Can You Save by Switching?

Most people will be able to save by switching, but sums need doing. First find out the following information – just call your existing lender and ask.

1. How much, including penalties, will it cost me to repay the loan in full? Answer equals REPAY amount (such as £3,200).

2. If I stick with this loan, how many repayments do I have left and how much are they? Multiply the number of payments left by the repayment amount and you get the KEEP PAYING total, (for example 32 months at £125 per month = £4,000).

IF YOU'RE SWITCHING TO ANOTHER PERSONAL LOAN

Ask the new lender 'How much is the total cost to borrow the REPAY amount over the same number of months as the existing loan has left?' (Or even pay it off sooner if you can afford to.) The answer is the NEW LOAN amount (for instance, 'How much will it cost me to borrow £3,200 over 32 months?' Answer: £3,600).

Now, quite simply, if the NEW LOAN amount is less than the KEEP PAYING amount, it is worth switching (for example, in this example you'd be £400 better off).

IF YOU'RE SWITCHING TO A HALF-PRICE PLASTIC PERSONAL LOAN

The calculation is the same, except it's more difficult to work out the NEW LOAN amount, as credit-card providers don't give this type of quote. If you're not a spreadsheet junkie, but have access to the internet, then use a loan-calculator, plug in the interest rate and the amount you think you can repay; this should give you the New Loan cost.

If not, the only other route is to call up the cheapest personal loan-provider you can find and ask for an uninsured loan quote. As the credit-card interest rate will be lower than this (or you wouldn't be doing it), if it's worth switching in the case of a personal loan, it'll be even more worth doing with the cheaper credit-card rate.

five

FOOD POISONING
DEBT CRISIS – WHAT TO DO

THERE'S ALWAYS A SOLUTION
NO MATTER HOW BAD THE DEBT

Debt Crisis isn't a title to inspire confidence. However, no debt problem is unsolvable. There's always a way back. Debt crisis has many causes – radical financial change such as losing a job, illness, divorce or death; an inability to plan; a tendency to overspend, and many more. Frankly, at this point I don't care how you did it; let's just work out how we get you out of there.

First, remember debt isn't isolated from your other finances. So use the rest of the Money Diet to minimise your costs. If you've crippling debt, though, don't just follow my 'cut bills without cutting back' advice – it's time to cut back! (See Financial Fitness, page 16.)

ARE YOU REALLY IN DEBT CRISIS?

Let me repeat my definition of debt crisis. If you have debts and you cannot meet the minimum repayments, this is a

411

crisis, even if it's only in the short term. Yet, anyone who spends more than they can afford is moving towards crisis and should consider taking stock and starting to act.

A common mistake is to think that missing a few months' payments isn't a big deal. It is – and the reason's simple: it can start a debt spiral.

*A **debt spiral**.* Miss payments and your credit score descends more quickly than Homer Simpson on a doughnut. Late-payment fines may be added, more interest piles up – on both the original debt and on the fines – and you owe substantially more. Then, even if the 'short-term bad time' ends, the debts are now much bigger, and you can't reduce the cost using new cheaper debts due to your now reduced credit score.

This isn't a scare story, but a call to action. If you can't meet your payments, sort things out. Right now. Today. The sooner it's done, the less serious it will be – and the quicker it'll be over. Some people wait years before dealing with their debts – by then the action needed is drastic and their ability to play the system is severely restricted.

WHAT TO DO
If it's Only Just Happening

If you think you're going to be unable to meet your minimum payments soon, then you may not yet have damaged your credit score. In that case, you may still be a 'Potential Player' and able to minimise the interest costs by shifting the debt, and by reducing expenditure using the Money Diet, forestalling the debt crisis before it happens. See pages 63 and 77.

If You're in the Quagmire

If you're reading this, you're worried! So let's take it step by step and work through all the different things you can do.

Traditional debt advice says 'never borrow your way out of a debt problem'. Yet this ignores the cost of debts. A more savvy approach is 'never borrow *more* to get out of a debt problem'. If it is possible to borrow elsewhere more cheaply to replace existing borrowing, then this can provide a huge boost.

Those with big debts may save thousands a year in interest by being savvier with their borrowing. This is a great start to debt rescue, though clever consuming should only be one part of a disciplined attempt to regain control of the situation – looking at your entire finances and spending habits is the other.

Being in debt can be a particularly dark time. Many people are scared to tell partners, friends or anyone. Yet, there is always a way out.

If you haven't told the people who count, read through the solutions first and go to them with an action plan. It's much easier that way and remember – if you are prepared to take action the question isn't 'will I ever get through this?' but '*when* will I get through this?' Good luck.

The Four Cornerstones of Dealing with Crisis Debts

Before I get into the nitty-gritty, let me give you the big picture.

Cut your expenditure
Do a Financial Blitz to cut all your costs and
cut back on everything you can.

Lower your interest
If possible move your debts to reduce the interest cost.

413

Pay the worst first
Prioritise paying off the debts with the highest interest rate.

Free help helps
If you need help, use the non-commercial
free agencies (details later).

It's very important to get on top of debts as soon as possible. Don't default or miss payments. Let your lender know if you are going to be unable to pay – it's always better to talk to them, though, of course, preventative measures such as reducing interest, expenditure, and being a smart consumer are the best form of action.

The 'Nightmare Debts – What Should I Do'? Checklist
The following methods can be used either separately or together.

■ *Budget, budget, budget and er, budget.* There's no point in going through this excercise unless you have a real understanding of your money situation. I don't mean a scrap of paper with your guesses either. Use 'Prepare Your Pocket' (page 28), and its Money Diet Monthly Calorie Counter to go through, step-by-step, every single item of expenditure.

■ *Credit card balance transfers, whatever your credit score.* Used correctly and with discipline, credit cards are the cheapest borrowings possible. If you can shift your debts to where they're cheaper, and if you can still get new debt, see 'Precision Plastic' (page 356). If not read the 'Credit Card Shuffle', page 391.

■ *Unsecured Loans:* Standard personal loans can give you a

consistent cheap debt, and as you must make the repayments each month, it helps provide structure to your repayments. Again this is primarily for those who still have a decent credit score.

- **Check credit reference files:** Those rejected from credit-card or personal-loan lending without an obviously poor credit history should check that their information held by the credit reference agencies Equifax, Experian and Call-Credit isn't erroneous.

- **Use savings:** The interest *paid* on savings is usually far less than that *charged* on borrowing, so paying off debts with savings makes sense. If this leaves you without savings, then don't cut the credit cards up; instead lock them away in case of a dire emergency. If one doesn't happen you're quids in; if it does you're no worse off than you are right now and you will have saved substantial interest charges in the meantime.

- **Remortgage:** Mortgages are simply a special type of loan with cheaper rates. Borrowing the money on your existing mortgage, or remortgaging to a new cheaper deal, is often, though not always, the best move as while the interest rate is lower you'll be borrowing for much longer. However, it may get you out of a temporary hole, although don't be tempted into using this as a consistent 'get out of jail free' plan – you'll end up losing your home!

- **Check your benefits:** You may be entitled to a range of benefits, tax credits or grants you aren't aware of. It's worth seeing what's out there. Your local benefits office or Citizens Advice Bureau will help.

- **Secured loans:** Secured loans are lending of last resort. Secured means secured on your home, so if you fail to

Money Diet Quick Fact Snack: Debt-consolidation Companies

These are the most palatable of the companies looking to profit out of debt crisis. They advertise for homeowners to loan to, and offer to pay off all your other loans so you owe them one easy, simple, low monthly payment. Let's examine just what this means:

Homeowners: These companies are actually giving you a 'secured' loan, so if you can't pay up they can make a claim on your home. In effect this is what a mortgage is, yet these companies may charge two or three times the mortgage rate. Why not first see if you can remortgage (see page 322) at their cheaper rate.

Consolidation: 'One nice, easy monthly payment.' This is a nice sell; it makes the whole thing seem harmless. Yet there is no benefit purely from having all your money in one place. You only benefit if the interest rate is reduced – yet often they don't mention their interest rates because they can be more expensive than other forms of lending. Five loans with cheap interest are better than one loan with high interest. Don't buy this spiel.

Low monthly payment: Though attractive, because you can meet the repayments, be aware of the consequence. The loan is usually spread over a much, much longer time than your current debts. It may mean paying it off for 10, 20 or 30 years and therefore thousands of pounds in extra interest with limited or low flexibility to change. Again, compare this to the cost of putting the money on a mortgage.

More available for a holiday: This makes me want to growl. It's unfair temptation. They're trying to get you to borrow even more. Of course, if you're in debt crisis the idea of a holiday to get away and forget it all seems wonderful – but doing it with their money will cost you for years.

Re-encouragement to spend: These companies tend not to do a budget. That's dangerous: you're often in crisis because you've overspent. Budgets are crucial. And please remember – even if they clear your credit cards, don't use them again. It'll get worse.

Lock-in penalties: No, you didn't hear this in the advert because it tends not to be mentioned. Some of these companies will lock you into the loan, with big penalties for repaying early, so you're stuck with them, and stuck paying interest year after year after year. Plus these penalties are on a secured loan and may mean even if you just want to move house, you have to pay a large Rule of 78 penalty (see page 402).

---

repay it you can lose your house. However, in certain circumstances it is the best option. Those with expensive debts and some (not too substantial) credit-history problems may be able to benefit by cutting their interest rates. However, if you're going to look at this, first investigate remortgaging, as a mortgage is a form of secured loan but with a cheaper rate.

While writing this checklist I've added and then deleted 'secured loans' three times, debating whether the tacit approval I give by including it does more harm than good. In the end I've kept it, as while for most they're a nightmare worse than getting stuck between two elephants on heat, in very specific circumstances it's a good move.

Only move debts to secured loans if the interest is substantially cheaper, get the shortest repayment time your budget can stretch to and always check what penalties you'll pay for early repayment. Websites MoneySupermarket and MoneyExtra have comparison services to help you find the cheapest.

The next bit's so important I hope my publisher has letters big and bold enough to do it justice. If you simply can't meet repayments, all the above just don't do the trick and you are in so far over your head that you're drowning

Quickly go and see a debt counsellor.

This really is very important. I'm not talking about any of those companies that advertise on the television, promising to consolidate your loans and fix your credit, no matter how glamorous the celeb promoting them. They can be hideously expensive, damage your credit score and leave you locked into unnecessary debt for years (see 'Debt-consolidation Companies', page 416).

Instead, a number of free debt-counselling charities or non-profit agencies will give you detailed, personal one-to-one advice on what to do.

Those I'd plump for are:

- The Consumer Credit Counselling Service. www.cccs. co.uk; 0800 138 1111
- National Debtline. www.nationaldebtline.co.uk; 0808 808 4000
- Citizens Advice Bureau. www.citizensadvice.org.uk
- Payplan. www.payplan.com; 0800 085 4298

All are completely free. They all operate in slightly different ways, so there's nothing wrong with trying more than one of them to see which you prefer. There is also a good range of local agencies that may be able to help – just ensure they're genuine advice centres and provide free, non-profit, unbiased advice.

Now you may be asking, 'Hold on, isn't he going to tell me what to do here? Isn't that what the Money Diet's about?' In this case, no, I'm not. And there's a simple reason. These folks are good, free, one-to-one advisers who will help you. They are not in it to make money out of you; they're just there to help you out of a problem.

And if I'm really honest, they're better than me at it. I'm a MoneySaving expert, a system player, yet at this point those in debt crisis move outside the system.

Debt crisis is tricky and can be complicated. There's nothing wrong with getting help. I'm a huge fan. Don't wait until you're in debt crisis; see them in conjunction with doing the Money Diet if it looks like you're going to have problems.

They aim not to be judgemental. They will help prioritise your expenditure. Often people assume that banks, doorstep loan collectors or credit cards are the first people you should pay. Actually you should focus on keeping the heat and electricity on, a roof over your head and food on the table.

On occasion, debt-counselling services will negotiate with lenders for you. This may involve freezing your interest, making agreements to pay the debt sooner or just buying you a bit of time and space. The dreaded terms 'Individual Voluntary Arrangements' and 'bankruptcy' may be mentioned.

Actually they're not so bad in reality. Going bankrupt stops anyone else demanding money and closes off any routes creditors have. The worst debt e-mail I've ever received was from a man who said he had £260,000 on credit cards and a salary of under £30,000. I don't understand how he was lent so much, but I directed him to the free debt counsellors. He was advised to go bankrupt. He did. A while later he got back in touch – his life wasn't brilliant, but the pressure was off his

> ### Why I Harp on so Much about Non-commercial Debt Help
>
> The best explanation doesn't come from me. It comes from a post on the Debt-free Wannabee section of the moneysavingexpert.com chat forum where many who are in debt get together, talk and support each other.
>
> *'We, my wife and I, are on a seven-year plan with the Consumer Credit Counselling Service, having recently changed from a commercial debt management company after listening to Martin. The simple action of swapping to the CCCS has shaved over two years off the length of our plan as the money we were paying the management company now goes to our creditors instead! Of course, that also means a financial saving of nearly eight grand over the term of the original plan's 10-year period.'*

shoulders and he was sleeping for the first time in years. It ain't no bed of roses, but I'd still call it a solution.

What Not to Do

Don't go to debt-consolidation agencies, debt-management companies, credit-repair companies, door-to-door lenders, loan sharks, cheque-cashing companies or any of the other businesses who prey on people in crisis. They may promise no-nonsense easy cash solutions, but in the long run you'll pay, and in the worst case you will have people knocking on your door, not taking no for an answer.

If you're already involved with such companies, still see the free debt-counselling agencies and get some advice. They may be able to extricate you, or at least help balance the payments.

Debt can be more than a financial crisis – it can be very dark. Let me be honest, I've never been in debt crisis. I don't know what it feels like. Yet I'm often asked for help by people who are. The following 'memory' is something I thought long and hard about before putting in. I hope I've done the right thing. I hope if you're in debt trouble it'll encourage you to talk to someone about it.

One day, a woman posted in the chat section of my website. She had run up debts without telling her husband, and he had just lost his job. She said she couldn't see any option other than killing herself. I was scared for her and didn't really know what to do – the money side, yes, but I'm not a counsellor. So I took advice from someone who was, and wrote a careful reply to try and say the right thing.

The first person to reply after me was Andrea, one of the site's regulars. She simply extended a hand of friendship, said things were never as bad as they seemed, and 'Why not send me a personal message? I'll bring the virtual coffee, if you bring the biscuits.' I'd be lying if I tried to pretend my eyes were dry after I read it.

More people replied. The following are a couple of posts I've selected. Their words, not mine ...

Light at the end of the tunnel: 'Just to let you know there is light at the end of that very dark tunnel. I, too, got into £8,000 worth of debt as a student. When I started working I added to this a further £7,000 bank loan thinking I could pay it all off with my newly acquired wage. I WAS WRONG – BIG TIME!!!! Solicitors' letters ensued, and so I contacted the Consumer Credit Counselling Service. With a debt management plan created by them I have slowly paid off £10,000 in three years. By the end of this year all my store cards and credit cards will have been paid off, and by 2005 everything else will be too. It was hard initially not to be able to buy 'things' and I didn't have a holiday for two years but instead saved up and went to Australia this March – yes, just by saving and not spending. I learned money-respect the hard way and I'm not going down that road again. Try the CCCS – it worked for me.'

The best decision I ever made: 'Over two years ago, I started getting into money troubles. I was earning in excess of £75k p.a!! I lost my contract and couldn't pay off loans. I was feeling the strain. The mortgage was falling behind. Just when I thought things couldn't get any worse, my wife announced she couldn't carry on like this and we separated. I moved back in with my parents and thought that maybe this would see an end to it all – nope. My half of the loans still left me with more than £20k of debt. I had a new job paying me £16k p.a - just enough to cover my outgoings and maintenance payments, leaving me little spare to go and see my son twice a month. I was advised the only solution was personal bankruptcy … the words alone filled me with dread. The day arrived for court, I was ushered in to see a judge. Five minutes later, I was officially bankrupt.

Now I am debt-free, but have tight constraints for another 2.5 years until the bankruptcy period is over. But it isn't all that bad. I know exactly what my salary will be and have no more worries about being chased by creditors. I come to the end of the month and know I have a little money left to go towards my son's birthday and take him away for a week. It has to be in the UK – not glamorous, but what the hell? My advice for anyone who is in a similar situation … Please do not make the same mistakes as me and leave everything, thinking it will all go away – it doesn't. The feeling I get now, knowing that there will be an end to all of this soon, is indescribable. Hopefully, someone reading this may make a similar decision – it is the best one I have ever made.'

I wish I could tell you I knew what happened to the suicidal woman. She never did post again. I pray she read the messages and advice and sorted the problems out. If you're in debt crisis, please deal with it – there are people who will help you for free. Use them.

A FINAL £ THOUGHT

... I Hope the Money Diet No Longer Works

Since the first edition of *The Money Diet* there is a growing number of financially savvy people. Companies have noticed and at the fringes have started to push existing customer offers and make rate tarting tougher. If the entire nation followed the Money Diet properly, this book would become worthless. There'd be no more 0 per cent credit cards, no more top-paying savings accounts; direct marketing would stop; branding consultants would have to change careers and start driving school buses. Providers would learn that marketing gimmicks fail, so they'd give up, and there'd be nothing for us to take advantage of any more. Yet that's sadly still a long way away. So I'll finish with an easier hope – the same one I started with ... I hope you save some money.

Martin

INDEX

car 284-9
critical illness 76
home 291-7
internet rates 114-15
mobile phones 67-9
Mortgage Payment Protection Insurance
(MPPI) 273-5
non-smoker savings 75-6
payment protection insurance (PPI)
282-4
permanent health insurance (PHI) 75
private medical insurance (PMI) 69, 75
risk factors and rates 66-9
'self-insurance' 68-9
travel 266-9
interest rates on borrowing 304-6
international phone calls *see* overseas phone
calls
internet
access to preferential rates 94
getting benefits if you don't have access
113-15
search engines 106
shopping robots 80
ways to find the best deal 105-9
see also specific subjects for websites
internet access
broadband 156-7, 184, 187, 196-200
dial-up 193-6
internet banking 239, 240, 242
internet price comparison services, fuel costs
175-9
internet purchases, your rights 133-4
internet service providers (ISPs) 195-6,
200
internet shopping 206-9
introductory offers, loopholes 153-4
investment advice 20-1
investment funds, discount brokers 233-5
investment versus saving 211-12
investments
past performance figures 89
shares 236-8
ISA-backed mortgages 328-9, 330
ISAs (Individual Savings Accounts)
fixed rate cash ISAs 224, 228-9
Guaranteed Equity Bond Cash ISAs 226-7
how they work 230-2

improving returns on existing cash ISAs
225-7, 232
internet rates for cash ISAs 114
mini-cash ISAs 212-13, 223-5
moving for better rates 161
unit trusts within ISAs 230-1, 233-5
where to buy 233-5
ISPs (internet service providers) 195-6, 200

January sales 29, 53

level-term life assurance 142-4, 275-8
see also life assurance; term assurance
life assurance
commission 159
finding the best deal 142-4
see also level-term life assurance; mortgage-
decreasing-term-life-assurance (MDLA);
term assurance
life changes, effects on finances 69-70
loan insurance (payment protection insurance,
PPI) 282-4
loans
asking for repayment 24
consolidation by increasing mortgage 326
from family 25-6, 324
internet rates 114
see also personal loans
loopholes, making use of 150-61
loyalty
brands 94-8
disadvantages of 91-8
importance to companies 90-1
moving outside your comfort zone 112-13
test yourself 99-100
to building societies 168-9
to co-operatives 168-9
loyalty cards 92

magazines
best-buy guides 109
cost of 58, 62, 145
mail order purchases, your rights 133-4
marketing, brand loyalty 94-8
married couples, savings 214
MasterCard 358-9
medical insurance *see* healthcare cashback
plans; private medical insurance